Regulating Employment Relations, Work and Labour Laws

KLUWER LAW INTERNATIONAL

BULLETIN OF COMPARATIVE LABOUR RELATIONS – 74

Regulating Employment Relations, Work and Labour Laws

International Comparisons between Key Countries

General Editor: Roger Blanpain

Guest Editors and Lead Authors: Greg J. Bamber and Philippe Pochet

Authors

Greg J. Bamber
Philippe Pochet
Cameron Allan
Richard N. Block
Frank Burchill
Joelle Cuillerier
Grant Fitzner
Ben French
Stacy Hickox

Berndt Keller
Michael L. Moore
Sofia Murhem
Gregor Murray
Asako Nakamichi
Werner Nienhueser
Erling Rasmussen
Hiromasa Suzuki
Hiroaki Watanabe

Wolters Kluwer
Law & Business

AUSTIN   BOSTON   CHICAGO   NEW YORK   THE NETHERLANDS

Published by:
Kluwer Law International
PO Box 316
2400 AH Alphen aan den Rijn
The Netherlands
Website: www.kluwerlaw.com

Sold and distributed in North, Central and South America by:
Aspen Publishers, Inc.
7201 McKinney Circle
Frederick, MD 21704
United States of America
Email: customer.service@aspenpublishers.com

Sold and distributed in all other countries by:
Turpin Distribution Services Ltd.
Stratton Business Park
Pegasus Drive, Biggleswade
Bedfordshire SG18 8TQ
United Kingdom
Email: kluwerlaw@turpin-distribution.com

Printed on acid-free paper.

ISBN 978-90-411-3199-7

Printed in Great Britain.

Summary of Contents

Table of Contents

Asako Nakamichi, Werner Nienhueser, Erling Rasmussen, Hiromasa Suzuki and Hiroaki Watanabe

Part III
An International Review of Key Issues 63
Greg J. Bamber, Philippe Pochet, Cameron Allan, Richard N. Block,
Frank Burchill, Joelle Cuillerier, Grant Fitzner, Ben French,
Stacy Hickox, Berndt Keller, Michael L. Moore, Sofia Murhem,
Gregor Murray, Asako Nakamichi, Werner Nienhueser, Erling Rasmussen,
Hiromasa Suzuki and Hiroaki Watanabe

Chapter 1
Work and Family 65

Notes on Guest Editors
and Lead Authors

Greg J. Bamber is Professor and Director of Research, Department of Management, Monash University (Melbourne, Australia). He has previously worked in Australia at Griffith University, the Queensland University of Technology, the University of Queensland and at the University of Durham (UK). He is a past president of the Australian and New Zealand Academy of Management and of the International Federation of Scholarly Associations of Management. He has been an arbitrator, mediator and advisor for the UK Advisory, Conciliation and Arbitration Service. He has direct experience of industrial-relations practice in many countries, especially Australia and the United Kingdom. He advises, researches and consults with international organizations, governments, employers and unions. His publications include many articles and such authored, co-authored or co-edited books as: *Militant Managers?* (Gower); *Managing Managers* (Blackwell); *Organisational Change Strategies* (Longman); *Employment Relations in the Asia-Pacific* (Allen & Unwin/Thomson); *New Technology* (Routledge); *International and Comparative Employment Relations* (Sage/Allen & Unwin); and *Up in the Air: How Airlines Can Improve Performance by Engaging their Employees* (Cornell University Press). His publications have been translated into French, German, Spanish, Indonesian, Italian, Russian, Chinese, Korean and Japanese. E-mail: GregBamber@gmail.com.

Philippe Pochet is a political scientist. He is General Director of the European Trade Union Institute (ETUI). He is an invited lecturer at the Catholic University of Louvain (Belgium) and an affiliate at the Centre of European Studies (Free University of Brussels). He is a former Adjunct Professor at Griffith University. He has published more than 250 articles and 30 edited books. His main research fields are: social impacts of the monetary union, social dimension of the European Union and social dialogue at sector and cross-sector levels, the open method of coordination and the new modes of governance, the social challenges of the globalization process and of climate change. E-mail: ppochet@etui.org.

Notes on Other Authors

Cameron Allan is an Adjunct Senior Lecturer at Griffith University. Until 2008 he worked as a Senior Lecturer in the Department of Employment Relations at the Griffith Business School at Griffith University (Brisbane, Australia). His research interests include: employment relations in the health, retail and fast food industries, management strategy, non-standard employment, workplace performance, working time arrangements, and teaching and learning in higher education. Dr Allan has been the joint recipient of several grants from the Australian Research Council. E-mail: Cameron.Allan@justice.qld.gov.au.

    Richard N. Block is Professor of Labor and Industrial Relations at Michigan State University (Michigan, USA). He has published extensively on industrial relations. Recent publications include: *Indicators of Labour Standards: An Overview and Comparison* in *Qualitative Indicators of Labour Standards: Comparative Methods and Applications*, David Kucera (ed.), Social Indicators Research Series (Springer); and *Industrial Relations in the United States and Canada* in *Global Industrial Relations*, Michael Morley, Patrick Gunnigle, and David G. Collings (eds) (Routledge). He has been a visiting faculty member at Columbia University, the University of Toronto, and the London School of Economics and Political Science. He is also an experienced labour-management neutral. E-mail: block@msu.edu.

    Frank Burchill OBE was appointed as the first Professor of Industrial Relations at the University of Keele in 1989 where he established a Centre for Industrial Relations and led the development of a full-scale Department of Human Resource Management and Industrial Relations. His research interests have been in Trade Union History and in Public Sector Industrial Relations with special emphasis on the Health Service. He has had books and articles published related to these interests, along with work on negotiating theory. Currently, he is in Australia and doing some work with the University of Tasmania. He was a leading arbitrator/mediator for ACAS; Deputy Chairman of the Central Arbitration Committee; member of the

Doctors' and Dentists' Pay Review Body; Chairman of the UK Fire and Rescue Service National Joint Council, where he chaired two industry-wide sets of partnership negotiations to successful conclusions – one in the Print Industry and one in the Paper Industry. He is currently pursuing his interests in partnership negotiations. E-mail: frank.burchill@yahoo.co.uk.

Joelle Cuillerier is completing a Master's Degree in Industrial Relations at the School of Industrial Relations, Université de Montréal, Canada. She holds a BA from the University of Ottawa. Her main interests focus on union organizing and renewal with reference to the retail sector. She is also a research assistant in the Interuniversity Research Centre on Globalization and Work (CRIMT). E-mail: joelle.cuillerier@umontreal.ca.

Grant Fitzner is Chief Analyst and Chief Economist at the UK Department for Communities and Local Government. He was formerly Director of Employment Market Analysis and Research at the UK Department for Business, Innovation and Skills. He has worked as a senior economist and currency strategist with HSBC, as a senior economist and policy analyst for the Australian government, and as principal researcher for a labour movement think tank. His interests include: the quality of work, job satisfaction, flexible working, unions and discrimination at work. E-mail: grant.fitzner@communities.gsi.gov.uk.

Ben French, LLB (Hons), B Bus (IR Major) (Griffith University), Grad. Dip. Legal Practice (Queensland University of Technology), is admitted as a solicitor in the state of Queensland, Australia, and teaches Equal Employment Opportunity Law and Employment Relations Law at Griffith University. His current research interests include: workplace relations law in Australia and disability discrimination law. E-mail: B.French@griffith.edu.au.

Stacy Hickox attended the School of Industrial and Labour Relations at Cornell University (New York, USA) and received her law degree from the University of Pennsylvania. She is currently an Assistant Professor in the School of Labour and Industrial Relations at Michigan State University. Prior to going to SLIR she practiced disability law at Michigan Protection and Advocacy Service. She also taught employment law and disability law for several years at MSU's law school. She has written a book on the Americans with Disabilities Act as well as several law review articles on employment law. E-mail: hickoxs@msu.edu.

Berndt Keller has a PhD (University of Bochum, Germany), a post-doc. (University of California, Berkeley), and Habilitation (University of Essen). He is Professor of Employment Relations, Faculty of Public Policy and Management at the University of Konstanz (Germany). He is co-editor of *Industrielle Beziehungen*, the German journal of industrial relations, associate editor of *Journal of Industrial Relations*, and a member of the executive committee of the International Industrial Relations Association (IIRA). His research interests include: public sector industrial relations, employment relations in the European Union, patterns of atypical employment/contingent work, and flexicurity mergers. E-mail: Berndt. Karl.Keller@uni-konstanz.de.

Michael L. Moore is Professor of Human Resources and Compensation, School of Labour and Industrial Relations, Michigan State University. He has published extensively, including: Hoshin Kanri Planning: The Five Alignments of the Toyota Production System in the *International Journal of Business Innovation and Research* and A Brownfield Conversion: A Case Study of Opel Belgium in the *International Journal of Productivity and Quality Management*. He has been a visiting professor at Griffith University, Australia, the University of Pretoria, S.A. and Thammasat University, Thailand. Prof. Moore is an experienced consultant in the private and public sector. E-mail: mooremm@msu.edu.

Sofia Murhem is an Associate Professor in the Department of Economic History, Uppsala University, Sweden. Her publications include: *Turning to Europe: A New Swedish Industrial Relations Regime in the 1990s*. Uppsala: Acta Universitatis Upsaliensis. Uppsala Studies in Economic History (diss.); *Les petites entreprises et la production des normes sociales, une comparaison Allemagne, France, Suède* (PIE-Lang); *Implementation of the Sectoral Social Dialogue in Sweden*, in Dufresne, A., Degryse, C. and Pochet, P. (eds.), The European Sectoral Social Dialogue. Actors, Developments and Challenges (PIE-Peter Lang); *European Integration and Nordic Trade Unions*, Götz, N. (ed.) (Routledge); *Swedish Trade Unions and European Sector-Level Industrial Relations – Goals and Strategies*; *EU Industrial Relations v. National Industrial Relations: Comparative and Interdisciplinary Perspectives*, Rönnmar, Mia (ed.), Kluwer Law. E-mail: sofia.murhem@ekhist.uu.se.

Gregor Murray is Director of the Interuniversity Research Centre on Globalization and Work (CRIMT – Université de Montréal, Université Laval, HEC Montreal <www.crimt.org>), Professor in the School of Industrial Relations at the University of Montreal, and Canada Research Chair on Globalization and Work. CRIMT is pursuing an interdisciplinary research program, involving more than seventy researchers internationally, on the challenges of globalization for work and employment. His work focuses on workplace organization, trade unionism, multinational firms, globalization and citizenship at work. His publications include: *La représentation syndicale; Le droit et les syndicats*; *The Social Regulation of the Global Firm*; *L'organisation de la production et du travail: vers un nouveau modèle*; *Work and Employment Relations in the High-Performance Workplace*; and *L'état des relations professionnelles* ('The State of Industrial Relations'). E-mail: gregor.murray@umontreal.ca.

Asako Nakamichi is a Research Associate at the Institute for Research in Business Administration, Waseda University. Educated in Japan (Tsukuba University) and in the US, she holds a Master's Degree in Law and Diplomacy from the Fletcher School of Tufts University (Massachusetts, USA). She is currently conducting research on skills and career development of temporary agency workers in France and Japan and on human resources management issues in Japanese call centres. Her recent publications include: Vocational Training toward Temporary Agency Workers in France, in *The Japanese Journal of Labour Studies* (*Furansu ni okeru hakenshain heno shokugyonouryoku kaihatsushien no torikumi, Nihon Rodo Kenkyu Zasshi*, Vol. 51 January 2009), Career Development through Temporary Agency Work (Call Center Operators), in *Research Paper Series, Department of Research on the Staffing Industry, Institute of Social Science*, University of Tokyo, July 2009, No. 14. E-mail: anakamichi@aoni.waseda.jp.

Werner Nienhueser has a PhD and a Habilitation (University of Paderborn, Germany). He has worked at the University of Mannheim and University Paderborn, at the German Research Foundation (DFG), and at the University of Konstanz. He is currently Professor of Business Administration and Human Resource Management, Department of Economics, University of Duisburg-Essen. He is co-editor of *Zeitschrift für Personalforschung*, the German human resource management journal. He is a member of the editorial board of *Management Revue* and *Industrielle Beziehungen*, the German journal of industrial relations. He is a member of the International Industrial Relations Association (IIRA). His research interests include: human resource management strategies, political theories of employment policies, patterns of atypical employment/contingent work – in particular temporary agency work. His recent publications include: 'Effects of the "Principle of Non-Discrimination" on Temporary Agency Work – Compensation and Working Conditions of Temporary Agency Workers in 15 European Countries' in the *Industrial Relations Journal*, 2006, Vol. 37, No. 1, Wenzel Matiaske (ed.); 'Flexible Work – Atypical Work – Precarious Work', *Management Review*, Special Issue, Vol. 16, No. 3. München, Mering 2005. E-mail: werner.nienhueser@ uni-due.de.

Erling Rasmussen PhD joined the Department of Management, Auckland University of Technology (AUT), New Zealand, as Professor of Work and Employment in 2007, after a career in academia and the public and private sectors. His teaching and research interests lie in the field of New Zealand and comparative employment relations, with a special interest in the effects of public policy changes. Besides being the co-author of New Zealand's leading textbooks on employment relations (see <www.employment.org.nz>), he is also the editor of the *New Zealand Journal of Employment Relations* (see <www.nzjournal.org.nz>), and is a former President of the Association of Industrial Relations Academics in Australia and New Zealand (AIRAANZ). E-mail: erling.rasmussen@aut.ac.nz.

Hiromasa Suzuki is Professor of Labour Economics at Waseda University's School of Commerce, Japan. He was educated at Waseda University, School of Economics and Political Sciences, and holds a doctoral degree from the University of Rouen, France. From to 1970 to 1986 he worked for the ILO, Geneva, mostly in the Industrial Relations Branch. He was appointed to his current position in 1986. His main focus of research lies in international comparison of employment, working time and industrial relations, in particular in the EU, East Asia and Japan. His recent publications include: *Ajia no shakaiteki hatten to shakaiteki taiwa* ('Social Development and Social Dialogue in Asia'); *Nihon hyouronsha, 2002* ('Changing Employment Relations in four East Asian Countries') Waseda Business and Economic Studies, No. 40. 2004; '*Senshinkoku no koyo senryaku*' ('Employment strategies in developed countries') in *Korekarano koyo senryaku* ('Towards a future employment strategy'), Japan Institute for Labour Policy and Training, 2007. E-mail: masa-suzuki@mbd.ocn.ne.jp.

Hiroaki Watanabe is a Senior Researcher at the Japan Institute for Labour Policy and Training. He excels in investigating labour issues in the field.

His current research covers a wide area of employment, including issues of atypical workers, distressed regions and foreign workers. His recent publications are: 'Gaibu jinzaino katsuyou no kakudai' ('Increasing recourse to external human resources'), *Japan Labour Review*, No.526, May 2004, and 'Gaikokujin roudousha' ('Foreign workers'), *Japan Labour Review*, No.531, October 2004. E-mail: hwata@jil.go.jp.

Acknowledgements

We express thanks to all the authors who are named on the title page. The volume also draws on various other sources and commentary. Therefore, the colleagues mentioned are not necessarily responsible for all of the content that relates to their jurisdictions.

We also appreciate various forms of help from many other people, including: Gerardo De Liseo, Sharon Ford, Anthony Gould, Paul Grieve, Eileen Hoffman, Nina Jaffe, Mark Mourell, David Prior, Penny Sara, Liz Todhunter, Gayathri Viswanathan, Wiebke Warneck, Lucy Yarrington and several members of the Australian Public Service; the original version of this project was commissioned by the Australian government. We also thank our current colleagues. Because it is not practicable to thank our various university colleagues individually, we are grateful to those at Griffith University, Australia and Monash University, Australia and the European Trade Union Institute, Belgium, for the help they and others provided to us.

We are most grateful to Roger Blanpain, Joeri Lauwers and Ewa Szkatula who encouraged us to publish this special issue of the *Bulletin* and helped us to improve the manuscript. We acknowledge Kluwer's editorial team for their kind support in the publication of this volume.

Our greatest debt is to our partners and families, who have endured our absence for too long while we have been working on this project.

Greg Bamber   Philippe Pochet
gregbamber@gmail.com   ppochet@etui.org

April 2010

List of Abbreviations

ACAS	Advisory, Conciliation and Arbitration Service (UK)
ADEA	Age Discrimination in Employment Act (US)
ACTU	Australian Council of Trade Unions
ADA	Americans with Disabilities Act
AFL-CIO	American Federation of Labor and Congress of Industrial Organizations
AFPC	Australian Fair Pay Commission
AHRC	Australian Human Rights Commission
AIRC	Australian Industrial Relations Commission
ALP	Australian Labor Party
ALRA	Association of Labor Relations Agencies (US & Canada)
APEC	Asia-Pacific Economic Cooperation
AWA	Australian Workplace Agreement
BCA	Business Council of Australia
BERR	Department of Business, Enterprise and Regulatory Reform (UK)
BIS	Department of Business, Innovation and Skills (UK)
BLS	Bureau of Labor Statistics (US)
BPIF	British Printing Industries' Federation
CAC	Central Arbitration Committee (UK)
CBA	Collective Bargaining Agreement
CBI	Confederation of British Industry
CEEP	European Centre of Employers and Enterprises providing Public services
CIPD	Chartered Institute of Personnel and Development (UK)
CME	Coordinated Market Economy
CTU	Council of Trade Unions (NZ)
DME	Developed Market Economy

EC	European Community
ECJ	European Court of Justice
EEOC	Equal Employment Opportunity Commission (US)
EEF	Engineering Employers' Federation (UK)
EES	European Employment Strategy
EFCA	Employee Free Choice Act (US)
EFO	European Federal Organisations
EHRC	Equality and Human Rights Commission (UK)
EMA	Employers and Manufacturers Association (New Zealand)
EPA	Equal Pay Act (US)
ETUC	European Trade Union Confederation
EU	European Union
Eurofound	European Foundation for the Improvement of Living and Working Conditions
EWCs	European Works Councils
FLRA	Federal Labor Relations Authority (US)
FLSA	Fair Labor Standards Act (US)
FMCS	Federal Mediation and Conciliation Service (US)
FMLA	Family Medical Leave Act (US)
FMW	Federal Minimum Wage
FWA	Fair Work Australia
FW Act	Fair Work Act 2009 (Australia)
FWO	Fair Work Ombudsman
HR	Human Resources
HRPA	Human Resources Policy Association
HSE Act	Health and Safety in Employment Act (New Zealand)
ILO	International Labour Organisation
IR	Industrial Relations
ITEA	Individual Transitional Employment Agreement (Australia)
JBF	Japan Business Federation
JCCs	Joint Consultative Committees (UK)
LDE	Less Developed Economy
LMC	Labour-Management Committee
LPC	Low Pay Commission (UK)
LSL	Labor Standards Law (Japan)
NES	National Employment Standards (Australia)
NLRA	National Labor Relations Act (US)
NLRB	National Labor Relations Board (US)
NMW	National Minimum Wage (UK)
OECD	Organization for Economic Cooperation and Development
OHS	Occupational Health and Safety
OML	Ordinary Maternity Leave (UK)
OSCAR	Out of School Childcare and Recreation
PPP	Purchasing Power Parity
PSA	Personal-Service-Agentur (Germany)

SAP	Statutory Adoption Pay (UK)
SE	*Societas Europaea* (European Company)
SMP	Statutory Maternity Pay
SPP	Statutory Paternity Pay
TOIL	Time-off-in-lieu
TUC	Trades Union Congress (UK)
UEAPME	European Association of Craft, Small and Medium-Sized Enterprises (EU)
UNICE	Union of Industrial and Employers' Confederation of Europe (EU)
WA	Workplace Authority (Australia)
WARN	Worker Adjustment and Retraining Notification Act (US)
WHD	Department of Labor's Wage and Hour Division (US)
WRA	Workplace Relations Act 1996 (Australia)

Preface

The objective of this special *Bulletin of Comparative Labour Relations* volume is to compare international information on important aspects of work, employment relations and labour law in various jurisdictions: the European Union (especially Germany, Sweden and the United Kingdom), Japan, the United States, Canada, Australia and New Zealand. These jurisdictions include a range of different types of industrial relations systems, forms of regulation and cultures.

This volume aims to contribute to the literature on and knowledge of international and comparative employment relations and labour law. It addresses key aspects of the regulation of employment relations and legislation that are topical in most jurisdictions: work and family provisions; individual agreements; forms of engagement; minimum wages and conditions; working hours; paid leave entitlements; employment protection; dispute settlement procedures; freedom of association and representative organizations; collective bargaining and industrial action. Each of these topics is the subject of a separate chapter.

The information gathered here provides an overview of these systems as a first step in understanding recent developments in these jurisdictions. A few tables summarizing and comparing the jurisdictions illustrate general trends and broad differences. Due to the differences in the data between jurisdictions (e.g., definitions and methodologies), the information is not always fully comparable and each table should be interpreted cautiously. We do not repeat such caveats, but they apply throughout this volume.

The volume provides an introduction to a broad field. For definitive accounts of the regulation of employment relations in the various jurisdictions, readers should consult original primary sources from each of those jurisdictions. A selection of primary sources is included in the references. More are included in Bamber, Lansbury and Wailes.[1]

---

1. Bamber, Lansbury and Wailes, 2010.

Of the nine jurisdictions, five are federal systems. In the European Union (EU), Canada, Australia and United States the responsibilities for employment relations are shared between the federal governments and the governments of the states or provinces. Germany is also a federal state, but most of the matters pertaining to the domain of employment relations (apart from a recent exception of the public sector) are regulated at the federal level. A more important distinction between the countries is in terms of varieties of capitalism,[2] which we discuss in Part I.

We could characterize the United Kingdom, United States, Canada, Australia and New Zealand as liberal market economies (LMEs). These can be contrasted with Japan, Germany, and Sweden (and the EU more generally), which are more coordinated market economies (CMEs). Since the 1980s, Australia, New Zealand and the United Kingdom have experienced dramatic changes to employment relations policies as governments shifted to and from being led by centre-left to centre-right political parties.

The other countries have displayed more continuity. In Sweden collective bargaining still covers more than 90% of the workers and is a central element to labour-market regulation. Lifetime employment with long-term commitments, remain key elements, at least for core employees in the Japanese system, even though more flexibility has been introduced. In Germany, although sector negotiations still prevail, there is more flexibility in terms of company specific contracts than hitherto. The United States is much less collectively regulated than in the immediate post-World War II period. The EU still has only a limited supranational jurisdiction, but its influence is growing. This paradox can be explained, first, by the fact that in most Member States there has been a trend towards deregulation, which has increased the importance of the minimum standards adopted at the EU level in the 1980s and 1990s; and second, this reflects that the EU has been a pioneer in legislating in new domains (e.g., equality between men and women, anti-discrimination and stress at work).

As the Canadian contributors to this volume, Gregor Murray and Joelle Cuillerier, put it:

> The workplace has changed significantly over the past decades and the pace of change appears to be ever accelerating. New information and communications technologies, the increasing internationalisation of the production of goods and services, a revolution in the management of production and work organisation, the dislocation and relocation of workplaces across both time and space and the multiplication and fragmentation of individual and collective social identities in and beyond the workplace are just some of the factors driving these changes. The extent of change, moreover, leads to an increasing 'disconnect' between, on the one hand, the prevailing institutional framework

---

2. Hall & Soskice, 2001; Dore, 2000.

for work and employment and the sets of assumptions that informed it, and, on the other hand, these current changes sweeping the world of work.

As this volume elaborates, public policy-makers and the employment relations partners are playing on contested terrain. At the same time, they try to accommodate each others' interests in the face of continuity and change in a world that is confronting increasing globalization in the aftermath of a global financial crisis.

This issue of the *Bulletin of Comparative Labour Relations* includes three parts. Part I is an introductory part by Greg Bamber and Philippe Pochet: 'Frameworks for Internationally Comparative Analysis'. This revisits important theoretical debates, for example, those about convergence, divergence and the varieties of capitalism. This discussion is important even though we do not select one best approach. Because this issue of the *Bulletin* deals with various countries from different continents, it is helpful to consider such theoretical frameworks that help us to comprehend the various processes of the different national systems. However those who are not interested in such theory may wish to proceed directly to Part II.

After examining recent changes in employment relations and related issues, Part II summarizes the main actors, the structure of collective bargaining and a few future challenges. This includes chapters that summarize the employment relations situation and context in each of the jurisdictions that this volume focuses on. Part III includes ten chapters comparing the main forms of individual and collective rights in each of these jurisdictions.

Currencies are specific to each context; for example, in sections that refer to Australia, the currency cited is Australian dollars, whereas in sections relating to the United States of America, the currency cited is United States dollars, and so on.

Part I

Frameworks for Internationally Comparative Analysis

Greg J. Bamber and Philippe Pochet

The jurisdictions that this volume focuses on are Germany, Sweden, Japan and the European Union more generally, as well as the United States, United Kingdom, Canada, Australia and New Zealand. These jurisdictions are characterized by a diversity of employment relations systems.

Comparative analysis of employment relations and labour law is challenging.[3] Each country has a particular historical legacy of institutions, procedures and customs. Particular policies and practices have to be understood in their historical and political-economy context ('path dependency') and in relation to the actors' strategies as well as the domestic and supranational institutions. Moreover, national systems are not static: External circumstances and internal factors contribute to and help to induce change. Several theories have been suggested to help understand the dynamics of comparative employment relations. Some scholars have revisited debates about the old convergence thesis under the label of 'varieties of capitalism'. The convergence thesis was also rejuvenated by the apparently increasing pace of globalization and of the apparent strength of deregulated capitalist economies in recent years (at least before the post-2008 global financial crisis). However, there are powerful arguments that such developed market economies (DMEs) as Japan and Germany[4] are still quite different from those such as the United States and United Kingdom.

---

3. Bamber, Wailes & Lansbury, 2010, Ch. 1; Blanpain, 2010.
4. Dore, 2000.

Arguments about the different varieties of capitalism and their strengths and weaknesses involve several academic communities (including political economists, political scientists, sociologists as well as international business and employment relations specialists). In this part, we review several approaches to considering varieties of capitalism. We distinguish between such possibilities as bipolarization between coordinated and uncoordinated ideal types, clustering around several models; and hybridization within each cluster. We start, however, by revisiting the convergence and divergence debates.

1.   DEBATES ABOUT
            CONVERGENCE AND DIVERGENCE[5]

When we consider questions of convergence and divergence, we should bear in mind that there are at least three different, but interrelated, levels of analysis. The first is the national level, which is shaped by national institutions and their supposed complementarities. Often, the comparison is between the performances of the various countries. The second level is the industry (sector). Each economic sector has its own characteristics; working in the steel industry is different from working in a bank or public sector. Such differences could be attributed more to the specificity of the sector than to the institutional infrastructure of a country. Third, the scope and the form of the enterprise – small and medium enterprise (SME), national, multinational, transnational and so on – are also important. These three levels are not all independent. There are linkages between the national, sector and enterprise levels, and the sector and type of enterprise in a particular country.

In most of the suggested typologies, employment relations are a key variable. To what extent are there useful typologies of the variety of employment relations systems? We begin by reviewing the convergence arguments.

1.1.   CONVERGENCE

The convergence thesis was developed in several branches of the social sciences in the post-1945 period. The proposition is that there is a tendency for technological and market forces to push national systems towards uniformity or 'convergence'. This proposition is based on the *logic of industrialism*. As more societies adopt industrial forms of production and organization, this creates 'common characteristics and imperatives' across these societies. Kerr et al.[6] applied this approach to employment relations. To accommodate these imperatives, Kerr et al.[7] argue that industrial societies had to cultivate a means of developing employment relations systems that embodied the 'principles of pluralistic industrialism', which, in turn,

---

5. For a more detailed discussion, see Bamber, Lansbury & Wailes, (2010)
6. Kerr et al., 1960.
7. *Ibid.*, 384–392.

played a central role in establishing consensus. They concede that total convergence is unlikely because of the persistence of political, social, cultural and ideological differences. Nevertheless, while these authors acknowledge that there were factors that could mediate the relationship between industrialism and the particular institutions that developed – including the timing of development and the nature of the modernizing elite – they also argue that the logic of industrialism tended to override these sources of difference and would produce convergence on a particular set of institutional arrangements of labour-market regulation.

This tradition is mirrored by discussions of modern capitalism, which, in turn, tend to suggest a convergence process at a broad level towards a political-economy model based on mixed public and private ownership, strong planning activities and neo-corporatist institutions.[8] It is relevant that these debates were taking place in a period when there was a 'cold war' between the United States and the Soviet Union and their allies and a conflict of ideologies promoted by the Western powers and the Eastern bloc.

Piore[9] doubts that the convergence thesis is a general theory. He observes that certain aspects of industrial societies tend to converge while others diverge, depending upon time and circumstances. An alternative approach, he suggests, is to focus on the role of regulatory institutions in the employment relations of different societies. He argues that capitalist economies pass through a series of regulatory systems in the course of their historical development. As technology and industry change, they outgrow the regulatory structures initially adopted, and the system is increasingly likely to remain in some kind of equilibrium. The result is an economic and social crisis that is settled only by the development of a new set of institutions.

Others question the basic assumption that common pressures will lead to common results. Even though there may be strong pressures associated with industrialism, this does not necessarily imply that there would be convergence on a single set of societal institutions, much less on a single set of institutions that resemble those that had developed in the United States.[10] Common pressures are mediated by national institutions and trajectories (path dependency). The pressures could be similar, but the outcomes may be different.

Kerr later modifies his views to take into account some of these criticisms.[11] He argues that convergence is a tendency that is not likely to precipitate identical systems among industrialized countries. He emphasizes that industrialization on a world scale is never likely to be total because the barriers to it in many less-developed economies (LDEs) are insurmountable. Nevertheless, he still holds to the central assumptions of the original study: that the basic tensions inherent in the

---

8. E.g., Shonfield, 1965; Galbraith, 1967.
9. Piore, 1981.
10. Berger, 1996, 2–4.
11. Kerr, 1983.

process of industrialization had been overcome by modern industrial societies and that there would be a growing consensus around liberal-democratic institutions and the pluralist mixed economy.

Since the collapse of the Soviet Union, the emphasis on globalization and continuing technological change induced a renewed interest in the convergence thesis, albeit one in a neo-liberal/financial paradigm. Among the factors leading to convergence, there has arguably been an increase in the international flows of information and capital, with more attention on shareholders' short-term interests and less emphasis on the longer-term horizon of patient capital (from the banks). Shareholders' short-term interests are strongly influencing managerial and corporate behaviour. The financial markets, including the stock exchanges and private equity are key players of this convergence process.

Again, there are two versions of convergence. The simplest is the total convergence towards a complete de-institutionalization and the apparent supremacy of market forces. The second is an inversion of the institutional hierarchy. The French school of regulation argued that the post-war (Keynesian) institutions were dominated by considerations of labour markets and wage costs. The more recent context is dominated by considerations of capital markets and finance, which tend to determine the relations between the institutions.[12] Similar criticisms apply to this post-1990 globalization thesis as applied to the earlier logic-of-industrialization convergence thesis.

1.2.   DIVERGENCE

Several studies suggest that rather than convergence, there is continuing divergence. Goldthorpe[13] argues that, far from converging, DMEs have followed divergent paths. On the one hand, there are countries in Europe like Sweden, Norway, Germany and Austria where inequalities between capital and labour have been mitigated by neo-corporatist institutions and state public policies. Such countries seek to balance, to a degree, the interests of employers, workers and the state. In the 1980s Japan also attracted a lot of attention at the micro-plant level[14] and also at the macro-level.[15] It was the success of the Japanese economy and of a series of leading firms that prompted a re-launch of debates about different forms of capitalism.

What explains the continuing diversity? We will discuss three approaches: the varieties of capitalism approach, the cluster approach, and, third, the hybridization and internal diversity approach.

---

12. E.g., Aglietta & Berrebi, 2006.
13. Goldthorpe, 1984.
14. E.g., on Toyotaism, see Womack et al., 1990; corporate governance, Gospel & Pendelton, 2005.
15. E.g., the interaction between different institutions; Dore, 2000.

4

2. VARIETIES OF CAPITALISM

What is the 'best' form of capitalism in the face of increasing international competition, at the micro-level (firms) and at the macro-level?[16] A catalyst to the debate was the book by Albert,[17] which distinguishes between two 'ideal types' (Rhineland and Anglo-Saxon). Hall and Soskice[18] elaborate a parallel distinction between 'LMEs' and 'CMEs' as two ideal types. The authors present ideal types and not precise designs for real national institutions. An ideal type is formed from characteristics of a given phenomenon, but it does not necessarily correspond to all of the characteristics of any particular case. Following Max Weber, an ideal type is a logical construct. It used to help us to understand and explain reality by selecting and accentuating certain elements of it.

Proponents of the varieties of capitalism approach argue against the notion of convergence and assert that there is more than one path to economic success; that it is not inevitable that CMEs will converge to a single Anglophone model. They take into consideration four dimensions: corporate governance, education and training, employment relations and inter-company relations (the governance system between companies). We can characterize the Anglophone countries (United States, United Kingdom, Canada, Australia and New Zealand) as LMEs. These can be contrasted with the CMEs (Japan, Germany, Sweden and most of the EU's institutions, more generally). Hall and Gingerich[19] support the varieties of capitalism thesis by using statistical analysis. Nevertheless, the thesis is still debatable. Kenworthy[20] arrives at different conclusions.

Focusing specifically on labour-market institutions, Freeman[21] questions the notion of a one best-practice approach compared with diversified forms of capitalism and the differing impacts in terms of economic performance. Such approaches conclude that the market is not the only efficient coordinating mechanism. They tend to argue that different configurations could reach similar results in terms of economic efficiency.

As Thelen and Kume[22] emphasize, 'Much of the writing in the varieties of capitalism literature[23] is based on a stylized and highly composite (national level) picture of employers' interests. In this literature, employers (at least within a given country) in CMEs are seen as having 'invested' in various institutions (e.g., wage-bargaining institutions), and from this it follows that they have an interest in maintaining these institutions, for instance, as the locus within which they can continue to coordinate among themselves, 'to the benefit of all'.[24]

---

16. Dore, 2000; Sopart, 2005.
17. Albert, 1991.
18. Hall and Soskice, 2001.
19. Hall & Gingerich, 2004.
20. Kenworthy, 2006.
21. Freeman, 2000.
22. Thelen & Kume, 2006.
23. E.g., Hall & Soskice, 2001.
24. Thelen & Kume, 2006, 13–14.

Thelen and Kume's study shows, on the contrary, that there is growing sector diversity, with some sectors having increased coordination and others moving in the opposite direction.[25] Further, Morgan and Kubo[26] distinguish the societal, sector, firm and individual levels of analysis, which reveal disjunctures or loosening of linkages both within and between the levels of analysis.

2.1.   CLUSTERING

Another criticism of the varieties of capitalism approach is that it includes only two poles. Pontusson[27] analyses differences between the Nordic countries and Germany, while Schmidt[28] reminds us that we can see at least one other variety of capitalism, a statist one (e.g., France, South Korea and to a lesser extent, Italy). Perhaps this category could also encompass developmental states, which are often apparent in newly industrializing economies. There are at least three possible coordination mechanisms (the market, the employers, the state).

A second stream of criticism focuses on the usefulness of having only a limited number of variables. Most of the countries' practices are far from the ideal types and the diversity of institutional complementarities could be lost. Whitley,[29] for instance, analyses business models with more variables; he considers eight aspects: the means of ownership control, the extent of integration of supply chains, the extent of integration of industrial sectors, the extent of alliance coordination of supply chain, the extent of coordination between sectors, the extent of employer-employee interdependence, the extent of delegation and the trust accorded to employees. Whitley distinguishes between six types of business models: fragmented, coordinated industrial district, compartmentalized, state-organized, collaborative and highly coordinated. Such an approach is valuable, but its degree of sophistication implies that each case seems to represent a particular type. Because Whitley focused on Asian countries (Taiwan and South Korea rather than Italy or France), his cases are more unusual. He also finds more diversity, because he uses more variables.

Others use statistical tools to delineate different clusters. Amable[30] first constructs a typology based on five domains: product-market competition, wage-labour nexus, finance and corporate governance, welfare state and education. Second, he conducts a statistical analysis (initially for each dimension and then regrouping all dimensions). The analysis confirms his typology so he proposes five models of political economy: a market-based, a social-democratic, a continental European model, a Mediterranean one, and an Asian model (Japan and Korea).

---

25. See also, Jacoby, 2005.
26. Morgan & Kubo, 2005.
27. Pontusson, 2005.
28. Schmidt, 2002.
29. Whitley, 1999.
30. Amable, 2003.

Other authors suggest broadly similar *clusters*. Cartapanis et al.[31] also use a statistical approach (principal component analysis and a hierarchical clustering method) to classify the ten transition-economy members of the EU. Their analysis tends to confirm the three types of welfare capitalism posited by Esping-Andersen[32] together with a fourth world (Southern Europe) as proposed by Fererra.[33] Begg et al.[34] present a typology of employment regimes, similar to that of the welfare-state. Other studies also confirm the prevalence of these four clusters for countries of Western Europe when focusing on different themes such as forms of work organization,[35] flexicurity policies[36] or employment quality.[37]

The notion of clustering is appealing, not least because it allows for much more diversity than the earlier, simpler approaches. Clustering is also a way to reduce the complexity and to consider specific institutional complementarities. Nevertheless a limitation of clustering is that, whereas it seems to make sense for most of the EU countries plus the Anglophone DMEs, it does not make as much sense for the range of newly industrializing economies, including the transition-economy members of the EU, and Asian countries. Therefore, the proponents of this approach try to assimilate emerging cases with the old categories (e.g., France and Korea, Italy and Taiwan) or to create ad hoc categories, for instance, for Asian countries or the EU's transition-economy Member States.

2.2.   HYBRIDITY AND INTERNAL DIVERSITY

Poole[38] identifies several factors, which operate in most DMEs to induce structural change, but holds that these are leading to diverse outcomes or 'divergent evolutionary trajectories'. This situation reflects the growing diversity in the use of technology and the structure of work organization. The trend has been described as an 'explosion' with different strands of development moving away from each other in different directions as opposed to 'implosive' convergence towards a single concept of 'best practice'.

One criticism of the national-model concept is highlighted by considering intra-national differences between sectors or industries. For example, Katz and Darbishire[39] examine six countries and conclude that there is increased diversity of employment patterns across the countries studied. They call this 'converging on divergence' and argue that it is characterized by the spread of four employment patterns: low wage, human resource management (HRM), Japanese-oriented and

31. Cartapanis, Koulinsky & Richez, 2005.
32. Esping-Andersen, 1990.
33. Fererra, 1996.
34. Begg et al., 1991.
35. Lorenz & Valeyre, 2005.
36. Tangian, 2005.
37. Davoine & Erhel, 2006.
38. Poole, 1986.
39. Katz & Darbishire, 2000.

joint team based. However, they also note differences in the distribution of these patterns between countries as well as within countries. In particular, they argue that differences reflect the varying impact of national-level institutions, the degree of centralization of bargaining, the extent of similarity of processes at a decentralized level and the degree of effective coordination between decentralized bargaining structures. Some argue, however, that the empirical evidence does not support their claim that four employment patterns are spreading across all six countries.[40] It is also arguable that these employment patterns are not mutually exclusive.[41]

One explanation of the continuing diversity is that transplanted institutions may react differently with their surrounding institutions in a new context and will necessitate adaptation of those 'imported practices'.[42] Most of the studies of the supposed Americanization of Japanese and German firms show a substantial adaptation and hybridization of the role of shareholder value.[43] Such literature illustrates the coexistence of various models within countries. Those researching the introduction of 'lean production' in the car industry tend to reach similar conclusions: that there is continuing internal diversity, rather than one common model.[44]

Others have developed an actor's perspective. They show that changes in the structure of employment are tending to weaken union power. Although these changes are widespread, they are likely to have different consequences for employers, governments and unions, depending on their organizational base. Freeman[45] identifies evidence of divergent trends in union membership and density across DMEs. He points out that there is by no means a convergence towards a single model of unionism. He reminds us that although this is the principal worker institution under capitalism, unionism has developed remarkably differently among DMEs.[46] Since the 1980s union density has been maintained at high levels in the Scandinavian countries and Belgium, but has declined significantly in the United States, Australia, United Kingdom, Japan and most of the other countries.[47] Where union density is low and there is change in the structure of employment, union density is likely to decline further. By contrast, where union density is already high, it is more likely to remain stable.

Streeck and Thelen[48] have theorized institutional change by distinguishing five modes of transformation: displacement, layering, drift, conversion, exhaustion. They add two elements to the debate. First, institutionalized rules are subject to reinterpretation by the actors; collective bargaining is typically an institutionalized process in which rules are reinterpreted regularly.

40. Giles, 2000, 476; Hancke, 2001, 306; Streeck, 2001.
41. Wailes, 2000; De la Graza, 2001.
42. Deeg & Jackson, 2006.
43. Jacoby, 2005; Gospel & Pendleton, 2005.
44. Boyer & Freyssenet, 2000.
45. Freeman, 1989.
46. *Ibid.*
47. Bamber, Wailes & Lansbury, 2010.
48. Streeck & Thelen, 2005.

Their second point is institutional diversity – there might be more than one institution in the same domain in one country.[49] This reminds us that the diversity within each country may counter apparent similarities between countries. The difference between hybridization and internal diversity is that hybridization deals with only one way in which the cases may deviate from types, and it is still very close to the idea of clear, macro-level types, because it sees these as the source of hybridization.[50] The hybridization thesis could also be seen as a form of convergence theory. If all national systems become hybrid – borrowing the most efficient institutions from other jurisdictions – we should eventually have only one global hybrid. Lorenz and Valeyre, analysing organizational change in Europe based on a survey by the European Foundation, concluded: 'One way of reading the evidence . . . on organisational diversity is that hybridisation is a pervasive phenomena across European nations'.[51] They also comment that much of the variety across Europe could have resulted from building on local traditions in work organization, which offer alternative ways of achieving flexibility and cooperation.

Heterogeneity is increasing not only between, but also within, national employment relations systems. The internal diversity thesis is based on two approaches. The first focuses on the meso-level and suggests that there is not really a national model. Sectors or regions are organized in different ways. For example, the network capitalism (district) in northern Italy differs from the car industry around Turin, which differs from the paternalistic capitalism that tends to prevail in the south of Italy.

The second approach underlines the role of the transnational companies and multilevel governance. 'One consequence of the multilevel governance is the growing heterogeneity among firms within national models – in short, "models within models". For instance, in many economies regulatory reforms offer distinct sets of rules for globally-oriented firms, which firms can opt into if they desire so.'[52] Internal diversity is increasing because, to an extent, actors are able to choose which practices they will observe. There is a coexistence of different coordination principles, even in LMEs. In the United States, for example, Silicon Valley, California, has a different set of practices compared with the car industry around Detroit, Michigan.

Crouch[53] proposes that 'empirical cases should be studied, not to determine to which (singular) of a number of theoretical types they should each be allocated, but to determine which (plural) of these forms are to be found within them, in roughly what proportions, and what change over time'. This is a tough proposal, but a lofty goal to aim for.

---

49. *Ibid.*
50. Crouch, 2005, 41.
51. *Ibid.*, 2–3.
52. Deeg & Jackson 2006, 14.
53. Crouch, 2005.

3.   FUTURE CHALLENGES

Following our discussion of theories and looking forward to the empirical material in the rest of this volume, we can start to formulate a few conclusions and raise a few questions.

Convergence theory draws attention to particular trajectories (e.g., industrialism or globalization). From this study of selected countries and the EU, in terms of employment relations the two varieties-of-capitalism ideal types are recognizable: LMEs and CMEs. In terms of collective bargaining, for instance, in both varieties of capitalism, we observe a general direction of change towards more decentralization, less power for the unions and more emphasis on shareholder value. Nevertheless this trend is by no means uniform. As Jacoby[54] observes, Japan became more liberal. But the United States under President George W. Bush became more liberal than it was under President Bill Clinton. Under President Barack Obama, this trend may be reversed.

Among the LMEs, in the United States and United Kingdom labour-market institutions (for example, unions and collective bargaining) were weakened by market forces and by political action (led by President Ronald Reagan and Prime Minister Margaret Thatcher). Australia, Canada and New Zealand are also LMEs, which many people assume are similar to the United States and United Kingdom. However, at least until the latter part of the 1990s, Australia still had labour markets that were more regulated than those of the United States and United Kingdom. While the United States and Australia became more liberal in the early years of the twenty-first century, Canada did not rush down this path and New Zealand reversed some of its earlier changes. Politicians and public policy makers have scope to make strategic choices to change institutions and the balance of power. It would appear that, within the clusters, internal diversity may be increasing.

We also observe more internal diversity among the CME cluster. Countries in the CME cluster seem to be getting less coordinated and their employment relations more flexible than before. Nevertheless, there is still an important role for governmental authorities, employers and unions in inducing and facilitating enterprises to promote good employment relations and 'decent work'.[55] We see firms in the CME cluster as more likely to be fostering 'high-road' rather than 'low-road' strategies towards employment relations. At various times the EU and most of the European CMEs have tried to adopt innovative and active labour-market policies, for example, 'flexicurity' in Denmark.[56] Such policies are less prevalent in LMEs and, when they are found, they tend to be less consistent and not as fully implemented.

---

54. Jacoby, 2005.
55. The ILO's conceptualization of decent work includes: creating jobs, guaranteeing rights at work, extending social protection, and promoting dialogue and conflict resolution with gender equality as a cross-cutting objective. See <www.ilo.org/public/english/bureau/inf/download/ecosoc/decentwork.pdf>.
56. Madsen, Due & Andersen, 2010.

Following the debates summarized earlier, we should distinguish between different levels of analysis. Although DMEs at the macro-level might appear to be similar, differences at the meso- or micro-level could be profound, as illustrated by our comparisons of collective bargaining in a few DMEs in this volume. It is important, when addressing issues of convergence/divergence, to specify the level of generality. For instance, there may be a tendency towards convergence around the idea of flexibility, active labour markets, new forms of organization or lean production. However, simultaneously, there may be diverse national, sector or enterprise policies, which remain 'path dependent'. Moreover, there may also be divergent trends from one sector to another or else in the implementation of specific measures at workplaces. Thus depending on the level chosen, there could be convergence at one level of analysis, while there is diversity around country/sector/enterprise-specific policies and also divergences at workplace level.

The internal diversity literature reminds us about the complexity of reality and the importance of institutions and the interactions between them. In other words are the different institutions aligned or are there misalignments between them? Those who seek to transplant institutions or laws to foreign contexts should bear in mind that non-complementarities between institutions can be problematic.

The clusters and ideal types of capitalism provide helpful frames of reference when evaluating approaches to employment relations in different contexts. Nonetheless, there is much scope for further research, for example, to develop additional tools of analysis that can apply to more countries. The concepts that we review in this part have generally been formulated from the perspective of a small number of DMEs. It fits the jurisdictions that we focus on in this volume. Therefore, the varieties of capitalism typology provides a valuable point of departure. However, we hope that this volume will provide a contribution towards more generally applicable theories and explanations of the international patterns of employment relations. France, Spain and Italy, for example, would seem not to fit the current varieties of capitalism typology. The only Asian country to be generally included in the varieties of capitalism literature is Japan.

Amable's[57] typology is a more sophisticated approach, which includes an Asian model but this still includes only Japan and Korea. These two countries are significant, though they represent only a tiny sample of the diverse range of Asian countries. So how are the debates about such ideal types, clusters and typologies relevant in Asia? It would be a worthwhile challenge for those of us who try to understand employment relations in Asia to try to develop better concepts, which would help us to explain Asian employment relations more satisfactorily. This is a particular challenge for at least three reasons.

First, Asia includes much more diversity than the DMEs, for instance, in terms of culture, religions, races, income levels, industry structure, and forms of political economy. Asia includes several distinct clusters of economies that are at different stages of economic development in terms of their contrasting levels of gross domestic product (GDP) per capita. For instance, Asia includes DMEs (Japan, Australia and

---

57. Amable, 2003.

New Zealand); more recently industrialized 'Asian Tigers' (Hong Kong, Singapore, South Korea and Taiwan), emerging economies (parts of China, India, Indonesia, Malaysia, Russia and Thailand) and lesser-developed economies, like Bangladesh, Pakistan, Nepal and Vietnam.[58]

Second, despite the expanding role of China, which has a Communist government, perhaps there is a greater tendency for there to be right-of-centre governments in many of the other Asian economies than in the DMEs. It is left-of-centre politicians and unions who have driven the development of the EU's social chapter and the coordination in most CMEs.

Third, in general, unions are weaker and more fragmented in Asia than they were in most of the European DMEs when the EU's institutions were being developed. Unions in most Asian economies are not well positioned to press for the inclusion of an EU-style social chapter in Asia-Pacific Economic Cooperation (APEC). Concerted union action was long constrained by a legacy of cold-war divisions between union confederations in Asia. If we consider the case of China, although unions there are changing, the notion of a union in China does not yet necessarily imply that it is an independent organization comparable to unions as we understand them in DMEs.

In terms of its economic power and its dynamism, Asia is one of the world's most important regions. The political economy and employment relations of Asia are worthy of more research and attempts at conceptualization. This process could be facilitated by drawing on lessons from, and criticisms of, various attempts to theorize about employment relations in DMEs.

---

58. Bamber & Leggett, 2001.

Part II

An International Review
of Key Jurisdictions

Greg J. Bamber, Philippe Pochet, Cameron Allan, Richard N. Block, Frank Burchill, Joelle Cuillerier, Grant Fitzner, Ben French, Stacy Hickox, Berndt Keller, Michael L. Moore, Sofia Murhem, Gregor Murray, Asako Nakamichi, Werner Nienhueser, Erling Rasmussen, Hiromasa Suzuki and Hiroaki Watanabe

In this part, we summarize the major political and economic developments; the main actors; the structure of collective bargaining; and the recent changes and future trends of Germany, Sweden, the United Kingdom, the United States, Canada, New Zealand, Australia and Japan. We start by considering the European Union (EU).

1.   EUROPEAN UNION

1.1.   MAJOR POLITICAL AND ECONOMIC DEVELOPMENTS

The EU has only limited 'competences'[59] in the social field and its main role is to support and complement the activities of the Member States. The guiding principle is the 'subsidiarity principle', which supports the role of self-regulation by the non-state actors and a decentralized approach. The EU should intervene only when the

---

59.   See <http://europa.eu/scadplus/constitution/competences_en.htm>.

action of the individual Member States is insufficient. The EU aims to foster social dialogue and partnership between employers and unions.

1.2.　　　　THE MAIN ACTORS

1.2.1.　　　EU Institutions

The EU treaty lists a series of competences that are shared between the Member States and the EU:

- improvement in particular of the working environment to protect workers' health and safety;
- working conditions;
- social security and social protection of workers;
- protection of workers when their employment contract is terminated;
- information and consultation of workers;
- representation and collective defence of the interests of workers and employers, including co-determination;
- conditions of employment for third-country nationals legally residing in the EU;
- the integration of people excluded from the labour market;
- equality between men and women with regard to labour market opportunities and treatment at work;
- combating social exclusion; and
- modernization of social protection systems.

The EU can adopt directives, with minimum requirements for gradual implementation, having regard to the conditions and technical rules that apply in each of the Member States. Such directives should avoid imposing administrative, financial and legal constraints in a way that would hold back the creation and development of small and medium-sized undertakings. Most of the directives to be transposed at national level can be adopted by 'a qualified majority' (around 70% of the weighted votes in the Council) in co-decision with the European Parliament.

1.2.2.　　　Unions

Workers are represented at the European cross-industry level by the European Trade Union Confederation (ETUC). Established in 1973, the ETUC represents eighty-two member organizations in thirty-six European countries, as well as twelve European sector-based industry federations.

1.2.3.　　　Employers

European employers are represented by three organizations: The Union of Industrial and Employers' Confederations of Europe (UNICE), established in 1958, represents forty employers' associations in thirty-four European countries. (UNICE changed its name in early 2007. It then became BusinessEurope.) The European Association of Craft, Small and Medium-Sized Enterprises (UEAPME) represents small and medium-sized enterprises and participates in the European social dialogue as part of the BusinessEurope delegation. European Centre of Employers and Enterprises providing Public services (CEEP) was formed in 1961 and includes enterprises and organizations from across Europe, both public and private, at national, regional and local levels, which are public employers or providers of services of general interest.

1.3.   STRUCTURE OF COLLECTIVE BARGAINING

The European-level cross-industry social dialogue started in the mid-1980s and has been developed considerably since then. The Maastricht and Amsterdam Treaties enabled the EU's social partners a de facto role as legislators by enabling them to conclude collective agreements, which can subsequently be transformed into directives by the EU Council of Ministers. Social dialogue is different from traditional collective bargaining at national level, for it does not cover wage bargaining.[60]

The Commission has a general duty to promote the consultation of social partners at the community level. It takes relevant measures to facilitate dialogue by ensuring balanced support for the parties. After the Lisbon treaty was adopted (December 2009), the EU institutions should support the social dialogue.

According to the EU Treaty, the procedure is as follows: Before submitting legislative proposals in the social policy field, the Commission shall consult management and labour on the possible direction of community action. If, after such consultation, the Commission considers community action advisable, it shall consult EU social partners on the content of the envisaged proposal. Social partners can submit an opinion.

Alternatively, the EU social partners can again decide to initiate a bargaining process. If so, 'the dialogue between them at community level may lead to contractual relations, including agreements. Agreements concluded at the community level shall be implemented either in accordance with the procedures and practices specific to management and labour and the Member States or ... by a Council decision on a proposal from the Commission' (Amsterdam Treaty).

When the Maastricht Treaty was adopted in 1991, the United Kingdom won an 'opt-out' in respect of social policy. In 1997, the (new) UK government belatedly endorsed the Social Policy Agreement. This has since been incorporated into the Amsterdam Treaty.

Moreover, this treaty contained a new section on European-level employment policy coordination. For the first time, the then fifteen EU Member States were obliged to see employment as a 'matter of common interest' and consequently resolved to devise coordinated job promotion strategies.[61]

---

60. Dufresne, Degryse & Pochet, 2006.
61. Zeitlin & Pochet, 2005.

In the second half of the 1990s, BusinessEurope, the ETUC and CEEP embarked on several rounds of negotiations with a view to reaching framework agreements. The first round, in 1995, was on parental leave. The second, in 1997, was on part-time work, and the third, in 1999, was on fixed-term contracts. All three of these agreements were transformed into community directives. The next attempt to reach a 'legislative' framework agreement, on temporary agency work, failed in 2001. Following that failed attempt there was a move towards 'autonomous' agreements. Such agreements are not implemented by community legislation, but by procedures and practices specific to the social partners and the Member States. An autonomous agreement on telework was signed in 2002 and another on stress at work in 2004, with a third, in 2007, on harassment and violence at work.

1.4.   CHANGES AND FUTURE TRENDS

In the EU discourse, the post-2008 global financial crisis precipitated a larger role for the social partners in an endeavour to mitigate the unemployment consequences. Two other changes merit our attention: the effects of the enlargement process and judgments of the Court of Justice. Both tend to weaken the unions.

The 2004 enlargement of ten new Member States (and later adding Bulgaria and Romania) brought much more diversity within Europe, particularly for social policies. Many of these new Member States opposed the development of a European social dimension. New structural problems arose, mainly for the social partners and for the possibility of collective bargaining as unions and employers' associations are weak in many of these countries. Collective bargaining in these countries is generally at plant level and there is no mechanism for extending agreements to the sector or national level.

The second events were the ruling of the European Court of Justice (ECJ; Viking, Laval, Rüffert and Luxembourg). For a summary and other relevant literature, see <www.etui.org/en/Headline-issues/Viking-Laval-Rueffert-Luxembourg>. There was tension between the free movement of services over issues of fundamental social rights and collective bargaining.

In 2004, Laval un Partneri, a Latvian construction company, posted workers from Latvia to refurbish a school and build an annex in Vaxholm, Sweden. The Swedish unions started negotiations with Laval to negotiate a collective agreement with regard to wages and other working conditions. The company announced that it had signed an agreement with the Latvian Building Workers' Union and it refused to sign an agreement with the relevant Swedish union. The union began a blockade of the building site, and Laval applied to the Swedish Labour Court to obtain a declaration that the blockade was illegal. The Swedish Labour Court sought a preliminary ruling from the ECJ. In December 2007, the ECJ ruled that, in the absence of a collective agreement declared to be applicable *erga omnes*, it is illegal for a union to blockade a building site to try to force a service provider established in another Member State to enter into negotiations on the rates of pay for posted workers and to sign a collective agreement with more favourable conditions than those resulting from the relevant legislative provisions. The main argument was that the freedom to provide services has to be guaranteed. If the provider had to apply all the provisions of a collective agreement, it would make it less attractive, or more difficult, for the service provider to work in another Member State. The ECJ emphasized that the Posted Workers Directive imposes an obligation on foreign providers only to respect the nucleus of working standards set out in the directive, in this case the minimum wage. The Court also emphasized the lack of certainty of the Swedish collective agreement system as the foreign enterprise is unable to know in advance all the conditions they would have to guarantee to their posted workers.

This and other related rulings had a significant impact and are considered by many observers to represent a victory for those who support liberal markets, rather than those who support more socially oriented integration.[62]

2. GERMANY

2.1. MAJOR POLITICAL AND ECONOMIC DEVELOPMENTS

At present Germany is Europe's most industrialized and populous country. Unification of the two halves of Germany in 1990 was unexpected but was a very important political event. The sudden integration of a socialist, centrally-planned economy into a capitalist, social-market economy (*soziale Marktwirtschaft*) has created long-lasting challenges for the political economy. Among others, unemployment has remained at comparatively high levels in the unified Germany, there has been migration from the east to the west, and employment relations are less institutionalized and established in the east.

After a long period of coalition governments between the Christian democrats and the Free democrats (1982–1998) political majorities changed in 1998 when a majority of Social democrats and the Greens won the general election. Between 2005 and 2009 there was a 'grand coalition government' of Christian democrats and Social democrats. Since 2009, the Christian democrats ended the previous awkward coalition with the Social democrats in favour of an alliance with the pro-business Free democrats. Changes of employment relations towards deregulation and more 'flexibility' were introduced by various governments. For example, there were significant changes in labour-market policies in 2003–2004 (*Hartz-Reformen*) that were initiated by a social democratic led government. Thus, the 'outcomes' of these policy changes cannot be attributed only to the composition of the government. There are likely to be further changes under the post-2009 coalition.

Germany was one of the founding members of the European Economic Community and its economy has become integrated into the EU. In the early 1990s the common market was completed (and included the free movement of labour as one of the fundamental liberties). In the late 1990s the European Monetary Union (EMU) was launched (and the national currencies of all participating countries

---

62. Wolfson & Sommers, 2006; Zeitlin & Pochet, 2005.

were abolished). In 2004 and 2006 the so-called eastern enlargement of the EU meant that ten new Member States joined the EU. These events have had major consequences for the development of national systems of employment relations (among others, the introduction of European Works Councils (EWCs), greater importance for social dialogues at sector and inter-professional level, the establishment of a European employment policy, and changes to national collective bargaining towards transnational coordination following the advent of the EMU).

The German collective bargaining system is still dominated by sector collective bargaining. In 2005, 41% of all establishments in western Germany and 23% of establishments in eastern Germany were covered by collective agreements. These establishments covered 67% of employees in western Germany and about 53% of employees in eastern Germany. The sector with the most comprehensive bargaining coverage is public and social insurance, whereas the lowest bargaining coverage is found in business services. In practice, however, the regulation of work and employment conditions results from an interaction between collective agreements at the sector level with works agreements at company or plant level reflecting the relative power of the social partners. Although the sector level agreements are still the most important form of collective agreements, there is an obvious tendency towards coordinated decentralization and, in some cases, even fragmentation. Between 1996 and 2005 the share of employees covered by sector collective agreements decreased by 14% in western Germany and by 25% in eastern Germany.[63] This reflects the moves towards Europeanization, globalization and greater flexibility in various ways.

2.2.   THE MAIN ACTORS

2.2.1.   Government

The government does not play an active role in the German employment relations system. The main corporate actors at the national level are the Confederation of German Employers' Associations (*Bundesvereinigung Deutscher Arbeitgeberverbände* – BDA) and the German Trade Union Federation (*Deutscher Gewerkschaftsbund* – DGB). The most important actors at sector or branch level are the Metal and Engineering Employers' Federation (EEF; *Gesamtverband der metallindustriellen Arbeitgeberverbände – Gesamtmetall*) and IG Metall (Union of Metal Industry Workers).

On the one hand, the system of employment relations has frequently been described as being highly legalized (*Verrechtlichung*); for example, all its parts are regulated by specific acts. On the other hand, the principle of bargaining autonomy (*Tarifautonomie*) is legally guaranteed and respected by all state authorities. There is no state intervention in the processes of collective bargaining. There were some attempts towards the development of corporatist forms of tripartite corporatism

---

63. WSI, 2005; Kohaut, 2007.

(concerted action in the late 1960s and 1970s, alliance for jobs in the mid- and late-1990s) but eventually these innovations failed.

Since the mid/late 1980s, governments led by the conservative as well as the social-democratic party have introduced various forms of 'deregulation' of the labour market and its institutions (among others, reduced employment protection, extension of limited contracts). Consequences of such ad hoc measures are difficult to evaluate but are usually rather limited.

In general, readers should keep in mind that Germany is a federalist state. However, in contrast to most other federalist countries, the impact of the federal states (*Bundesländer*) on the system of employment relations is limited. There are no major regional differences due to different political circumstances.

2.2.2. Unions

Since their reconstruction after World War II unions have been based on the organizational principle of industrial unionism (*Industriegewerkschaften*). Therefore, the number of unions has been low from a comparative perspective. Between the mid-1990s and the early 2000s, a wave of mergers and takeovers reduced the number of DGB-affiliates further (from sixteen to eight). By far the biggest unions are the IG Metall (about 2.3 million members) and the Unified Service Sector Union (*vereinte Dienstleistungsgewerkschaft – ver.di*) (about 2.2 million members). Together they organize almost 70% of the membership of all DGB-affiliated unions.

There was a short period of major growth after German reunification (from eight to almost 12 million members). Since the early/mid-1990s, however, unions have lost more than 30% of their members – a more significant decline than in most comparable countries. Today, density ratios are not much more than 20%. This decline has led to a major loss of financial resources and legitimacy for the unions.

In the German institutional context 'other forms of representation of workers' interests' means, of course, co-determination. The Works Constitution Act (*Betriebsverfassungsgesetz*) has been described as 'the' characteristic feature of the German system of employment relations. It defines a specific set of rights and duties, or opportunities and constraints, for employee participation in managerial decision-making. From a strictly legal point of view, works councils represent the interests of all employees independent of their membership in unions. In empirical terms, less than 60% of works councillors are members of a union. This percentage has been decreasing. The density at company level has been relatively stable over time but is only at about 50% of all employees. This makes the implementation and monitoring of collective contracts difficult for unions, especially where they do not have works councils as their agents.

2.2.3. Employers

From a comparative perspective, Germany belongs to a small group of countries that have interrelated forms of interest representation. There are general business or trade associations (*Wirtschafts- or Unternehmensverbände*) as well as specific employers' associations (*Arbeitgeberverbände*). The first group represents more general economic interests, whereas the second is responsible for social policy issues and employment relations, including collective bargaining. There is a division of labour, then, between both forms of interest representation.

Since the early/mid-1990s some employers' associations, although not business associations, have lost members. A frequent counterstrategy has been either the foundation of an alternative type of association or the development of so-called split membership within associations. In both options enterprises remain members of the associations without being obliged to stick to the collectively agreed standards of employment. It is too soon to judge whether this strategy is the solution of an old problem or will create a new problem.

2.3.   STRUCTURE OF COLLECTIVE BARGAINING

Within the dual system of employment relations, and in contrast to unified systems of employment relations, the enterprise level is separated from the sector level. Peaceful and high-trust cooperation between management and works councils at the lower level has to be distinguished from collective bargaining between unions and employers' associations, which include the options of strikes and lockouts at the upper level. Collective bargaining has usually taken place at the sector-regional level. There were few exceptions of bargaining either at the national level (among others, in the public sector) or at the enterprise level (Volkswagen being the most prominent example). In many bargaining rounds the engineering sector was the 'pattern setter', followed by most of the other sectors. Thus, there was generally a comparatively high degree of intersectional coordination.

Since the mid/late 1980s this traditional system has been changed. The trend is towards more 'flexibility' at the company level to be reached by 'coordinated decentralization' and/or 'regulated flexibility'. First, various forms of so-called opening clauses (*Öffnungsklauseln*), which allow individual companies to deviate from collective contracts under specific circumstances, have been introduced. These procedural arrangements are often used in various sectors not only for working time arrangements, but also for wages and salaries. One of their consequences is the growing importance of the company level in general, and an increasing impact of works councils, in particular.

Furthermore, enterprise specific contracts (*Firmen- or Haustarifverträge*) between unions and individual companies have increased since the mid-1990s. The practical relevance of this trend towards 'single employer bargaining' is difficult to evaluate yet. Since the early 1990s there has been a significant rise in the number of such contracts. However, they only cover a small percentage of employees (less than 10%, with higher percentages in the east than in the west).

Recent figures indicate a gradual decline in the overall rates of collective bargaining since the mid-1990s. Currently they are at an unexpectedly low level (of not much more than 60% of employees). It is arguable that German employment relations are less of a 'dual' system than often assumed. The interconnectedness between the upper, regional-sector and the lower, enterprise or company level is increasing.

Another trend, the so-called tacit escape from collective bargaining results (*stille Tarifflucht*), has to be considered. This development means that companies remain members of employers' associations but do not comply with their collective contracts even though they are legally obliged to do so. This behaviour, which is difficult to evaluate, can take place with or without the more or less tacit consent of works councils and/or unions. It is more frequent in the east than in the west.

Another relatively new form of bargaining has grown in importance. So called alliances for work and productivity (*Bündnisse für Arbeit und Wettbewerbsfähigkeit*) are negotiated at the enterprise level and are characterized by a form of quid pro quo bargaining. Certain concessions from the employees' side (the standard length of the working week, salaries, Christmas and vacation bonuses) can be met by employers' guarantees of employment security for a specified period. These enterprise-specific pacts have been of a short-term, more defensive character in times of economic slow-downs but, most recently, they have also been of a more long-term character ('productivity coalitions'). The number of pacts has significantly increased in the recent past.

As well as the specific system of co-determination as the other comparable form of job regulation, another important element is the regulation of industrial disputes, in particular the mediation system. There is a legally-based distinction between conflicts of rights (about the interpretation and enforcement of existing contracts) and conflicts of interest (about the conclusion of new collective contracts). Within the highly 'legalized' system of employment relations, all individual as well as collective conflicts of rights are settled by peaceful means. This can happen either at enterprise level by a special dispute settlement body (*Schiedsstelle* or arbitration committee) or by binding decisions of specialized labour courts at the local, federal state and state levels. There are not legally-based mediation procedures for conflicts of interest and such procedures have never been taken into consideration because they would constitute a violation of the principle of free collective bargaining (*Tarifautonomie*). There are mediation agreements (*Schlichtungsabkommen*), however, in all major sectors of the economy. These instruments of conflict resolution are not introduced by legal interference (like the state), but are agreed by the social partners on a voluntary basis. In a comparative perspective with other EU or Organization for Economic Cooperation and Development (OECD) Member States, Germany has always been characterized by a low level of industrial conflict, such as strikes and lockouts.

2.4.   CHANGES AND FUTURE TRENDS

Predictions about trends suggest that the gradual decline of the main actors and key institutions will continue, and that forms of 'disorganized' instead of 'organized' decentralization will probably become more important. The former German system of employment relations will be less integrated and less 'dual' than in the past but more heterogeneous and fragmented. Consequently, the importance of enterprise-level bargaining, and works councils as institutions of co-management, is likely to increase. The number and quality of company or enterprise agreements (*Betriebsvereinbarungen*) as more 'flexible' forms of adjustment will grow as the processes of decentralization continue.

Union density is likely to continue to decline leading to further losses (not only financial) of resources, bargaining power and legitimacy (in the eyes of the general public). There are no clear indicators at present that these trends towards de-unionization, which can be traced back to the early/mid-1990s, could be reversed in the near future. Management and employers' associations and not works councils and unions are the prime movers in employment relations. The balance of power has decisively shifted.

Differences between sectors (industrial-production versus private-service sectors) will probably increase. This development will also include a further decrease of coverage rates of collective bargaining and the importance of poorly regulated sectors will increase in quantitative as well as in qualitative terms. The so-called white spots on the collective bargaining map ('non-union' sectors) have been growing to a greater extent than formerly expected.

One characteristic feature is that Germany still has to cope with the long-lasting consequences of unification. Major differences between the old (West) and the new (East) federal states continue, even though the same legal-institutional framework has been in place in both parts of Germany since the 1990s. As mentioned in the introduction, rates of unemployment are significantly higher in the east than in the west; density ratios on 'both sides of industry' and coverage rates at company as well as at sector level are much lower in the east than in the west. The problem of the 'working poor' can no longer be ignored in certain sectors.

Co-determination or employee participation in managerial decision-making takes place at two interrelated levels. Works councils and their increasing importance at the enterprise levels have already been mentioned. At the upper (or company) level, employees' interests are represented within the governing bodies, especially the supervisory board (*Aufsichtsrat*). Germany has, in contrast to the unified structure of the Anglo-Saxon countries, a characteristic two-tiered board structure of corporate governance consisting of a management board (*Vorstand*) and a supervisory board.

After political debates and subsequent legal controversies had been settled in the 1970s, this part of the employment relations system was not controversial in the 1990s and early 2000s. More recently, however, a heated and unexpected political controversy about its impacts and 'necessary' major changes was launched by some employers' associations and their public supporters. In late 2006, a review body, which was installed by the government, recommended only minor changes in Germany's system of co-determination in its official report. Nevertheless the controversy continues. Possible decisions depend on future political majorities and the composition of the government.

The composition of the workforce with regard to employment contracts has to be taken into account if we want to predict trends and the directions of change. Since the 1980s, the so-called regular employment relationship (*Normalarbeits-verhältnis*) has lost importance. The extent of various forms of atypical employment (or contingent work) has significantly increased (regular part-time work, petty or marginal time employment, fixed-term employment/limited contracts, temporary agency work, and new self-employment). We can assume that they will continue to grow to a degree. Exact figures are difficult to estimate, but it can be conservatively calculated that these atypical groups account for about one-third of the labour force.

Changes to the legal framework (*Hartz-Reformen*) have tried to extend these forms. It is unclear if these politically motivated steps will prove to be an effective means of labour market reform and if they will increase the existing opportunities of employment or employability. It is difficult to predict the long-term consequences for the employment-related systems of social protection, especially pensions, but one consequence could be a further segmentation of labour markets.

3.   SWEDEN

3.1.   Major Political and Economic Developments

Sweden was severely affected by the international recession of the 1990s and for the first time since the 1930s depression, this caused severe unemployment. During the 1970s, when most European countries faced high unemployment, Sweden avoided this by expanding the public sector, implementing active labour- market policies and supporting industries in trouble. As a result, unemployment in Sweden was low. For example, between 1980 and 1992, less than about 2.5% of the workforce was registered as unemployed. From a European perspective, this percentage was low. However, to this percentage should be added the number of people participating in active labour-market measures. By the end of 1992, unemployment rose to 7% and to well over 10% in 1993–1995. In contrast to the 1970s, the social-democratic government launched a budget-balancing program, which meant cutbacks in the public sector instead of expansion. As part of this program, unemployment benefits were cut, from 90% of the working wage to 80% in 1993 and 75% in 1996. The benefits were restored in 1997 to 80% (up to a certain income level). Unemployment peaked in 1995–1996. In 2000–2004 unemployment was about 5%. However, the labour force diminished from 4.5 million in 1992, to 4 million in the middle of the 1990s.

The Swedish economy recovered in the late 1990s, but the labour force size did not fully recover. Until the post-2008 global financial crisis, the Swedish economy was very strong, unemployment had decreased further, and there was a shortage of labour in some sectors. During the last century and beyond, large corporations were the base of the Swedish economy. Most, such as Ericsson, are based on innovations and inventions, but there are also a few retail-based corporations, such as H&M and IKEA, and some that are based on Swedish natural resources such as timber and metals. These large corporations have been very profitable, taking advantage of the favourable global economy. The strong Swedish dependence on international exports meant that Sweden was exposed to the drop in demand in 2008. For instance, both Swedish car manufacturers, Volvo and Saab, owned by Ford and GM, respectively, were threatened by bankruptcy. The Swedish government did not support failing industries financially in the way that, for instance, the French did, but agreed to support companies if they applied for grants from the European investment bank.

The developments since 2008 have again caused high Swedish unemployment, especially affecting young people. In addition, a considerable proportion of the labour force has been on long-term sick leave or has taken early retirement. Various political measures have aimed to decrease that proportion. The right-wing government, elected in autumn 2006 has, for example, introduced tax incentives to employ people who have been long-term unemployed. This was part of an election promise, to get more people into work. Among measures introduced are tax cuts for working people and on household services, such as cleaning. The post-2008 global financial crisis has also prompted the government to expand tax cuts on household services to include repairs and construction work.

3.2. THE MAIN ACTORS

The social partners had long played an important role in Swedish political life. Unionization has been high for a long time but has declined in the twenty-first century. However, unionization in Sweden is still above 70%, and is one of the highest density levels in Europe. The drop is nevertheless dramatic and is discussed further later. The reasons for the high unionization are partly that Sweden retains the Ghent system.[64] This means that in contrast to most other countries, workers who become unemployed tend not to leave the union. There are other contributing factors as well. As in the other Nordic countries, white-collar workers, academics and the public sector are highly unionized. In addition, Swedish unions are strong, both on a central level, and on a local level. According to Swedish labour law, the unions are, in most cases, legal entities. Hence, the unions' position is strong. In fact, all employee representation is via the unions.

Swedish union organization is industry-based: All employees in an industry or branch tend to belong to the same union irrespective of their various occupations. However, there is a division between blue-collar, white-collar and professional employees. In 2009, the Swedish Trade Union Confederation

---

64. This means that the unions administer the unemployment insurance funds. The system was named after Ghent, Belgium, and Belgium still retains the system. The Ghent system was introduced in Sweden in the 1930s, and earlier in the other Nordic countries. Sweden, Denmark and Finland still maintain the Ghent system, whereas Norway has abandoned it. As a result, unionization has decreased in Norway, whereas it is still very high in Sweden, Denmark and Finland.

(*Landsorganisationen, LO*), founded in 1898, had fourteen affiliates. The largest LO unions are *Kommunal*, the Swedish Municipal Workers' Union (512,000 members) and *IF Metall* (385,000 members). In all, the LO unions have about 1,700,000 members, which is about 70% of all blue-collar workers.

White-collar workers became unionized at a later stage than blue-collar workers, and the present organization was the result of a 1941 merger: *Tjänstemännens Centralorganisation – TCO* (Swedish Confederation of Professional Employees). TCO has 16 member unions, which have about 1,200,000 members. This makes union density for white-collar employees about the same as for blue-collar employees. The largest TCO union is Unionen, whose members work in the private sector. Unionen has approximately 500,000 members. *Sveriges Akademikers Centralorganisation – SACO* (Swedish Confederation of Professional Associations), was founded in 1947, and has twenty-three member unions and almost 600,000 members.

Importantly, there is also a high density of organization in employers' associations. Swedish employers are better organized than their peers in many other countries. The reason is probably because the Swedish economy is dominated by large corporations. Also, the high degree of unionization has prompted employers to organize to a considerable extent. As for the unions, the employers' associations are also industry-based. The Swedish Employers' Confederation (*Svenska Arbetsgivareföreningen, SAF*) was founded in 1902. In 2001 SAF and *Industriförbundet*, the Federation of Swedish Industries, merged to form *Svenskt Näringsliv*, the Confederation of Swedish Enterprise. *Svenskt Näringsliv* represents 54,000 Swedish companies and consists of 50 trade and employers' association members, thereby making up for 70% of the private sector. In all, the member companies have about 1,700,000 employees.

3.3.   STRUCTURE OF COLLECTIVE BARGAINING

Many matters that are the object of legal regulation in other countries are determined in Sweden by collective agreements. For instance, there are no statutory minimum wages. Instead wages are determined by collective agreements.

According to Swedish legislation, a collective agreement is a written agreement between an employers' association or an employer and a union concerning employment conditions for employees, or the relations between the employer and the employees. Hence, collective agreements in the legal sense include both collective agreements (agreements between employers' organizations and unions) and substitute agreements (agreements between a union and an employer, which is not a member of an employers' association). If even one employee demands a collective agreement, the company has to sign. A collective or substitute agreement signed in a workplace is valid for all employees in that particular workplace, not only for the union members. However, when Swedish collective agreements are made at the enterprise level, they cannot be extended to other companies.

Although there are no comprehensive statistics on the coverage of collective agreements, we estimate that about 90% of all employees are covered by a collective or substitute agreement, ranging from about 70% in the private sector to 100% in the public sector.

During the 1990s, the problems with a decentralized bargaining process became evident, because there were relatively high wage increases in spite of high unemployment. Thus, the unions, which organized many of those unemployed, needed a way of moderating the demands for higher wages. At the same time, global competition increased, as did international interdependence and European economic integration. Hence, competitive wage levels were crucial for employers.[65] In 1996, the government demanded new models for bargaining, which would make it possible to determine wage levels that were internationally competitive; otherwise it would contemplate legislation. The unions in the manufacturing sector, which had begun to cooperate more closely, invited employers to come to a new type of agreement. The result was the Industrial Agreement,[66] *Industriavtalet*, of 1997, which meant the beginning of a new close cooperation at a sector level and a common view on economic and industrial policy. It was a new way of negotiating and mediating, and a return towards centralization, though at the sector level.[67] As the Saltsjöbaden Agreement of 1938, which laid the foundation of the well-known so-called Swedish model, and which still is the main basic agreement for the Swedish labour market, the Industrial Agreement denotes that the social partners take responsibility for the labour market without the need for government interference.

The Industrial Agreement has been a role model for other sectors of the labour market to the extent that such agreements have been made to cover most sectors, including the local- and regional-government sector. However, such agreements are missing from several important bargaining areas, including retailing, the construction and transport industries. Areas not covered by collaboration agreements can be subject to mediation from The National Mediation Office, which is an agency for central government activities in dispute settlement. Apart from mediating in labour disputes, the agency has to promote an efficient wage formation process and is responsible for public statistics on wages. The National Mediation Office was established in 2000.

In 2007 when Swedish Enterprise invited the central union organizations to begin negotiating a new general agreement more suited to the contemporary reality, attempts were made to replace the Saltsjöbaden Agreement. The Employers' Federation stated its goal was to strengthen mutual confidence between employers and employees. The reform should aim at international competitiveness as well as providing employee security and development. The agreement should include

---

65. Elvander, 2002.
66. The Agreement on Industrial Development and Wage Formation is usually abbreviated as *Industriavtalet*, the Industrial Agreement – the term that we use in this volume.
67. Elvander, 2002.

regulation of negotiations of collective agreements and industrial disputes. The aim was also to replace the law on employment protection (LAS), which employers have described as anachronistic. The unions agreed to discuss the matter but declared that industrial action and LAS were not up for discussion. Discussions began in 2008 but were not successful due to irreconcilable opinions. Although LAS has been discussed for many years, and on the agenda mainly for the employers' organizations and right-wing political parties, the right-wing coalition, elected in 2006, has declared that it does not intend to revoke LAS.

3.4.   RECENT CHANGES AND FUTURE TRENDS

Since the 1980s, the Swedish employment relations regime has changed but is still consistent with the 'Swedish model' of employment relations, at least so far. Some of these changes have been the Industrial Agreement 1997 and its successors. Other significant factors inducing change include the Europeanization or internationalization process, changes within the production processes and the reduction in union density.

The Industrial Agreement induced a re-centralization but at a sector level. In addition, new mediation procedures were launched, either in the form of agreements such as the Industrial Agreement and its successor or for those not included in those agreements, by the National Mediation Office. Attempts to renew the Saltsjöbaden Agreement and make a new basic agreement for the Swedish labour market failed in 2008. Nonetheless, the 'Swedish model' is still alive, albeit not in as healthy a state as it was in the 1950s and 1960s.

The internationalization or Europeanization, not only of employment relations, but also other aspects of political decision-making has prompted unions to change their strategies. The increasing international economic dependence has also affected employment relations, mainly through mergers with foreign companies and the increase of foreign ownership of Swedish companies. This was evident during the global financial crisis, when managers and owners may have been located far away from the employees and unions, affecting the ability of unions to influence decisions.

Structural and technological changes, sometimes called 'the third industrial revolution', have led to a rise in the importance of service-sector companies and small businesses with new production processes and more demands for flexibility. Hence, the law on employment protection has been the subject for debate but so far without result.

Perhaps the most dramatic change is that the LO union has lost 25% of its members since 1985, while TCO has lost almost 10%. The only peak organization to have gained members is SACO, whose increase is substantial – more than 50%, probably reflecting the increase of higher education in Sweden. In sum, these changes mean that Swedish unions have lost 12% of their members since 1994, or approximately 474,000 people. The decline is increasing rather than slowing. Union officials have been concerned but also self-critical. In 1996, 87% of all blue-collar workers were unionized. By 2009, the number had fallen to 71%, and for the first time, more white-collar workers were unionized: 72%. Union officials attribute the decrease in unionization to new production methods, fewer blue-collar workers and increasing costs for unemployment insurance due to government legislation. The latter was designed to make unemployment insurance costs based more on the potential risk of unemployment. The new production methods have resulted in more small companies and more temporary employment, both of which tend to be less unionized. The recession in the 1990s led to the introduction of more forms of employment, opening up the possibility of more temporary employment and employment agencies. In 1997, legislative changes allowing 'temporary employment without a cause' were introduced by the social-democratic government. Temporary employment has increased considerably in Sweden from about 10% in 1990 to about 15% in 1998; since then it seems to have stabilized.

Traditionally, blue-collar workers have been the most highly unionized category, but in the twenty-first century, there are more white-collar jobs. There is discussion about how the unions have failed to show how employees can benefit from being union members. Increasing costs for unemployment insurance, which due to the Ghent system is closely associated with union membership, have probably caused the unions to lose members. This is a change that took place after the 2006 elections, but unions began losing members long before then. In the long run, if the decline continues, it will fundamentally alter the post-1945 Swedish model of employment relations.

4.   UNITED KINGDOM

4.1.   MAJOR POLITICAL AND ECONOMIC DEVELOPMENTS

There have been important changes in UK employment relations. The post-1979 Conservative governments led by Margaret Thatcher implemented radical change in the regulation of employment relations. These changes helped to precipitate a decline in the union movement in terms of its size, shape and role in job regulation and the national polity.

The post-1997 new-Labour governments led by Tony Blair and Gordon Brown did not generally reverse Mrs Thatcher's changes. Nevertheless, the Labour governments added a foundation of minimum standards in the workplace. The main innovations are: a national minimum wage (NMW); a right not to work more than forty-eight hours a week; four weeks' paid leave; a discipline and grievance procedure (and a right to be accompanied by a union official or work colleague); a right to no-discrimination on grounds of religion, belief, sexual orientation, or age; a right to union recognition for collective bargaining in specified circumstances; equal treatment for part-time and fixed-term employees compared with their full-time colleagues; protection for public-interest disclosure (whistleblowers); paternity leave, adoption leave, parental leave and time-off for domestic emergencies; a right for parents of children up to 6 years of age to request flexible working with an obligation on employers to treat the request seriously. Earlier rights to maternity leave were extended. In terms of consultation, in 2005, employees gained new legal rights to be informed and consulted on a regular basis about developments in their workplace through the National Information and Consultation of Employees Regulations, which now apply to undertakings with fifty or more employees. This allows for employee representation through the establishment of works councils.

4.2. THE MAIN ACTORS

4.2.1. Government

The government sets employment relations policy and legislation through its Department for Business, Innovation and Skills (BIS); it was formerly called the Department of Trade and Industry. Other portfolios, notably the Department for Work and Pensions, regulate wider labour market policy. The EU and the ECJ both play a significant role in the determination of UK employment law.

The government funds several statutory agencies, which relate to the labour market. These include Employment Tribunals, the Advisory, Conciliation and Arbitration Service (ACAS), which incorporates the Central Arbitration Committee (CAC), the Low Pay Commission (LPC), the Health and Safety Commission and the Equality and Human Rights Commission (ECHR).

4.2.2. Unions

The Trades Union Congress (TUC) is the central union federation in the United Kingdom. It has sixty-six affiliated unions representing nearly 7 million working people. TUC policy is determined by its annual Congress, but between congresses this responsibility is held by its General Council, which includes leaders elected from among the TUC's affiliated unions.

4.2.3. Employers

There are national employer associations. The Confederation of British Industry (CBI) represents larger employers who affiliate through their employers' organization: for example, the Engineering Employers' Federation (the EEF), the British Printing Industries' Federation (BPIF) and others. Such associations offer support to employers on employment and related matters, and represent employers in European Federal Organisations (EFOs). There is also the Institute of Directors, which supports the professional needs of directors, the Federation of Small Businesses, and the British Chambers of Commerce (which are more concerned with trade, price and competition issues). The Chartered Institute of Personnel and Development (CIPD) supports the professional needs of human resource (HR) managers and professionals.

4.3.   STRUCTURE OF COLLECTIVE BARGAINING

Around 45% of British employees have their pay levels influenced by collective agreement.[68] Collective bargaining is much more widespread in the public sector, which contains approximately 20% of the UK labour force, and in larger workplaces and organizations. Collective bargaining coverage varies widely across different industries. Approximately 70% of public-sector employees are covered by collective bargaining with 22% of private-sector employees covered. Union membership density also varies between the sectors: It is about 16% in the private sector, 56% in the public sector; there is an average density of 28%.

The Workplace Employment Relations Surveys (WERS) research series is an invaluable source of information. WERS were conducted at roughly five-year intervals between 1980 and 2004. The sixth WERS is planned to take place in 2011. WERS show that the proportion of workplaces setting pay through collective bargaining has been in decline since the mid-1980s. In the private sector, the biggest change has been growth in the percentages of workplaces, where all pay is set by management at workplace level. However, most private-sector pay is determined at company level with the company deciding on local variations in the light of market conditions at such levels. The pay of many public-sector workers is influenced by the recommendations of national pay review bodies.

Britain has a voluntarist approach to employment relations with no national system of co-determination. Since the 1990s, government ministers and officials generally do not become involved in the settlement of industrial disputes. However, before the 1980s, there was more such involvement.

4.4.   RECENT CHANGES AND FUTURE TRENDS

British employment relations have changed greatly since the 1980s. Before the early 1980s they were characterized by robust unions engaged in collective bargaining with individual employers or employers' associations and even with workplace management. There was a considerable degree of multi-union workplace bargaining. Collective bargaining has become less fragmented with the decline in multi-unionism, the growth of single-table bargaining and the reduction in the number of unions.[69] The focus has also increasingly shifted from collective to individual employment rights in terms of employment law. Employers' associations and unions hold less sway than formerly. There is much less industrial militancy and this is usually confined to relatively small pockets of employment.

What have been the wider labour-market trends? The employment rate rose and unemployment rate fell to low levels.[70] The United Kingdom is one of the few EU members to exceed the three Lisbon employment rate targets set for 2010.

---

68. Burchill, 2008.
69. Brown et al., 2009.
70. See Dickens, Gregg & Wadsworth, 2004.

However, the global financial crisis had a bigger impact on the United Kingdom than most other countries. This crisis induced an increase in unemployment in 2009.

Women's labour force participation has risen strongly, and the gender pay gap narrowed. Part-time work is much more widespread, especially among women. The proportion of workers who are foreign-born has risen to account for one in eight of the British workforce. Likewise, there has been a steady increase in those from non-Caucasian ethnic minority backgrounds. Whereas in the 1980s, policy-makers saw early retirement as a possible counter to high unemployment, in the twenty-first century they are encouraging later retirement.

The trend towards individualization of employment relations is likely to continue. There are also signs of growing public concern over vulnerable workers, and efforts to achieve more effective compliance with and enforcement of employment law can be expected. Concerns about work-life balance and equality and diversity at work will continue, along with greater awareness of the importance of health and well-being at work. Migration and the need to improve the skills of the workforce will likely remain as major policy focuses.

5.   UNITED STATES OF AMERICA

5.1.   MAJOR POLITICAL AND ECONOMIC DEVELOPMENTS

From 1980 through 2008, the major political trend in the United States was a narrowing of the role of the government in regulating economic activity, including employment relations. The centre-right Republican Party, which generally supports limiting government involvement in the economy, was successful in five presidential elections: 1980, 1984, 1988, 2000, and 2004. This Republican success was interrupted only in 1992 and 1996. This is in contrast to the period from 1932 to 1980, when the New Deal/Post-Great Depression legacy of government involvement in the economy was dominant. During that period, the centre-left Democratic Party won eight presidential elections, whereas the Republican Party won only four.

Congress, the bicameral legislative branch, shows similar trends. From 1933 through 1980, the Democratic Party controlled both houses of Congress for forty-four years, whereas the Republican Party controlled both houses for only four years. From 1981 through 2006, however, the Republican Party controlled both houses for ten years, whereas the Democratic Party controlled both houses for eight years. The houses were split for eight years.

Starting in 2007, however, the Democratic Party regained control of both houses for the first time since 1995 and increased its majority in 2009. In addition, the Democratic presidential candidate, Barack Obama, was elected to the American presidency in November 2008 and was inaugurated in January 2009. These political trends may suggest an increased willingness on the part of voters in the United States to accept government intervention in the economy, including the labour market.

31

With regard to collective bargaining rights, attempts since 1974 to amend the legislation that governs most private-sector labour relations – the National Labor Relations Act (NLRA) – so as to expand the rights of unions have been unsuccessful. This has been primarily due to the opposition of employers who have been supported by sympathetic Republican influence over the legislative process. Between 1980 and 2006, the most notable of such legislative initiatives were bills proposed in 1990 and 1993 to prohibit employers from permanently replacing striking workers.

It is also important to note that interpretations of the NLRA that have erected barriers to union organizing and bargaining can be traced to the mid-1950s, when employers were permitted to speak against unions during campaigns without giving unions the right to respond. They were also able to bar union organizers from their property, and exclude various business decisions from bargaining even though those decisions may have affected employment. The collective bargaining rights of employers, unions and employees are also affected by presidential appointments made to the National Labor Relations Board (NLRB) and the courts.

With regard to individual employment rights, although no employment protection that was enacted prior to the late 1970s has been repealed, because the president nominates federal judges and generally controls the administration of laws, much of the existing legislation has been re-interpreted such that rights of employees and unions are narrowed, and rights of employers expanded. For example, the Americans with Disabilities Act (ADA) was enacted in 1990 to protect the rights of employees with disabilities. Yet since then, the US Supreme Court has interpreted the coverage of the ADA so narrowly that it does not protect many employees who have a disability. For example, in 1999 the US Supreme Court limited the definition of major life activities, which could establish a disability, and gave only limited coverage for employees who have disabilities even with medical treatment.

Similarly, although the Family Medical Leave Act (FMLA), enacted during a Democratic presidency in 1993, generally allows employees twelve weeks of leave for a serious medical condition of themselves or a family member, the amount of family-related leave provided by law in the United States is less than that provided in all other DMEs. Extensive regulations interpreting the FMLA, which became effective in January 2009, before the inauguration of President Obama, have tightened up the availability even of unpaid leave.

Although unionization in the United States has declined since the 1980s, this decline started in the mid-1950s. From a post-World War II high of approximately 32% in the mid-1950s, union density steadily declined through 2006 to 13%. Although density stabilized to 13% in 2007 and 14% in 2008, it continues to be low by historical and comparative standards.

American unions have often been flexible in their collective bargaining responses even though they have faced continuing difficulties in recruiting new members. In large unionized industries experiencing financial difficulty, such as manufacturing and airlines, unions have accepted concessions or innovative agreements in order to ensure the financial viability of firms, or as in the case of the automotive assembly and supply industries, to help the firms through bankruptcy proceedings. Reflecting diversity, however, other unions have been successful in winning gains for low-wage workers in service industries.[71]

The changing political climate, along with the continuing decline in unionization, has had the expected effect on workers. Using 1982–1984 as the base year, for the period 1964–1979, the average real hourly wage for production workers in the United States was USD 8.79 per hour. For the period 1980–2008, the average real hourly wage for production workers was USD 8.06 (US Bureau of Labor Statistics, undated). Average real weekly earnings for production workers, which take into account hours worked, show a similar trend. Using 1982 as a base, for the period 1964–1979, average real weekly earnings were USD 325.22; for the period 1980–2008, they were USD 276.85 (United States Bureau of Labor Statistics, undated).

With the inauguration of a Democratic president in 2009, following large Democratic majorities in both houses of Congress, the probability of changes in the NLRA to expand the rights of unions appears greater than at any time since the mid-1930s. The Employee Free Choice Act (EFCA), currently before the Congress, and supported by the US labour movement, would expand the rights of unions to organize through the use of employee signatures, rather than solely through the election process. It would speed up the processing of cases involving employer discrimination against employees, increase the penalties applicable to employers who discriminate against workers on the grounds of union activity, and require first-agreement arbitration between an employer and a newly organized union.

With regard to employment relations, in late 2008, a Democratic-controlled Congress passed broad amendments to the ADA, including reversing the effects of the 1999 Supreme Court decision. In 2009, the Democratic-controlled Congress enacted and President Obama signed legislation reversing a 2007 US Supreme Court decision that employees could not recover for unlawful employment decisions made more than 180 days before filing the claim, because they had been underpaid for years without filing a complaint. Thus, victims of unequal pay can now recover damages based on any payment of unequal wages. Other claims of discrimination, however, continue to be limited by the 180- or 300-day limitations period for filing claims. In a similar effort to expand the rights of employees with disabilities, proposed regulations interpreting the 2008 amendments to the ADA are expected to greatly enhance the coverage of that Act.

---

71. Hirsch & Macpherson, 2000; Block & Belman, 2003; Dresser & Bernhardt, 2006; Bailey, 2007.

5.2.   THE MAIN ACTORS[72]

5.2.1.   Government

The NLRA, the basic labour relations/collective bargaining legislation covering nearly all private-sector employees in the United States (employees in railroad and airlines are covered by the Railway Labor Act and employees in agriculture are not covered), was enacted in 1935, with substantial amendments in 1947. The NLRA model consists of six attributes: employee choice; majoritarianism; decentralization; exclusive representation; bargaining power; written, legally-enforceable collective bargaining agreements (CBAs); and administration by a specialized agency.

Employee Choice:

Employees in a state-determined 'bargaining unit' determine whether they wish a union to represent them for collective bargaining purposes. Once employees choose representation, the representation stays with the bargaining unit, even if some of the original employees leave, until and unless the current employees indicate a desire no longer to be represented for collective bargaining purposes.

Majoritarianism:

The choice to be or not to be represented by the union is based on a majority decision of the employees in the bargaining (actually 'election') unit. Sector bargaining and corporatist structures do not exist. The typical method of determining representation is via a state-supervised 'representation' election in which the employees in the unit vote for or against union representation.

Decentralization:

The bargaining unit can be a firm, a facility or facilities within a firm, or a craft or occupation within a facility. This unit-based bargaining results in a decentralized system with bargaining agreements establishing terms and conditions of employment at the bargaining unit level.

Exclusive Representation:

If a union is chosen by a majority of employees, it represents all employees in the unit, whether they voted for the union or not. The employer must negotiate with that union, and no other union may represent those employees.

The Role of Bargaining Power and Industrial Conflict:

In general, outcomes are determined by the bargaining power of the parties with power exercised by use or threat of a strike or lockout. The state has very little formal influence in determining the terms and conditions of employment for employees.

---

72. For more details, see Block, 2006.

Written, Legally Enforceable Agreements:

The parties must reduce their agreement to writing. This is legally enforceable for the duration of the agreement and cannot be changed unless both parties agree to a change.[73]

The NLRB administers collective labour law under the NLRA.[74] Because the NLRB is composed of presidential appointees serving five-year terms, albeit with the advice and consent of the US Senate, its decisions often reflect the shifting political trends of the United States as indicated in presidential elections.

Collective bargaining in public employment in the United States is not regulated by national law, but by each of the fifty states. Legislation and executive orders regulate collective bargaining for employees of the national government. Public employees in the United States are generally not permitted to strike. Twenty-six states permit at least some public employees, generally public-safety employees, to submit unresolved disputes to final and binding arbitration.

The United States has a system of laws protecting individual employee rights. These include federal and state laws prohibiting discrimination based on various personal characteristics, as well as federal laws regulating wages, overtime payments, and worker health and safety. States regulate unemployment insurance and workers' compensation (for worker loss of wages due to work-related injury or illness).

Allegations of violations of individual employment rights will first go to the federal Equal Employment Opportunity Commission (EEOC) or comparable state agencies if they involve allegations of discrimination. Other government agencies, such as the US Department of Labor, address violations of labour standards. Most administrative decisions can be appealed to a court. The use of alternative dispute resolution has expanded to settle discrimination claims, both as part of the EEOC's dispute resolution process and through arbitration agreements adopted by employers, with or without the presence of a union.

5.2.2.   Unions

Union structures reflect decentralized bargaining. The basic organizational component of the union structure is the national or international union, which is responsible for negotiating with employers, either directly or through the local unions it charters. The largest peak labour organization in the United States is the American Federation of Labor and Congress of Industrial Organizations (AFL-CIO), with fifty-six affiliated unions. Seven unions left the AFL-CIO in 2005 in a dispute over political and organizing strategy and established a new peak organization: Change to Win. Some large labour organizations, such as the National Education Association and the American Nurses Association, are independent.

---

73. Ruben, 2003.
74. Block, Beck & Kruger, 1996.

The local union is generally responsible for day-to-day workplace representation of union members and workers represented by unions. In general, local unions represent employees on a plant/facility-wide, enterprise-wide, or geographic, multi-unit basis.

5.2.3. Employers

Due to decentralized bargaining structures and the general absence of multi-employer bargaining, employers generally do not join multi-employer associations. There are industries, however, such as longshoring and local construction, in which there is voluntary multi-employer bargaining, and in these specific industries, firms have developed collective associations of employers.

Other broad-based management structures generally perform political and/or educational roles for managers. For example, the Human Resources Policy Association (HRPA) educates its members and the public on employers' perspectives on various public-policy matters affecting employment relations (HR Policy Association, undated). The HRPA, however, does not bargain for employers. Also relevant are organizations that indirectly support employer interests in weakening unions. These include the National Right-to-Work Foundation, which claims to oppose compulsory unionism, and the Center for Union Facts, which uses its funds to advertise regarding allegations of union abuses.

5.3. STRUCTURE OF COLLECTIVE BARGAINING

In the United States, each plant or enterprise is generally a separate bargaining unit. As new firms are established or as older firms establish new facilities, the employees in these new firms or establishments will generally not be unionized initially. If these firms or establishments are to be unionized, they must go through the unit-by-unit majoritarian processes discussed previously. The time period before the election (usually one to two months) is often characterized by an intense employer campaign against unionization, because the election rules permit the employer to present its point of view at the workplace while at the same time barring the union from the workplace.

There is a bargaining obligation for a unit only when a union has been certified or legally recognized in accordance with these majoritarian processes. Parties have a legal obligation to negotiate in good faith, which incorporates an obligation to meet at reasonable times, to listen to the positions of the other side, and to disclose relevant information to support their respective positions. Although there is generally no obligation to agree to a proposal of the other side, or to make a concession, neither can the employer or the union engage in a 'take-it-or-leave-it' approach to bargaining that refuses to recognize the institutional legitimacy of the other party. Ultimately, however, because the parties may use economic weapons and engage in industrial conflict, the bargain on which the parties agree is often heavily influenced either by a strike or lockout, or more frequently, by the expected results of a strike or lockout that does not occur.

In the public sector, the impasse procedures many states have established as 'strike substitutes' result in far more government involvement in the process and outcomes of bargaining than occurs in the private sector. In states in which state-mandated compulsory arbitration is incorporated into the impasse procedure, the arbitrator, who is in a sense an arm of the state, has the authority to impose terms and conditions on public-sector parties when they are unable to agree.

The law generally requires the parties to negotiate only over 'terms and conditions' of employment, or 'mandatory subjects of bargaining'. An employer that must negotiate with a union may not act unilaterally with respect to any mandatory subject of bargaining unless that subject has been a topic of negotiations between the employer and the union and the parties have reached an 'impasse'. Typical matters addressed in CBAs include management rights, pay rates, seniority, criteria for promotion and lay-offs, vacations, health insurance and other fringe benefits, grievance procedures and sick leave.

Over a period of almost thirty years, from the mid-1960s to the early 1990s, the law developed to give employers the right to make changes in the capital structures of their business without being required to negotiate those changes with the union, unless the change resulted solely in production relocation; such changes were not considered to be mandatory subjects of bargaining. This development of the law has given employers wide latitude to restructure their businesses with little union involvement.

A key feature of the collective bargaining systems in the public and private sectors is the wide use of grievance procedures ending in arbitration as alternatives to the strike or lockout to settle disputes that arise during the CBA. The typical grievance procedure incorporates multiple steps designed to involve representatives of each side who are further removed from the parties involved in the dispute. If the parties are unable to resolve the dispute at the lower levels, the dispute is referred to an arbitrator, whose decision is final and binding. Typical grievances cases involve discipline or discharge, work assignment, health and welfare plans, and pay rates.[75] The overwhelming majority of disputes that arise under collective agreements are settled by the parties without arbitration.

5.4.   RECENT CHANGES AND FUTURE TRENDS

There is no 'extension', and there is a principle that employees are not represented by a union unless the unit in which they are employed chooses by a majority vote to be represented. This does not produce a favourable context for union growth. This is evidenced by the long-term decline in the percentage of the workforce that is unionized in the United States. In the short term, the prospects for collective bargaining in the United States are gloomy. The courts are generally more supportive of employers' property rights, rather than rights of unions and their members; the emphasis placed on individual rights also tends to favour the interests

---

75. Federal Mediation and Conciliation Service, 2004.

of employers. In the absence of legislative change, the conditions that have caused the downward trend of union density are likely to persist. Even if there is legislative change that favours unions and collective bargaining, the effects are not likely to be immediate.

On the other hand, because the structure of collective bargaining is based on the bargaining unit rather than the individual employee, and because bargaining units, once unionized, tend to remain unionized, most of the decline in union density has occurred because of a rise in the never-unionized sector rather than from substantial employment declines in the unionized sector. Thus, the decline in union density has not been associated with a proportional decline in union membership. Between 2000 and 2008, the percentage of 'covered' employees declined by 8.1%, while absolute union membership fell by only 2.2%. But the growing never-unionized sector represents a continuing challenge for unions, and collective bargaining in general.

There has also been a substantial decline in industrial conflict since the 1970s. In 1974, there were 425 strikes that involved more than 1,000 workers. This number fell to eighty-one in 1983, thirty-one in 1993, and only fifteen in 2008. Whether this decline is the result of legal doctrine making it less likely that strikes will be successful, or whether globalization is reducing the returns from striking, the eschewing by labour of its major weapon suggests additional problems for unions in the future. Even if the NLRA is changed in a way that is favourable to unions, it is too early to judge whether such legislative changes, combined with the recent increase in the representation rate, indicates the beginning of a long-term growth in unionization in the United States.

6.   CANADA

6.1.   MAJOR POLITICAL AND ECONOMIC DEVELOPMENTS

Canada's decentralized federal political structure exerts a significant influence on the regulation of employment, employment relations and labour law. The combination of ten decentralized provinces (each with the major jurisdiction over labour and employment issues), three northern territories and a separate federal government, results in a patchwork of approaches to labour and employment issues. At any one time, there will usually be a combination of social-democratic, liberal (or centrist), conservative and nationalist (autonomist) governments in key provinces with differing orientations. Conservatives were in power at the federal level from 1979 to 1980, from 1984 to 1993 and from 2006 to the present, whereas centrists ruled from 1980 to 1984 and from 1993 to 2006.

Another distinguishing characteristic of Canada is the co-existence of founding 'peoples' or 'nations' in a federal structure, resulting in institutional bilingualism at federal level but pronounced differences between regions within the country. According to the most recent 2006 census data, the mother tongue of the Canadian population is distributed as follows: 57% English, 22% French and

20% a third language; 4% are aboriginal peoples. The importance of third languages also reflects the continuing high levels of immigration that characterize Canadian workplaces and society. The balance between English and French has been shifting as a result of increased population growth in English-speaking Canada and a continuing shift in the economic balance towards the west of the country, with particularly high levels of economic growth in Alberta and British Columbia.

More than 80% of French language speakers in Canada reside in Quebec province. This provides the backdrop to continuing tensions over Quebec's political status. The *Parti québécois* (Quebec Party), a Quebec based political party committed to establishing a sovereign or separate status for Quebec, was first elected in 1976 and ruled from 1976 to 1985 and from 1994 to 2003. During that time, referenda seeking a mandate to pursue Quebec sovereignty were defeated in 1980 and 1995, albeit very narrowly in the latter case. Canadian politics continues to be dominated by calculations of political and linguistic status. When the Canadian constitution was repatriated from the United Kingdom in 1984, it resulted in a new charter of fundamental rights and freedoms for individuals and groups and was done so without the express consent of Quebec province, resulting in a constitutional imbroglio. Successive efforts to fix an amending formula and/or to secure Quebec autonomy have all failed. The emergence in the federal parliament of a separate Quebec party (the *Bloc québécois*), which seeks representation only in that province, is an expression of continuing tensions within Canadian federalization and further accentuates the regional fragmentation in the Canadian federation.

Canada has one of the more open economies in the world. Exports and imports account for a significant proportion of GDP. However, roughly 85% of trade is concentrated on exchange with the United States. Canadian integration in the US economy was reinforced by successive treaties: first, the Canada-United States Free Trade Agreement and, second, the North American Free Trade Agreement (it also includes Mexico), which came into effect in 1989 and 1994, respectively. Subsequent smaller bi- and multi-lateral trade agreements have facilitated commercial exchange with Caribbean, Central and Latin American countries. The overall pattern of these free trade agreements is that, unlike the EU, they are restricted to commercial exchange and do not entail social dimensions, except in as much as individual countries are expected to implement their own labour legislation and, in the case of developing countries, to technical and capacity-building exchanges.

Before 2008, Canada was in a strong economic position, fuelled by a world boom in commodity prices and an advantageous position of the Canadian dollar relative to the US dollar. On the policy side, there has been a sustained effort to improve its fiscal position (through the introduction of a goods and services tax in the 1990s) and to limit public expenditure, while maintaining relative to the United States a relatively wide range of public health and education services. This has resulted in repeated annual financial surpluses and a considerable reduction in the overall public debt ratio. Somewhat perversely, these improvements in economic fundamentals have sparked a significant appreciation in the value of the Canadian dollar, thus sparking concerns about the export implications for Canadian international trade, notably with the United States.

The global financial crisis of 2008–2009 has had mixed implications. Although a tradition of relatively extensive regulation of the financial sector limited the exposure of the Canadian economy to some of the more egregious excesses of rampant financial capitalism, its heavy dependence on the fortunes of the US economy, where the effects of the crisis were much more serious, has translated into declining levels of employment and a sharp rise in unemployment. The manufacturing sector has proved particularly vulnerable to declining demand, the appreciation of the Canadian dollar and a global shift of manufacturing activity towards low-cost countries. The rosy prospects for government expenditure have also changed. On the revenue side, the diminution of economic activity and a federal Conservative Government commitment since its election in 2006 to reduce the goods and services tax from 7% to 5%, have reduced government tax income. At the same time, Canada's participation in the effort to spur global economic activity through stimulus spending has resulted in rising deficits for governments at all levels and increasing pressures to limit or freeze public-sector employee wage increases.

While Canada exhibits many of the major characteristics of LMEs, its emphasis on social safety nets (including fiscal transfers to the low paid) and universal access to publicly-funded health care and education remain an important distinguishing feature relative to its southern neighbour. Moreover, strong public support for these social-policy orientations inhibits the capacity of conservative governments to steer social policy orientations in a more neo-liberal direction.

6.2. The Main Actors

6.2.1. Government

The Canadian Parliament and the provincial legislatures all have the power to enact labour laws. The jurisdiction of the federal and provincial governments arises from the Constitution Act 1867. Judicial interpretation of these sections gives provincial legislatures a large scope with federal authority limited to a narrow field of law-making in labour and employment matters.

The Canada Labour Code of the federal jurisdiction applies to:

a. works or undertakings connecting a province with another province or country, such as railways, bus operations, trucking, pipelines, ferries, tunnels, bridges, canals, telephone and cable systems;
b. extra-provincial shipping and services connected with such shipping, such as longshoring (wharves);
c. air transport, aircraft and airports;
d. radio and television broadcasting;
e. banks;

f. defined operations of specific works that have been declared by Parliament to be for the general advantage of Canada or of two or more provinces; and

g. federal Crown corporations.

Provincial authority is derived from the 'property and civil rights' subsection of the Constitution. The right to enter into contracts is a civil right, and because labour laws impose certain restrictions on contracts between employers and employees, they fall within provincial authority as property and civil rights legislation. Provinces also have the right to legislate on 'local works and undertakings'. This division of powers means that approximately 90% of employees are under the jurisdiction of provincial labour legislation with the other 10% under federal jurisdiction.

Given the high degree of decentralization and the potential for competitive social policy benchmarking between jurisdictions, there is some attempt at harmonization. The Canadian Association of Administrators of Labour Legislation is an association of federal-provincial-territorial departments of labour and heads of occupational safety and health agencies that discusses trends and problems in the field of labour relations. The federal jurisdiction has historically taken the lead role in labour-policy reform, notably in terms of providing a template for the smaller provinces. The importance and permeability of local states to different political tendencies also means that provinces sometimes compete for jobs on the basis of labour and social policy. There is increasing evidence that provinces are seeking to make their social frameworks 'more competitive'. It is an historic irony that free trade beyond the Canadian borders has only recently begun to induce attempts to reduce trade barriers, particularly non-tariff barriers, between Canadian provinces.

It is beyond the scope of this volume to consider all of the various provincial jurisdictions. However, to illustrate the diversity and similarities between the jurisdictions, the volume generally includes information on the two largest and most important provincial jurisdictions (Ontario and Quebec) as well as the Canadian national (federal) jurisdiction.

6.2.2.   Unions

The Canadian Labour Congress (CLC) represents approximately 71% of unionized workers in Canada. Three other union organizations in Quebec province – the *Confédération des syndicats nationaux* (CSN), the *Centrale des syndicats du Québec* (CSQ) and the *Centrale des syndicats démocratiques* (CSD) – account for a further 10% of union members in Canada, with the bulk of the remaining members in non-affiliated public-sector organizations. The Canadian Labour Congress – the major peak organization – is quite decentralized in terms of highly autonomous federated national and international unions, and distinct provincial labour federations.

A unique feature of unionism in Canada is the historical legacy of so-called international unions, which are US-based unions such as the United Steelworkers of America and the Teamsters that have members in both the United States and Canada. Although there has been a long-term decline in the overall proportion of such 'international' unions, half of the ten largest affiliates of the Canadian Labour Congress are such international unions. The major unions are divided between private and public sectors. Long-term trends favour the growth of public-sector unions, such as the Canadian Union of Public Employees and the National Union of Public and General Employees (the two largest unions to the Canadian Labour Congress) and the consolidation and merger of major private-sector unions into larger groupings.

In the absence of formal mechanisms for bi- and tripartite discussions between governments, employers and worker representatives, other types of organizations are increasingly part of the public policy landscape. For example, in the case of workers who fall outside the areas of the economy where union representation is the norm, advocacy groups increasingly make the case for the low paid. Other non-governmental organizations, often in wide-ranging coalitions that include labour unions, are active on issues of international labour rights and trade issues.

6.2.3.   Employers

There is not a single peak organization for employer representation in Canada. A series of employer and business organizations aspire to represent particular interests on issues of public policy. None of these organizations are engaged in collective bargaining on labour-relations issues. Major firms will typically belong to several employer and trade organizations. The Canadian Manufacturers and Exporters represents core manufacturing and international trade interests. It tends to be an authoritative voice on major competitiveness issues. Whereas local Chambers of Commerce play an important role in voicing business interests at municipal level, the Canadian Chamber of Commerce plays a lobbying role at federal level. The Canadian Federation of Independent Business is a voice for small business, tending to promote less regulation and lower taxes. The Canadian Council of Chief Executives is an association to voice the views of major business leaders on public policy issues. Although an independent research organization supported by its members and clients, the Conference Board of Canada is also seen as a prominent public-policy voice by the business community. At industry level, in addition to lobbying on public policy and trade issues, a few associations will provide labour-relations services and advice to member firms, but these organizations are generally not involved in bargaining with unions. The Canadian Employers' Council is a voluntary organization that brings together Canadian employer interests for the purposes of representation at international level, for example, the employer delegation to the ILO.

6.3.   STRUCTURE OF COLLECTIVE BARGAINING

The basic legal regime for collective representation is similar in Canada and the United States. The right to belong to a union for the purposes of collective bargaining is a positive right that can be exercised only when a union is recognized as the exclusive bargaining agent for a group of workers. A union gains exclusive bargaining rights when it demonstrates that it has majority support from the workers in the particular unit that it seeks to organize. There is inevitably some form of administrative determination as to what the 'appropriate bargaining unit' might be in a particular case and, therefore, whether the union has secured majority support in that particular unit. In contrast to the United States, where the most common method of determining majority support is a certification election, the predominant method in Canada is the verification of membership cards, though some jurisdictions are shifting to an electoral determination. This process is generally overseen by an administrative tribunal (known as a labour board or labour relations commission), which is also charged with the determination of the certification or bargaining unit.

Bargaining units are typically highly decentralized, a single establishment being the norm, unless it can be demonstrated that many separate units of a larger firm are effectively managed as a single unit or that there is a significant commonality of interests. The parties may ultimately agree to conduct bargaining at a higher level, meaning that the effective bargaining unit could be made up of many certification units. In general, however, bargaining structure is decentralized and the patchwork system of representation further contributes to this decentralization.

Where the union is not recognized as a majority agent, workers are effectively disenfranchised from collective representation rights and fall under the jurisdiction of minimum standards legislation rather than provincial or federal labour codes. Access to collective representation is also restricted in other important ways. Workers generally must be deemed to be salaried or waged employees; independent workers do not, therefore, qualify for union representation rights. Collective representation rights are further restricted to employees who do not exercise a managerial or supervisory function.

Once the union is designated as the monopoly bargaining agent, it is the exclusive agent for all workers covered by that particular unit. All workers generally pay union dues, whether they are a member of the union or not. Employers are obliged to deduct the union dues at source. Unlike in the United States, this union shop provision is a legal requirement in most jurisdictions in Canada. The union must conduct membership votes in order to undertake strike action and to ratify collective agreements. Workers also have the right to alter the bargaining agent or to renounce their collective representation rights during a specified period before the end of the collective agreement. A system of compulsory arbitration during the life of the collective agreement limits industrial disputes to the terms of the agreement.

There are significant differences between the public and private sectors in bargaining structures. The norm in the private sector is decentralized establishment level bargaining. In some cases, for example in automobile assembly, employers and unions agree to bargain at company level for all of their Canadian establishments. In a few, very exceptional cases, employers and unions bargain at a single table for the industry as a whole. The public sector tends to have more centralized negotiations, varying from single tables for major issues (as in Quebec) to bargaining that covers a single type of service across the province. In certain provincial jurisdictions, the right to strike is severely curtailed and the parties are subject to compulsory (interest) arbitration. Other provincial jurisdictions maintain the rights to strike and lockout but curtail those rights through an obligation to maintain 'essential services' for the duration of conflicts.

There is only a marginal difference (approximately 2%) between union and collective bargaining coverage in Canada. In other words, an employee is either in the unionized sector or not, because only a small proportion of non-unionized employees have their terms and conditions of work determined by a collective agreement if their workplace is not already unionized.

There are no legislative obligations in Canada concerning employee consultation and involvement at the level of the workplace or firm, nor do there remain any national institutions that ensure labour-management dialogue on labour-market and workplace-innovation issues. There are, however, such institutions in some provinces and, with regards training issues, in some industries.

6.4.   RECENT CHANGES AND FUTURE TRENDS

The trend in union density over the last two decades is one of relative decline: from 36% in 1986 to 29% in 2009. However, this overall trend merits further qualifications.

Unlike in some other countries where unions have experienced considerable decline in their membership, absolute levels of union membership in Canada have either remained stable or expanded slightly since 1986. This is a significant trend because it means that unions have not experienced a particular weakening in their capacities. They remain highly resourced and strong players in the industries where they are most present.

The increasing divergence between the private and public sectors is, however, also significant. Union membership in the public sector rose from 61% to 71% over the 1986–2009 period, whereas private sector density declined from 27% to 16%. In particular, the 1990s were characterized by a significant growth in private services, a sector where union membership is very sparse. This trend means that collective bargaining is largely absent from so-called new economy industries. It also points to a relative weakening of collective bargaining power in private-sector industries where unions have to contend with a strong non-union presence.

The gender composition of the labour movement has also experienced important change. Male union density has declined markedly (from 40% to 28% from 1986 to 2009), whereas female union density has remained relatively stable (at 31%). This translates into an increasing influence of women in the labour movement and also the greater presence of women in the unionized public sector. Although some unions have adapted to this transition, and Canadian unions have fared better than those in many other countries on this account, many unions in Canada still remain in a 'male-wage earner' mindset.

The overall system of collective representation also faces challenges. The workplace has changed significantly over the past decades and the pace of change appears to be accelerating. Factors driving these changes include: new information and communications technologies, the increasing internationalization of the production of goods and services, transformations in the management of production and work organization, the dislocation and relocation of workplaces across both time and space and the multiplication and fragmentation of individual and collective social identities in and beyond the workplace. The extent of change, moreover, leads to an increasing 'disconnect' between, on the one hand, the prevailing institutional framework for work and employment and the sets of assumptions that informed it, and, on the other hand, the changes sweeping the world of work.

Bargaining at the level of the workplace, which is usually the private-sector norm in Canada, remains highly vulnerable to larger economic trends and this is all the more evident since the economic and financial crisis of 2008. As many observers from more centralized bargaining regimes remark, this type of bargaining is a flexible mechanism for ensuring economic and organizational adjustments. However, the coordination and institutionalization of innovation in such a decentralized and fragmented way can also be a significant challenge. This is the case, for example, with vocational and occupational training and also with innovative work practices. The challenges posed by these types of innovation – and they often fall beyond the parameters of the collective bargaining relationship – underscore the inability of management policy or collective bargaining alone to achieve key workplace objectives. They highlight the importance of the interface between public policy and workplace outcomes and also the importance of mechanisms to ensure social dialogue on these types of issues. This is also the case with increasing pressures on pension plans in unionized workplaces, faced with insolvency in some cases, the move from defined benefits to defined contributions in others, and the general challenge of the complex interface between decentralized privately negotiated regimes and public policies. There are challenges, then, to ensure the integrity and viability of pension plans relative to public-policy objectives.

A key future question, therefore, concerns the interface between private practices and public policy and the development of mechanisms of broader social dialogue to ensure debate around achieving the twin objectives of fairness and efficiency at work. This challenge also informed a key report on the future of federal labour standards in Canada.[76]

---

76. Arthurs, 2006.

7.   NEW ZEALAND

7.1.   MAJOR POLITICAL AND ECONOMIC DEVELOPMENTS

New Zealand, a DME, has two main cultural groups: people of European descent, and the minority Maori, whose Polynesian ancestors arrived on the islands around 1,000 years ago. New Zealand has had three great 'waves' of reforms that have attracted international interest: the reforms in the 1890s, the post-1936 reforms and the post-1984 reforms. This analysis will focus on the post-1984 reforms, which can be divided into three distinct phases – the 1980s, the 1990s and the new millennium. Following years of disappointing economic growth and external balance problems, the 1984 Labour Government started a comprehensive overhaul of public policy. Economic deregulation opened the New Zealand economy to international competition and numerous restrictions were abolished.[77] There was great international interest in the public-sector reform, which – under so-called New Public Management thinking – restructured, corporatized and privatized public-sector organizations.[78]

In the early 1990s, reforms of the social, health and employment relations areas overhauled the New Zealand welfare state, which created social and political divisions of a previously unseen scale. This probably boosted the support for electoral reform, which was decided in a referendum in 1993 (see later). The Employment Contracts Act 1991 abolished the century-old conciliation and arbitration system, introduced voluntary unionism and facilitated a shift towards workplace bargaining.[79] Besides a marked decline in unionism, the shift towards workplace and individual bargaining was also supported by restricting access to benefits and a rise in individual employee rights.[80] The changes of the 1990s still have a major influence on current employment relations in terms of legislative frameworks and decentralized, individualized employment arrangements.

Whereas the 1980s and 1990s saw a dramatic swing away from state intervention and collective bargaining, the new millennium witnessed a swing back towards a 'social democracy' public policy approach with more state intervention and the encouragement of collective bargaining.[81] The Employment Relations Act 2000 made the support of unions and collective bargaining an explicit aim and this act has been further enhanced by many changes to statutory minima – including a 60% lift in the minimum wage, a week's extra annual leave, paid parental leave and public holiday penal rates – during the 1999–2007 period.[82] Changes to social welfare and public investments in health and education have further buttressed employment relations changes.

---

77. Kelsey, 1997.
78. Boston et al., 1991, 1996.
79. Dannin, 1997; Harbridge, 1993.
80. Geare & Edgar, 2006; Rasmussen, Hunt & Lamm, 2006.
81. Davenport & Brown, 2002; Rasmussen, 2004.
82. Rasmussen, 2009.

Following a referendum in 1993, the electoral system shifted from 'first-past-the-post' towards a proportional electoral system and this has transformed public-policy making in New Zealand. The first-past-the-post electoral system – with its characteristic dominant government having a secure parliamentary majority – facilitated the rapid introduction of public-policy reforms in the post-1984 period. Under the new electoral system, where minority governments and unstable parliamentary majorities are the norm, rapid change is less feasible. Thus, there has been a slow-down in radical public-policy changes since 1996. Still, the Labour-led governments managed to introduce significant reforms in the 1999–2007 period.[83]

7.2.   THE MAIN ACTORS

7.2.1.   Government

The government has always had a major influence on employment relations issues. State intervention has been the prevailing order since the conciliation and arbitration system was introduced in 1894 and, since then, it has been further bolstered by a comprehensive array of legislative interventions. While the level of state intervention in collective bargaining and employment conditions has been diluted following the deregulation of employment relations in the last two decades, the state is still prevalent in setting statutory minima, providing efficient and low-cost employment institutions (Mediation Service, Employment Authority and Employment Court). Also illustrative of the increased interaction between government, employer organizations and unions in the post-1999 period has been the collaboration at national level to improve employer-union relationships at organizational or workplace level. There are also employer-union attempts to tackle skill development and industry specific issues. The centre-right National Party won the 2008 general election, thereby ending nine years of Labour-led government. However, in comparison with the National Party-led coalition governments of the 1990s, the post-2008 National Party-led coalition government seems to be less hostile towards unions.

7.2.2.   Unions

Unions recovered to an extent following the advent of the Labour-led government in 1999. Under the Labour governments, unions tend to have a higher profile in public-policy discussions. Besides general discussions of legislative changes, the unions were involved in industry specific initiatives and social welfare improvement (Rasmussen 2004; <www.nzctu.org.nz>). On the other hand, the unions' progress, in terms of membership gains, and collective bargaining coverage has been very slow. There was some optimism amongst the unions following

---

83. See Rasmussen, 2004.

substantial gains in the post-2004 period and with successful union negotiations in difficult-to-unionize service industries such as retail and fast-food. Public-sector unions also made considerable gains and national agreements have become important in education and health. Nonetheless, because there is a National Party-led coalition government again, the relatively small union presence in many private-sector enterprises is a worry for unions, especially because there are increases in unemployment following the 2008 global financial crisis.

7.2.3.   Employers

Business New Zealand has been the leading employer 'voice' since it was created through a merger of the Employers' Federation and the Manufacturers' Association. Business New Zealand is often in the news because of its participation in public policy debates, its collaboration with unions or its many surveys of employer opinions (see <www.businessnz.org.nz>). The regional employer organizations – the constituting members of Business New Zealand – are often featured in national and local media coverage of employment relations issues. The regional employer organizations – for example, Employers and Manufacturers Association (EMA) Northern (see <www.ema.org.nz>) – have considerable influence through their service, information and consulting links with their member businesses. It also means that these employers' organizations have a good understanding of the issues faced by their members.

In the 1980s and 1990s, the Business Roundtable was a crucial 'voice' of large businesses and their quest for deregulation. The Business Roundtable is an 'invitation only' lobby organization where CEOs of major New Zealand enterprises are invited to join. The Business Roundtable had significant influence on the public sector and labour-market changes – epitomized by the Employment Contracts Act (1991). However, the public disquiet over the fallouts associated with these policies, as well as the search for other, more efficient policies, have meant that the Business Roundtable had less influence on public-policy debates since the mid-1990s.[84]

7.3.   STRUCTURE OF COLLECTIVE BARGAINING

The current collective bargaining structure and its level have been heavily influenced by the employment relations changes of the 1990s.[85] The traditional conciliation and arbitration system was often combined with union-preference status and this combination ensured that union density and union membership stayed relatively high until the 1990s. The conciliation and arbitration system did support unionism and collective bargaining through the award system and 'blanket coverage', whereby collective agreements obtained legal status and

---

84.   See Deeks & Rasmussen, 2002, 276–277.
85.   Geare and Edgar, 2006; Rasmussen 2009.

enforcement and 'blanket coverage' extended these agreements/awards to all employees in a particular industry or of a particular occupation.

The Employment Contracts Act 1991 made union membership voluntary and prohibited preferential treatment being associated with union membership or non-membership. Furthermore, the Act's abolition of the conciliation and arbitration system promoted a shift towards workplace and individual bargaining. Finally, the sole focus on collective bargaining was changed when the Employment Contracts Act 1991 covered collective and individual employment contracts.[86] With the introduction of personal grievances for all employees, individual employment agreements gained another support structure.

The changes introduced by the Employment Contracts Act 1991 resulted in a sharp decline in union membership and union density. Associated with the decline in union density and collective bargaining was a major increase in employer-driven flexibility, which brought about significant changes to overtime payments, penal rates, working time norms, pay differentials and individual employment disputes.[87] It is important to stress that the decline in union membership and union density varied across industries and occupational employee groups. This meant that many workplaces would have no union representation or collective bargaining and collective bargaining became the exception for low-paid service-sector employees in, for example, retail, hospitality, age care and tourism.[88]

The Employment Relations Act 2000 and its support of unionism and collective bargaining has prompted a rise in union membership. Union membership has grown by around 25% in the 1999–2006 period, but union density has been stagnant since strong employment growth matched the growth in union membership. At the same time, collective bargaining levels have declined as many collective employment agreements have become individual employment agreements. This is partly caused by the phenomenon of 'collective contracting' – that is, collective employment contracts without union participation – being outlawed by the Employment Relations Act 2000.[89] It is also problematic that the variation across industries and occupations has continued. Collective bargaining and union membership have been strong in the public sector, but it is estimated that union density has declined to around 10% among private-sector employees and many service sectors have considerably lower membership or, in many segments, no union members.[90]

7.4.   RECENT CHANGES AND FUTURE TRENDS

It is too early to evaluate fully the impact of the Employment Relations Act 2000 and the associated changes to other employment relations legislation that ensued.

---

86. Harbridge, 1993.
87. Deeks & Rasmussen, 2002, 86–92.
88. Dannin, 1997; Tucker, 2002.
89. Dannin, 1997; Rasmussen, 2004.
90. Blackwood, Finberg-Danieli & Lafferty, 2006.

Although the support of collective bargaining and high-quality employment relationships has yet to prompt major changes, employment relations were influenced by the 'social-democratic' shift in public policy and, in particular, a tight labour market with pronounced skill shortages.[91] The post-2008 government announced, while in opposition, that it would only make some limited adjustments to the legislative framework and, thus, wholesale changes appear less likely.[92] However, it has already made two significant changes. First, the personal grievance rights for new employees in small enterprises allow for an agreed 90-day 'probationary period' during which employers would be able to terminate an employee without notice. Second, the pay equity unit at Department of Labour has been abolished and no pay equity cases will be pursued.

To what extent will the post-1999 public-policy approach lead to more productive employment relationships? Lack-lustre labour productivity growth has been an issue for some time and it prompted two different legislative approaches in the Employment Contracts Act 1991 and the Employment Relations Act 2000. The dominant focus of public policy has been on how to facilitate higher productivity growth and creating the elusive high wage, high skill economy. This has prompted a focus on workplace employer-union partnerships (including public-sector collaboration and the implementation of a tripartite Partnership Resource Centre – see <www.dol.govt.nz>) and on the role of employee participation and influence.[93]

The quality of employment relations was buttressed by a broadly based increase in statutory minima and through research and development projects in the areas of decent work, equal employment opportunities and work-life balance. To what degree will this facilitate a major long-term shift in future employment relationships? The answer is not yet clear, but the changing gender, ethnic and age distribution of the workforce are also challenges (see <www.stats.govt.nz>). A tight labour market encouraged employers and policy makers to consider how they can productively integrate a more diverse workforce. Creating a dynamic and inclusive labour market that can also overcome the long-term skills and productivity issues is a key employment relations issue. This will also be important for the wider New Zealand society.

8. AUSTRALIA

8.1. Major Political and Economic Developments

Since the early 1980s, there have been three different periods of national political leadership in Australia. The first period was from 1983 to 1996 during the tenure of the Australian Labor Party (ALP) government, led by Bob Hawke and then

91. Rasmussen, Hunt & Lamm, 2006.
92. See Rasmussen, 2009, 166–167.
93. Haynes, Boxall & Macky, 2005.

Paul Keating. The Labor Party is the centre-left party in Australia with links to the union movement. The Labor government came into office in 1983 during a period of high inflation and high unemployment. As part of a strategy to combat inflation, it entered into an accord with the central federation of Australian unions, the Australian Council of Trade Unions (ACTU), to moderate wage inflation. In exchange, the Labor government was able to deliver to the union movement improvements in the 'social wage'; a national superannuation scheme, elements of a national health system, and improved pensions, to mention a few. During the 1980s, this form of wage moderation helped reduce inflation and unemployment.

The Labor government also sought to reform other areas of the economy. The Australian dollar was floated and financial markets were de-regulated. To boost competitiveness, there was a reduction in tariffs and other forms of industry assistance. Furthermore, the government sold selected publicly-owned enterprises such as the Commonwealth Bank, Qantas and Australian Airlines. Additionally, the Labor government introduced targeted industry plans to reform key sectors of the economy. Following the urging by key employers' associations and with support from the ACTU, the government led moves towards enterprise-based collective bargaining.

The Labor government's monetary policy produced high interest rates in the late 1980s, which induced an economic recession and high unemployment. Unemployment peaked at about 11% in the early 1990s. Despite the corrective efforts of the Labor government to boost economic growth during the early 1990s and reduce unemployment to 8% in 1996, it lost political office to a conservative Liberal/National coalition government.

The second period of political leadership began with the conservative Liberal/National coalition government in 1996. The coalition government, led by John Howard, had strong links with the business community and also a rural lobby. This government preferred a free-market approach to economic management, including the privatization of more publicly-owned enterprises and deregulation in some markets.

Economic performance was mixed, with strong economic and employment growth, due to favourable international economic conditions and a minerals boom. Productivity growth, however, was muted. The Howard government produced large budget surpluses through restraint on public spending and new forms of taxation, principally a goods and services tax (GST), which was introduced in 2000. In terms of trade performance, Australia's net foreign debt rose sharply from 34% under Hawke/Keating to 45% under Howard.

Industrial relations regulation was the most controversial area of economic reform initiated by the 1996–2007 conservative government. Among other things, it sought to regulate private-sector employment relations at a national level. This responsibility was previously shared with State governments. The Howard government also sought to promote individual employment contracts rather than collective bargaining. The Howard Liberal/National government lowered the floor of basic labour standards and sought to reduce the role of unions at workplaces and in national policy making. It also restructured the key labour-market institutions, and set about dismantling the award system.

In November 2007, Australia elected another Labor government, led by Kevin Rudd. This government softened the hard edges of the conservative government's legislation.[94] The new employment relations act, *Fair Work Act* 2009 (FW Act) repealed the *Workplace Relations Act* 1996 (Cth) (WRA). The role of the Australian Industrial Relations Commission (AIRC) has been replaced by a new statutory agency, Fair Work Australia (FWA). The Workplace Authority (WA), established under the WRA, continues, but as the Fair Work Ombudsman (FWO).

The FW Act framework builds on the minimum labour standards by introducing the National Employment Standards (NES) that applied from 1 January 2010, covering the following entitlements: maximum weekly hours; parental leave; personal/carer's leave and compassionate leave; long service leave; notice of termination and redundancy pay, flexible work arrangements; annual leave; community service leave; public holidays and the Fair Work Information Statement. The NES underpins new federal modern awards and enterprise agreements. High income employees may contract out of elements of the ten NES.

The FW Act provides for collective bargaining at workplaces. Industry-wide agreements are not permitted. The FW Act repeals some of the anti-union provisions of the WRA 1996 and applies to most private-sector employment. New South Wales, Queensland, South Australia and Tasmania referred their private sector industrial relations powers to the federal government in 2009. Victoria had already referred its powers in 1996, so Western Australia became the only State that has not supported the national system under the FW Act.

8.2. THE MAIN ACTORS

8.2.1. Government

Australia has a federal political system with a national Federal government and six State governments (plus two territories). Under the Constitution, industrial-relations powers were shared between Federal and State governments, each of which operated their own employment relations systems – except the State of Victoria, since 1996. However, in 2006, the Liberal/National Federal government introduced the 'WorkChoices' (WRA) legislation, which took over most private-sector employment relations powers from the other five States. According to the Constitution, the federal government has always controlled the workplace and rights of territory employers and employees.

Under the 'WorkChoices' legislation, the Federal government controlled private-sector employment relations covering up to about 85% of workers.

---

94. The Australian commentary in this volume is based on the federal system as governed by the WRA, amended by the Workplace Relations Amendment (WorkChoices) Act 2005 and the Fair Work Act 2009.

This percentage is similar under the FW Act.. State industrial-relations systems cover State-government employees, some charities and unincorporated small businesses.

Although the conservative government had promised to deregulate labour markets, its legislation introduced more 'law' regulating the Australian industrial-relations system than before. The conservatives' rhetoric claimed the legislation created more jobs and simplified regulation under a centralized unitary employment relations system. Nevertheless, the legislation further de-unionized the workforce and weakened the Labor Party, which draws much of its financial support from the unions.

The post-2007 Labor government has further extended the influence of the Federal government on industrial-relations matters. After a more than a century of shared jurisdiction of employment relations between the State and Federal governments, the Federal Labor government entered into negotiations with State governments to refer their private-sector employment relations powers (see 8.1 above) and possibly also their public-sector powers to the Federal government.

8.2.2.   Unions

In the nineteenth century, the Australian group of British colonies imported a craft-based model of unionism complemented by industry and general unions. This structure of unionism was modernized in the 1980s and 1990s when the ACTU rationalized union coverage approximately along industry lines – inspired partly by German and Scandinavian examples. As in many other countries, Australian unionism has declined markedly in recent decades. Union density fell from 50% in 1980 to less than 20% in 2009. The declining density has been attributed to changing industry and occupational structure, increasing casualization of employment and a growing employer opposition to unionism, as well as to the anti-union policies of the conservative governments.

8.2.3.   Employers

The main employer associations in Australia include the Business Council of Australia (BCA) (representing the interests of large business), the Australian Chamber of Commerce and Industry (the main national employers' association), the Australian Industry Group (representing the engineering and related industries) and the National Farmers Federation (representing rural employers).

The BCA was a most important lobbyist on employment relations in the 1980s and 1990s. The BCA was influential in shifting the industrial relations system away from the system of compulsory conciliation and arbitration towards an enterprise-based model. The BCA was also instrumental in shaping the main elements of the WorkChoices legislation: a national system of private-sector employment relations; national minimum standards rather than industrial awards; and the promotion of enterprise-based collective bargaining and individual employment contracts.

8.3.   STRUCTURE OF COLLECTIVE BARGAINING

For most of the last century, the industrial tribunals played a significant and distinctive role in regulating employment relations. A tribunal operated in each of the states, with the exception of Victoria, after 1996. Additionally there was a federal tribunal – the AIRC – responsible for settling industrial disputes that could extend beyond the boundaries of any one state. The AIRC was the national regulator of employment relations in Australia.

The tribunals' purpose was to prevent and settle industrial disputes through a process of compulsory conciliation and arbitration. Unions, in dispute with an employer, could lodge the matter with a tribunal and the employer would be legally compelled by the tribunal to attend compulsory conciliation. If the parties could not reach agreement, the tribunal would arbitrate the matter and issue an 'award' – a legally enforceable document including rates of pay and conditions of employment.

This system promoted unions by giving them compulsory 'recognition rights' with employers. The system also promoted employers' associations who undertook much tribunal work representing their members. Reflecting the structure of unionism, many awards were based on occupations, regions and industries. In addition to individual unions, central union federations could lodge disputes with a tribunal to establish state-wide or national basic labour standards. Over the twentieth century, awards were progressively enlarged until they provided a comprehensive range of basic entitlements, including aspects such as pay rates, job structures, duty statements, hours of work, overtime, penalty rates, shift work arrangements, sick leave, annual leave, long service leave, redundancy provisions, various allowances and other benefits.

In the 1980s, employers' interest groups criticized the system of compulsory conciliation and arbitration as an impediment to productivity. Such critics argued that the system was too centralized and bureaucratic to accommodate the needs of industrial parties that wanted to negotiate productively-efficient employment arrangements at the enterprise level. In response to calls for enterprise-based bargaining, the then Labor government introduced legislation to create a separate stream of productivity-based, enterprise bargaining as the main mechanism of wage determination. Collectively-negotiated agreements could not disadvantage employees compared to award pay and conditions. The AIRC was given the role of making periodic modest wage adjustments to awards to protect those workers who were unable to bargain collectively.

After the conservative government won the election in 1996, it introduced legislation to further dismantle the tribunal system by reducing the role of the AIRC, the unions and awards. The role of the AIRC to settle disputes was greatly restricted. Awards were reduced to only twenty allowable matters, whilst industry (pattern) bargaining was prohibited. Union preference clauses and closed shop arrangements were also outlawed. The conservative government promoted a system of individual contracts (known as Australian Workplace Agreements (AWAs)) or collective bargaining as the preferred forms of wage determination.

A new entity, the Workplace Authority, was established to promote individual contracts.

In 2006, the conservative government introduced a second wave of industrial relations reform with its WorkChoices amendment legislation to the WRA. As mentioned already, the legislation stipulated a maximum of five minimum statutory labour standards as a replacement for industrial awards, which were to be phased out. The role of the AIRC was further reduced and the new agency, Australian Fair Pay Commission (AFPC), was established to review and adjust minimum wages periodically. The legislation also further restricted the activities of unions.

The post-2007 Labor government overturned many features of the conservatives' industrial relations legislation. Individual contracting was restricted – although individual contracts are still available for high-income earners. Minimum standards of employment have been expanded to include a comprehensive list of protections. The role of the regulator, FWA, has been expanded in terms of dispute resolution, managing collective bargaining and maintaining wage levels for the low paid. Key anti-union provisions have also been removed and good-faith bargaining is mandatory.

However the Labor government continued the previous government's commitment to modernizing the award system. 'Award Modernisation' is the process of reviewing and rationalizing awards to create a system of 'modern awards'. The AIRC began this process in 2008 following a formal request from the Australian Government. By the end of 2009 the AIRC had consolidated and standardized entitlements from a number of current state and federal awards. These modern awards were effective from 1 January 2010 but most include transitional provisions to phase in changes in wages, loadings and penalties over a five-year period.

8.4.   RECENT CHANGES AND FUTURE TRENDS

Employment relations in the twentieth century involved a high degree of state intervention and an idiosyncratic conciliation and arbitration tribunal system, which generated strong protections for employees and provided a major role for collective organizations of employers and employees. In the twenty-first century, the picture is likely to be quite different. There is a general acceptance from both sides of politics that, rather than conciliation and arbitration, enterprise-level regulation, is the preferred method of job regulation. The Labor Party supports collective bargaining and stemming the growth of individual contracts. The conservative parties are strong advocates of individual contracts. The political parties are divided on their views about the best arrangements for the many employees who are not covered by CBAs. Whereas the ALP supports a comprehensive safety net of basic labour standards, the conservative parties would prefer a small number of minimum standards.

There will be a major challenge in the twenty-first century for collective organizations of employers and employees. Although the decline in union membership is partly explained by government and employer hostility and structural factors, one of the chronic weaknesses of the Australian unions has been a reduction in union density in traditional industries. Developing and maintaining dynamic systems of workplace unionism will be a major priority if unions are to reverse declining union density. This task was particularly difficult in the context of the WorkChoices legislation, which favoured individual contracts and inhibited union organizing activity. Under the post-2007 Labor government, it remains to be seen to what extent unions will be able to reverse the decline in density.

Employers' associations have also been affected but not as severely as unions. Employers' associations have lost some of their relevance insofar as they have a diminished role representing members in industrial tribunals. Employers' associations have had to face competition from some law firms offering specialized industrial relations advice. Some employers' associations have also had to refocus on human-resource and general management training to supplement their industrial relations advisory functions. But employer associations are likely to retain their currency, because they still have an important advocacy function in political and economic affairs more generally.

The post-2008 global financial crisis prompted the Labor government to introduce Keynesian economic stimulus policies. Although Australia experienced a mild increase in unemployment, unlike most of the other DMEs the Australian economy did not enter into a recession.

9. JAPAN

9.1. MAJOR POLITICAL AND ECONOMIC DEVELOPMENTS

In a sense, Japan's political stability is impressive; the same conservative party, the Liberal Democratic Party (LDP) was in power, except for a short period, for more than fifty years, until August 2009. However, there were some changes in the style of government and policy direction, particularly since the start of the twenty-first century.

For a long time, Japanese politics were dominated by the LDP. The fragmented opposition consists of several parties – the socialist party, the social-democratic party, the communist party and the Buddhist party (*Komeito*) – which in combination usually held 40%–45% of seats in the Diet.

The LDP is a constellation of personalities and factions ranging from the progressive to the ultra-conservative. By establishing a balance of power between the factions, the LDP arrived at a consensual approach, but this resulted in a rather weak Prime-Ministership. This situation changed considerably in the 1990s. After the collapse of the Soviet Union and the Eastern bloc, the opposition parties, dominated by the predominantly Marxist socialist party, lost momentum. Seeing a vacuum in the opposition, some factions of the LDP split from the main party and formed new political parties. Thus, in 1994, a new coalition government headed by a former socialist, Murayama, held power for a short time only to be overtaken by a series of LDP governments (led by Hashimoto, Obuchi, Mori, Koizumi, Abe, Fukuda and Aso).

Beyond the frequent changes of leadership within the LDP, there were major shifts of policy direction, in particular, during the Koizumi government (2001–2006). In 2001, Junichiro Koizumi won a significant victory at the election for the Diet. His personal popularity gave him a strong platform for pursuing policies of economic liberalization and deregulation. He created an advisory council (Council on Economic and Fiscal Policy) with a limited number of personalities headed by the economist, Minister Heizo Takenaka. This council was instrumental in by-passing the coalition of politicians and bureaucrats. The Koizumi government endorsed the recommendation of the council to privatize many public corporations and organizations (there were privatizations of turnpikes, universities and, it also proposed to privatize postal services).

The lasting effects of Koizumi's deregulation policies are yet to be seen, but the way he utilized the advisory council, sometimes against the voice of certain factions in the LDP, was reminiscent of Yasuhiro Nakasone who conducted the privatization of railways and telecommunications in the mid-1980s.

Mr Hatoyama and his centre-left Democratic Party of Japan (DPJ) won a landslide victory in a snap general election in August 2009. This was a major defeat for the long-ruling LDP. The DPJ promised a more humane society and much change that would curtail the power of the bureaucracy and put the quality of life of ordinary people ahead of big-business interests. It also criticized American-style 'market fundamentalism'. Its promises also included a higher minimum wage, free high-school education and a promise not to raise sales taxes. This prompted critics to ask how the DPJ would pay for its policies.

Japan is the world's second-biggest economy. It achieved an 'economic miracle' in the post-1945 period. Recent economic developments have been shaped by two major factors: recessions and global competition. Government economic policies, as well as the strategy of Japanese firms, have revolved around these two inter-related factors. As for the chronology of the business cycle, the Japanese economy has experienced three distinct phases since the 1980s.

Initially, the Japan of the 1980s was ascendant with its dominant manufacturing sector and the stability of the yen. It was a period when the so-called Japanese model of management and employment relations attracted much international attention. Eventually, overheating of the Japanese economy and much liquidity provided by banking institutions led to a speculative 'bubble', which burst in 1990–1991.

After 1991 there was a series of recessions and deflationary pressures. Assets, collaterals and stocks lost most of their value, creating huge bad loans, not only for financial institutions, but also for the construction industry. In the post-bubble period, successive governments applied more or less Keynesian recipes of large-scale public spending. As a result, long-term public debt (for instance: government bonds and provincial government bonds) reached alarming levels. In comparative terms, long-term public debt represented around 70% of GDP in 1990; but by 2006 it had reached 150% of GDP. Such levels of public debt were relatively greater than those of other DMEs.

In 1996–1997, the bankruptcy of two major financial institutions (Yamaichi securities and Hokkaido Takushoku Bank) revealed that Japanese banking institutions, which had hitherto played a guiding role in the post-war economic growth, were in a critical condition.

Between 1996 and 2000, there was almost no GDP growth (a mere 0.1% over the five years), with the worst performance recorded in 1998: negative growth of 1.5%. The official unemployment rate during this period also reflects the economic stagnation. In 1991, it was only 2.1%, but by 1998 it had risen to 4.1% and in 2002 it reached a peak of 5.4%.

The third phase was a period of gradual recovery and growth. This started in 2003 and continued until 2007, albeit at a very modest pace. The major factor behind this recovery was exports, particularly exports to the booming Chinese economy. The manufacturers of machinery, steel, electronics and electrical appliances showed a high rate of profit while investment was also picking up in the domestic economy.

From the third quarter of 2008, the global financial crisis affected the previously booming manufacturing sector by creating a sudden drop in demand from overseas markets. The downturn in the business climate was too rapid for many firms to handle, so that many large firms recorded considerable losses for the fiscal year ending March 2009. Toyota, for example, in late 2008 had forecast a profit of more than ten billion dollars, but actually registered a large loss of 4 billion dollars at the end of March 2009 – the first such loss since the post-war reconstruction period. Many Japanese firms tried to reduce production levels sharply and downsize their workforce by terminating the contracts of temporary agency workers and seasonal workers. The issue of job insecurity, in particular for temporary agency workers, has attracted a considerable debate about the adequacy of the social safety net for retrenched workers.

The Japanese economy presents some curious features that seem to be at odds with traditional patterns. First, total wages were not increasing in spite of the economic recovery. This was in contrast with the clear improvement in the earnings of enterprises (operating profits, net profits). The decreasing share of economic rewards for labour may be explained partly by a shift in the governance structure, whereby firms tend to review rewards policy for stockholders, even though they did not embrace the full extent of the American model. Moreover, given the recessionary market and competitive pressures from East Asian economies, Japanese enterprises have reduced to a minimum the recruitment of permanent (regular) employees in favour of atypical forms of temporary employment (part-time workers, temporary agency workers and fixed-term workers). Thus, the increase in atypical employment has had a lasting influence, not only on wage movements but also on employment relations.

Second, price movements were still very weak. The CPI of the third quarter of 2006 stood exactly at the same level as in 1995. Combined with a declining labour share and price stability, total wages and domestic consumption were excluded from the growth recovery, jeopardizing in turn the fragile macro-economic expansion.

The globalization strategy of Japanese enterprises enjoyed significant progress, despite political frictions and cost disadvantages. The first major wave of moving production to other DMEs (e.g., United States and Europe) was in the 1980s. Electrical appliance and car manufacturers had to build or buy factories in developed countries to try to mitigate import restrictions. Moreover, the appreciation of the yen at the end of the 1980s accelerated this trend.

In the slump of the 1990s, many Japanese enterprises relocated much manufacturing to mainland China and other Asian countries for a different reason. Thanks to trade negotiations, the Japanese market has become more and more open to global competition. To remain competitive in Japan, as well as in global markets, Japanese enterprises had to relocate labour-intensive processes to China, where economic growth was accelerating through foreign investment.

The investment in China and other industrialized countries has been enhanced by the relative slump of the domestic market and good profitability of the US market. This helped the large 'blue-chip' manufacturers to earn large profits from US sales. Some big enterprises, such as Toyota and Canon, formulated global marketing strategies.

Thus, the Japanese economy has undergone significant changes. Once it had enjoyed the advantages of trade protection (provided by tariff and non-tariff trade barriers), which were underpinned by support from the central bureaucracy and the main banking system. More recently, however, Japanese enterprises have had to battle for their survival in a context of recession and tough global competition.

9.2.   THE MAIN ACTORS

9.2.1.   Government

Traditionally, the employment relations roles of the government were mainly behind the scenes, but included a de facto active role of consultation and negotiation with employers' and workers' organizations. On issues of labour law, tripartite commissions composed of representatives of employers and workers and independents are consulted on draft bills. The Ministry of Health, Labour and Welfare (in 1999, the Ministry of Labour was combined with the Ministry of Health) generally draws up the first draft of bills after consultation with the organizations concerned. This was the case with important pieces of legislation such as the Equal Employment Opportunity Law (1986); revisions of the Labour Standards Law (hours of work, 1987; dismissals, 2003); and revision of the Temporary Workers Law (dispatch workers law, 2003).

In the formulation of labour policies, the Koizumi government established a new approach by framing budgetary constraints fixed by the Council on Economic and Fiscal Policy. This Council was, on the whole, a strong advocate for deregulation and free markets, but subsequent governments appear to have been more sceptical about deregulation.

9.2.2.   Unions

As in many other DMEs, union density has decreased during the past twenty-five years. In 1980, there were 12.5 million union members and a union density of 31%; however, in 2006, membership had fallen to roughly 10 million, with a density of 18%. This decline had two distinct phases. Between 1980 and 1996, the total number of members remained at a constant level, whereas after 1997, unions lost some 2.5 million members.

Union density varies according to sectors. In 2006, it was 50% in civil services and 57% in public utilities such as electricity, gas and water. By contrast, union density was only 10% in the wholesale and retail sectors and 26% in the manufacturing sector. There are very few unions in small enterprises that have fewer than thirty employees (the density is not much more than 1%).

The decline of unionization has several causes. First, an industrial shift from manufacturing to the service sector is probably the main cause. Second, unionization is almost negligible in newly-created businesses (financial services and care-related business). Third, downsizing of established enterprises (such as steel, shipbuilding, telecommunications and railways) leads to a declining union membership. Fourth, the increase of atypical employment, in particular part-time workers, has presented a serious challenge to unions.

At the end of the first decade of the twenty-first century, 24% of the total workforce consists of part-time workers; these are mostly female workers in the services sector. Union density among part-time workers was a modest 4.3% in 2006, in spite of the efforts of some major union federations. Nevertheless, Japanese unions retain some strongholds in large manufacturing enterprises, as well as in the transport sector and the public sector.

Most unions in Japan are organized, not by occupation or by job, but by enterprise or establishment. An enterprise union consists of permanent (regular) employees of a single company, without distinction between white-collar and blue-collar workers, up to the lower management level. In many large enterprises, a 'union shop clause' is included so that all newly-recruited 'regular' employees automatically join the enterprise union. Excluded from this arrangement are workers of non-regular status (part-time workers, fixed-term workers) and workers of sub-contracting companies.

Most union activities, such as wage negotiation or representation on consultative committees, for example, take place at the enterprise level. Enterprise unions within the same industry join an industrial federation of unions. These industrial federations (there are more than a hundred) are generally loosely constituted organizations for the purpose of consultation and information-sharing. Only a few federations (UI Zensen, Electric workers' union) play a significant role in policy-making matters.

There are two national federations, the most important is Rengo (Japan Trade Union Confederation) with 6.5 million members and the Zenroren (National Confederation of Trade Unions) with 0.7 million members. Rengo was established in

1989 to create a united front for the labour movement and to regain political and social influence. Rengo replaced two competing confederations – Sohyo and Domei.

Rengo has generally pursued a cooperative approach to labour-management relations. It participates in consultation and negotiation on labour matters at the national level and formulates guidelines for the annual rounds of wage negotiations. In recessions and in face of the Koizumi government's advocacy of the deregulation of markets, Rengo was in a defensive position on employment relations issues (such as hours of work for white-collar workers, conditions for temporary agency workers).

9.2.3.   Employers

In 2002, a central employers' organization, the Japan Federation of Economic Organisations, was created by the amalgamation of the Federation of Japanese Business (Keidanren) and the Japan Federation of Employers' Associations (Nikkeiren). Before the amalgamation, Nikkeiren, created in 1948 amidst industrial strife, acted as the specialized and independent arm of the Federation of Japanese Business, because the same senior-level executives occupied positions in both organizations. But after the industrial relations parties tended to become more cooperative, the business sector considered that two separate federations were no longer necessary.

Japan Business Federation (JBF) does not participate in collective bargaining, which is generally carried out at the enterprise level. However, before the beginning of annual wage negotiations in spring, it releases guidelines for employers to follow when dealing with demands from the various unions during collective bargaining. Because JBF includes most large enterprises, these guidelines tend to play a major role.

9.3.   STRUCTURE OF COLLECTIVE BARGAINING

In Japan, collective bargaining focuses on pay agreements, which are concluded during annual negotiations every spring. Formal collective agreements specify general rules and procedures, hence, are seldom modified. In the unionized sector, it is almost a ritual to submit wage demands at the beginning of the year, based on the CPI, the profitability of the enterprise and the wage levels of similar enterprises. Industrial federations may fix a target for wage increases. In some sectors, such as the private non-government railways, the steel industry and the electricity industry, negotiations are coordinated so as to fix industry-wide rates. In other industries, pay negotiations are carried out with little coordination at the industry level.

The spring wage negotiations used to provoke national concern due to their macro-economic effects. However, in the 1990s, they became less important, partly because wage levels increased little if at all, and partly because negotiations were conducted at the enterprise level and took account of the profitability of the enterprise.

Apart from the annual spring pay negotiations, the parties may negotiate other matters such as bonuses, overtime rates and shorter working hours.

Industrial stoppages have almost disappeared: In 2004, only fifty-one stoppages involving about 7,000 workers were recorded. However, it seems that individual dissatisfaction is not handled well by enterprise unions, because there seem to be an increasing number of individual grievances in many enterprises. Further, there is widespread criticism that enterprise unions are only concerned to protect the interests of regular employees, often at the expense of part-time and temporary workers.

9.4.   RECENT CHANGES AND FUTURE TRENDS

The problems of the Japanese labour movement have long been discussed by employment relations specialists as well as by union leaders. The main issues of concern are:

(a) the steady decline of union density;
(b) the lack of militancy at all levels of the unionized sectors;
(c) the shortage of motivated union leaders;
(d) the limited participation of rank-and-file workers in union activities; and
(e) the bureaucratization of unions (most union activities are scheduled yearly)

In the context of public support for deregulation and free-market mechanisms, the union movement will be facing even more difficult times.

On the other hand, there are some positive signs for the labour movement. For instance, the framework of labour legislation, which was built after 1945, is still largely intact despite some modifications (Labour Standard Law, Trade Union Law and the Employment Insurance System). Moreover, where unions exist, their role and performance are usually well regarded by employers as well as by the workers. Attitudinal surveys tend to show that unionized workers view union activities favourably, although few of them participate actively in union activities.

Unions appear to be facing a difficult challenge of identifying the preferences and demands of the collective voice, due to the divergent composition and characteristics of their members (including white-collar and blue-collar workers, differences in age, sex and region). Before the 1970s oil crises, a demand for better wages and living conditions seemed to characterize the common interests of most workers. Subsequently, such a demand seems to be impractical (in the context of differences of profitability of individual enterprises) and less appealing (in the context of greater affluence). Nevertheless, unions at different levels still have a useful role to play as the voice of employees and to foster workers' participation.

Finally, there is an urgent need for unions to enlarge their membership base, particularly by including temporaries, part-time employees and retired workers. If they are to thrive again, Japanese unions might have to reinvent themselves as a broader social movement.

Part III

An International Review
of Key Issues

*Greg J. Bamber, Philippe Pochet, Cameron Allan,
Richard N. Block, Frank Burchill,
Joelle Cuillerier, Grant Fitzner, Ben French,
Stacy Hickox, Berndt Keller, Michael L. Moore,
Sofia Murhem, Gregor Murray, Asako Nakamichi,
Werner Nienhueser, Erling Rasmussen,
Hiromasa Suzuki and Hiroaki Watanabe*

This part includes ten chapters covering various aspects of individual and collective rights at work.

Chapter 1

Work and Family

This chapter covers maternity leave, parental leave, childcare policy and flexible work arrangements.

Attempts to reconcile family life and working commitments are high on the employment relations agenda in most of the countries. Ageing populations and debates about gender equality issues are two drivers. Nevertheless, there is still much variation from country to country. In the United Kingdom, Australia and New Zealand, this issue is a major focus for social policy and has led to the adoption of new legislative proposals. In the European Union (EU), the Scandinavian countries are often seen as a preferred model.

Comparing paid maternity (parental) leave is complicated. There are two main dimensions: the level of benefit and the length of the paid leave. Remuneration is not necessarily the full salary that applied before the parental leave. There are various options for extension of such leave. It is also possible for leave to be unpaid or partially paid. There is a diverse pattern of provision, but the trend is towards an increasing number of paid leave days. At the EU level, the parental leave directive has been revised (June 2009) with the minimum length of leave increased from three to four months. The most favourable parental situation is in Sweden with 480 days of paid leave (of which 60 are paternity leave).

The USA and Australia are among the few DMEs without statutory paid maternity leave. In Australia the most recent conservative government initiated a scheme that lasted for a few years whereby mothers were paid a cash bonus for each birth. All employees in Australia can access up to one year of unpaid parental leave. From 2011 it is proposed that most Australian women who have worked for at least twelve continuous months with their current employer (except certain casuals) will have the right as primary carers to access eighteen-weeks paid leave, paid at the rate of the Federal Minimum Wage (FMW).

Parental leave, including paternity leave, is also becoming more widely available, but it appears that many fathers are not fully taking full advantage of these new benefits (for example, Japan, where less than 0.5% of fathers take childcare leave compared with nearly 80% of mothers). Paid parental leave was a major issue in New Zealand in the late 1990s.

Sweden has often been recognized as having one of the most family-friendly policies among the developed countries as well as an extensive system of publicly funded childcare. Germany is lagging behind in terms of childcare (but there are proposals for improvement connected to reforming the school system). Childcare is an important issue in other European countries; the EU has set a general target for children attending childcare facilities by 2010 (see section 1.1 following page). In Canada, Quebec was the leading province in childcare policy. By contrast, this matter is not addressed at the federal level in the USA.

Flexible working-time arrangements are offered by some employers in the various countries, but there has not yet been a systematic analysis of such arrangements. As a generalization, public-sector employers seem to be more likely to have such innovative schemes. In the United Kingdom and New Zealand, parents with children under 6 years of age or parents of disabled children can make a request for flexible working arrangements, and the employer must give serious consideration to such employees' requests.

1.1.   EUROPEAN UNION

The Parental Leave Directive negotiated by the EU social partners provides a minimum of three months leave. The eligibility criteria and the procedures for making an application for parental leave are to be defined by law and/or collective agreement in the Member States, subject to compliance with the minimum requirements of the directive. The Member States may introduce more favourable provisions than those stipulated in the directive. The minimum requirements of the agreement are that male and female workers have individual entitlements to parental leave in respect of the birth or adoption of a child. The period of leave is at least three months; they are protected against the termination of their employment on the grounds of having requested or taken parental leave. Employees who have taken parental leave have the right to return to the same job at the end of the period of leave or, if that is not possible, to an equivalent or similar job consistent with their employment contract. Any accrued seniority rights are to be maintained. The Member States and/or the social partners are to allow workers to take time off from work, in accordance with national legislation, collective agreements and/or practice, for unforeseen circumstances arising from a family emergency relating to illness or accident, which necessitates immediate attendance of the employee. This agreement was revised and improved in June 2009. Amongst the main changes were:

An increase in the length of parental leave from three to four months and strengthening it as an individual right, by making a part of it fully non-transferable; a right to request flexible working arrangements when returning from leave; calls on Member States and/or social partners to establish notice periods to be given by workers who propose to take parental leave. It also recognizes to a greater extent increasingly diverse family structures and promotes an equal sharing of family responsibilities. The social partners have requested that their new agreement be extended universally by a directive in the same way as the original accord.

The part-time agreement foresees the equal treatment of employees regardless if they are working full time and part time and the right to change from full-time to part-time work and vice-versa (see Chapter 7). Other legislation (currently under review) protects pregnant workers by ensuring a minimum maternity leave of fourteen weeks and prohibiting the dismissal of pregnant workers and workers on maternity leave.

The European Employment Strategy (EES) calls on Member States to promote reconciliation policies, notably through the provision of accessible and affordable childcare facilities for children and other dependents. The 'Barcelona targets' in 2002 called for access to childcare for at least a third of children aged up to 3 years old and 90% of children aged from 3 to mandatory school age in 2010. These targets also promote suitably innovative and adaptable forms of work organization.[95] Guideline 18 of the employment strategy is devoted to this issue.

1.2.   GERMANY

Maternity leave is regulated by legislation (*Mutterschutzgesetz*), which applies to all women in paid employment, regardless whether they are part-time or full-time. Maternity leave covers the six weeks prior to and eight weeks after the birth. During maternity leave, employees are entitled to receive their average earnings paid by the employer. For women in a statutory health insurance scheme the employer has only to pay the difference between the allowance of the health insurance and the average earnings. Women covered by statutory health insurance are entitled to maternity benefits, which include pharmaceuticals and medical treatment in hospital or at home. Social-insurance contributions are maintained during maternity leave. The employee is protected against dismissal during the period of pregnancy and for four months after the birth. Although there is no special statutory entitlement for paternity leave as such, there are provisions for parental leave (*Elternzeit*). The family is entitled to an income-related child-rearing benefit (*Elterngeld*). The period of leave can be divided between the mother and father. Both parents are entitled to be paid the benefit, at a rate of 67% of a parent's former average net income and it is paid for twelve months. If the father takes more than two months of leave, the length of benefit payment is extended from twelve to fourteen months. The minimum benefit is EUR 300 per month and the maximum is EUR 1,800.

Parental leave to care for children (including leave for family reasons, leave to care for sick children or children with disabilities, and leave for family

---

95. For a recent evaluation, see Commission, 2008.

emergencies) is generally regulated by law and not by collective agreements. Both parents have the right to take parental leave for up to three years after a child's birth. Both parents are allowed to take parental leave concurrently.

The Federal Childcare Payment and Parental Leave Act (*Bundeselterngeld- und Elternzeitgesetz*) entitles parents on parental leave to childcare payment; the amount depends on the parents' household income. Employees are protected against dismissal during parental leave. Employees who are members of a statutory health insurance fund are entitled to sickness benefits if their child is sick or disabled. The entitlement is limited to ten working days per child per year and to a total maximum period of twenty-five working days per year. Single parents have extended entitlements.

Compared to other European countries, there is a relatively poor supply of childcare facilities for working parents. Only a small percentage of children attend a kindergarten or school until 4.00 p.m. There are initiatives to reorganize the German childcare and school system to provide childcare or school 'from 8.00 a.m. to 4.00 p.m.', in particular, for full-time working parents and working mothers. The outcome of current political discussions about the extension of child-care provisions is difficult to predict.

The supply of childcare facilities by employers is inadequate. Across the EU, only between 1% (industry/manufacturing) and 3% (services) of enterprises offer childcare facilities: In Germany, these percentages are much lower. Only 32% of working women, compared to 42% of male workers, say that their working time arrangements correspond with their personal family needs.[96]

Childcare is not seen as an important issue in collective bargaining. The traditional 'male breadwinner' model still dominates bargaining policy. Some larger enterprises have started to offer childcare facilities for working mothers. But this is limited to a small proportion of working parents and is an attempt to reduce labour turnover, especially for highly qualified personnel. For some enterprises, offering such facilities is in an attempt to enhance their reputation, but these facilities do not represent a substantial contribution to Germany's social services.

1.3.   SWEDEN

The law on equality declares that employers should make it easier for men and women to combine family and work. Pregnant women are not to be discriminated against in terms of remuneration, nor can they lawfully be dismissed or passed over for promotion.

Parents have the right to full parental leave until the child is 18 months old, but the maximum paid leave is 480 days for both parents, taken together. For 390 days, the parent receives 80% of their salary up to a cap, and for 90 days, minimum pay. Of the paid leave, sixty days are reserved for each parent. Parents also have the right to shorten their working time by 25% until the child has finished the first

---

96.   Klenner, 2004.

year in school or turns 8 years old. Following the implementation of EU Directive 92/85, female employees have the right to take maternity leave for at least seven weeks before the child's birth and at least seven weeks after the birth. There are also generous systems for carer's leave. If the child is ill, the parents have the right to stay at home with the child, up to 120 days per year, receiving 80% of their salary up to a cap.

Sweden has ratified ILO Conventions 156 and 165. Most of the initiatives to make it easier to combine family and work, however, are administered through the welfare system rather than under labour laws. Sweden has the world's most extensive system of childcare. For instance, municipalities must provide childcare services for any parent who requests them. There is a government subsidy to the municipalities to help cover part of the costs and there are limits on the fees which can be charged. In combination with generous provisions for parental leave and carer's leave, combining family and work in Sweden is comparatively easy.

1.4.   UNITED KINGDOM

The government aims to help working parents balance work and family life in ways that are also advantageous to business. Measures to support working families were Labour Party Manifesto commitments in 2001 and 2005. A package of improved laws for working parents was implemented in 2003:

(a) Parents with children under 6 or disabled children under 18 can make a request to work flexibly and their employers have a statutory duty to consider their requests seriously.

(b) Ordinary Maternity Leave (OML) of twenty-six weeks for all employed mothers is usually paid, followed by the possibility of twenty-six weeks' unpaid Additional Maternity Leave (AML) for mothers who have worked for their employer for the required qualifying period. Most mothers can choose to take up to one year off work.

(c) Payment of Statutory Maternity Pay (SMP) and Maternity Allowance (MA) for twenty-six weeks. Six weeks paid at 90% of average weekly earnings and twenty weeks at a flat rate (GBP 108.85 per week from April 2006).

(d) New fathers can take up to two weeks' paternity leave with Statutory Paternity Pay (SPP) paid at the same standard rate as SMP.

(e) An adoptive parent can take up to one year's adoption leave with six months' Statutory Adoption Pay (SAP) along similar lines to maternity leave.

(f) Parents of young children can qualify for thirteen weeks' unpaid parental leave, which they can take up to their child's 5th birthday. Parents of disabled children are able to take eighteen weeks' parental leave up to their child's 18th birthday.

(g) All employees have a right to a reasonable amount of unpaid time off work to deal with any emergency involving a dependent.

Mothers and fathers are taking their paid leave. The *Maternity and Paternity Rights and Benefits: Survey of Parents*[97] found that three-quarters of mothers take their full entitlement to paid maternity leave. This is up from two-thirds in 2002. In addition around 93% of fathers take time off around the date that their child is born, with 79% taking up their entitlement to paternity leave.

All businesses can claim from the government 92% of the amount they pay out in SMP/SPP/SAP, but businesses that pay less than GBP 45,000 in National Insurance contributions in a year are able to reclaim 100%, plus an extra 4.5%. Businesses can also claim the money in advance to help with their cash flow.

In the decade after 1997, the standard rate of SMP almost doubled, from GBP 55 to GBP 108.85. However, SMP and SPP should not be seen in isolation. Working Tax Credit supports working households on low incomes by topping-up earnings. Parents on paid maternity, paternity or adoption leave retain their eligibility for Working Tax Credit and the childcare element of Working Tax Credit. This means they receive additional financial support and can continue to receive help with the costs of childcare during paid leave. From 2007 SMP, combined with other government financial support for families was worth more than GBP 8,000 for many families during a child's first year, up from GBP 2,600 in 1997.

New provisions are being put in place through the Work and Families Act, which was enacted in June 2006. It contains measures to improve the arrangements for parents to take paid leave after the birth of a child, and extends the scope of the existing right to request flexible working. Specifically, the 2006 legislation:

(a) Extends the period for SMP/SPP/SAP payment to a maximum of fifty-two weeks. As a first step, the government extended the current entitlement of twenty-six weeks to thirty-nine weeks from April 2007. This will benefit around 400,000 mothers per year.

(b) Gives fathers a new right to more paternity leave, which will enable them to benefit from paid leave, if the mother returns to work after six months, but before the end of her maternity leave period. Between 240,000 to 280,000 fathers will benefit. The aim of the government is to introduce Additional Paternity Leave by 2010, the end of the current Parliament, alongside the further extension of maternity leave to fifty-two weeks.

(c) Extends the right to request flexible working to carers of adults from April 2007, which could benefit up to 1.5 million carers.

(d) Provides a one-off power, to increase the maximum amount of a week's pay affecting compensation payments in connection with, in particular, redundancy, unfair dismissal and insolvency.

---

97. DTI, 2005.

1.5.   UNITED STATES OF AMERICA

An increasing number of employers, including the federal government, provide for flexible work schedules that allow parents to better balance work and family responsibilities. Regarding statutory protection, the federal Family and Medical Leave Act requires employers to provide employees twelve weeks of unpaid leave for various reasons, including family illness and maternity. California and New Jersey are the only states that provide for paid family leave. There is no statutory provision specifically for paid maternity or paternity leave.

1.6.   CANADA

The Labour Code in the federal jurisdiction and the provinces provides for maternity-related leave, parental leave and compassionate care leave. In most jurisdictions, these provisions are being reviewed with a view to promoting better work/family balance.

Maternity leave and parental leave (for the care of newborn or adopted children) are available for a period of thirty-seven weeks. An important tool is the use of the Employment Insurance Commission, to which payments are made by employees and employers, to finance periods of unemployment, including parental leave. This Commission is in the federal jurisdiction. Provinces make arrangements to enhance the access of employees in their province. The province of Quebec recently improved its parental leave (maternity and paternity provisions). It provides an opportunity for either parent to take extended leave to care for newborn children. The financial contribution by the Commission is topped up by a Quebec government contribution through general taxation. Minimum-standards legislation ensures the articulation between these forms of income support and the right of individual employees to access their rights without fear of discrimination in their jobs.

Apart from income insurance, there are few other specific forms of legislated protection relative to parental responsibilities. Collective agreements sometimes seek to facilitate work-family balance issues through the introduction of clauses stipulating a degree of time flexibility. Continuing demographic pressures (reflecting at least in part the decline in the birth rate) are likely to prompt more legislative initiatives on this issue in the years ahead.

1.7.   NEW ZEALAND

Paid parental leave was a major issue in the late-1990s and it became a legislated entitlement in 2002. The current maximum entitlement is fourteen weeks paid parental level. Work-life balance, long working hours and work-related stress are amongst the most debated current issues in New Zealand. Government initiatives and union campaigns have played an important role, though the main driver has probably been the changes to work organization, employment participation and working-time patterns. Traditionally, work-life balance was underpinned by a support of standard employment patterns (including restrictions on non-standard employment patterns and/or additional payments) and legislative provision of leave entitlements. This traditional situation was built on the award system; and the changes introduced in the 1990s by the Employment Contracts Act precipitated a different situation when the traditional patterns of working life were changing.

Besides legislative changes, the post-1999 Labour-led governments relied mainly on three other levers. First, there were considerable changes in welfare policies and, in particular, a major increase in the levels of financial support to beneficiaries. This included, for example, subsidized childcare programs – Out of School Childcare (OSCAR) – to enable parents to work longer days, and transport subsidies as part of a comprehensive back-to-work package.

Second, the government used its role as a major employer in support of work-life balance initiatives. Public-sector employers have been trend-setters in promoting employment participation and career advancement for women and ethnic minorities. For example, research on call-centres has shown that public-sector call centres are leading the way in facilitating the return of mothers to paid employment.

Third, the government resourced research and information initiatives to make work-life balance part of mainstream employment relations (<www.dol.govt.nz/worklife/index>). It has also supported the EEO Trust that has been a key organization in making work-life balance and employment concerns – including a focus on the mature workforce – an area of interest for private-sector employers.

Work-life balance issues are newsworthy because there have been many problems in achieving suitable work-life balances. There are some contradictory factors. While the government advocates work-life balance, it also sees increasing productivity levels as a key public-policy goal and it aims to improve New Zealand's relative economic position amongst OECD countries. Similarly, enterprises are in a bind when they try to increase productivity, profits and competitiveness and, at the same time, try to be 'good employers' and promote work-life balance and equal opportunity policies. Research on work-life balance practices in the banking sector found that there was a considerable gap between the avowed policies and actual practices – a gap caused by management pressure on workers to achieve performance targets.

1.8.   AUSTRALIA

The federal Labor government has promised to introduce an eighteen-week paid parental leave scheme from January 2011 as mentioned above. Employees are entitled to twelve months unpaid parental leave, though paid maternity leave is more common in the public sector than in the private sector. Mothers are currently paid a cash bonus on the birth of each child. This will continue only for mothers who are not in employment. One of the new minimum National Employment

Standards to introduced in Australia on 1 January 2010 was the right of employees to request flexible working arrangements. Employers will be obliged to give due consideration to any such requests and must provide written reasons if the request is refused. However, after giving the request due consideration, there is no obligation on the employer to agree.

1.9.   JAPAN

The difficulty of combining work with childcare for women is seen as a major reason contributing to the decline of fertility rates in Japan. Although the number of double income households has steadily increased since 1980 to overtake (in 1997) the number of single-income households based on the traditional male-breadwinner model (Cabinet Office: White Paper on Gender Equality, 2008), the working environment for employees with family responsibilities is still relatively unaccommodating, in spite of the following legislative measures.

The Law Concerning the Welfare of Workers Who Take Care of Children or Other Family Members Including Child Care and Family Care Leave (enacted in 1991 and amended in 2004) was introduced in an attempt to ensure that employees with childcare and other family responsibilities could continue working. Under the childcare-leave legislation, employees who are rearing a child under the age of 1 year can take childcare leave for up to one year (one year and six months under certain conditions, for example, if they could not secure childcare) by submitting a request to his/her employer. Leave to care for a sick child before elementary school up to five days per year should also be granted upon request of the employee. Employees on fixed-term contracts and who were not eligible for childcare leave have been eligible since the 2004 amendments, after satisfying certain conditions (the contractual term should be for more than one year). Under the family-care leave legislation, an employee can apply for leave for a period of up to ninety-three days per year to provide care to a spouse, parent, child, or spouse's parent who is in need of assistance from a family member. Both forms of leave are limited to once per childcare recipient. The employer cannot reject a leave application from an employee who meets the requirements and cannot dismiss employees because they have applied for childcare, carer's leave or family leave.

Although an employer does not need to pay wages during the period of leave, the amendments to the Employment Insurance Law (in 2007) provided employees with benefits equivalent to a maximum of 50% of their wages during periods of childcare leave. For family-care leave, the benefits amount to 40% of the employees' wages. Moreover, payments of social insurance contributions during childcare leave can be waived on request of the employer (they cannot be waived for family care leave).

According to a Survey of Women's Employment Management (Ministry of Health, Labour and Welfare, 2004 (<www.mhlw.go.jp/english>), among the employees meeting the requirements to take childcare leave, less than 1% of male employees and 73% of female employees took childcare leave in 2003.

73

A major issue with regard to which workers utilize childcare leave is the gender imbalance. This is evidenced by the finding that, for every 100 employees who take the leave, 97 are females and only 3 are males. The imbalance also reflects the corporate culture of many Japanese companies, which makes it difficult for male employees to undertake such family responsibilities. Long working hours are also an issue, making it difficult to work as a regular employee while also assuming family responsibilities. Despite the legislation summarized previously, the situation of female employees with family responsibilities is deteriorating as a consequence of the 2008 economic crisis. In particular, the increasing number of cases of *ikukyu-giri* (dismissal or forced resignation by employers of employees who take childcare leave) is becoming an urgent problem, together with the shortage of childcare facilities for working parents.

Chapter 2
Individual Agreements

In Australia, under the post-1996 conservative government, Australian Workplace Agreements (AWAs) were a form of individualised employment arrangement. After the advent of the post-2007 Labor government, AWAs survived for a limited period. No new AWAs were permitted to be made after March 2008. Individual Transitional Employment Agreements (ITEAs) continued to be made until the end of 2009. This chapter explains how so-called individual agreements relate to laws or collective agreements in the other countries reviewed.

2.1.   EUROPEAN UNION

The main regulation is the directive (October 1991) on an employer's obligation to inform employees of the terms and conditions of the contract of employment (91/533). The directive applies to any employment relationship that is subject to prevailing legislation in a Member State, other than casual work, jobs involving no more than eight hours of work on average per week, and those not exceeding a month in all. An employee who is not given a written contract or a document referring to a collective agreement must, not later than two months after the commencement of employment, be given a written statement including: the identity of the parties; the place of work; a job specification or description, and the classification of employment; the duration or term of the employment relationship, and of any probationary trial period where applicable, and the periods of notice; the standard working hours and the amount of paid leave; the rate of pay and arrangements for payment; the applicable social security scheme, and any supplementary scheme where appropriate; and reference to applicable collective agreements.

Any subsequent change to the terms of employment must also be made in a written document. The employment contract for employees required to work in another country must also include: the duration of the employment abroad; the currency to be used for the payment of remuneration; any fringe benefits; and, where appropriate, the conditions governing the employee's repatriation. These are minimum requirements.

2.2. GERMANY

Because the terms and conditions of employment in Germany are mainly fixed by law, collective agreements and works agreements, there is little scope for individual agreements, except for senior managerial employees (*leitende Angestellte*). Any individual contracts may not deviate from the provisions of statute law, collective agreements or works agreements to disadvantage the employee.[98]

2.3. SWEDEN

An employer cannot have individual contracts and collective agreements for the same group of employees. If the employer is a member of an employers' association or has signed a collective agreement for a particular sector, then individual contracts are prohibited.

2.4. UNITED KINGDOM

Approximately two-thirds of employees are not covered by collective bargaining and may, therefore, be covered by individual agreements. However, there is no provision for individual agreements which could override collective ones.

Because of the growth of equality and non-discrimination legislation, individual agreements are difficult to sustain. They can easily be categorized, not only as failing the equal-pay-for-work-of-equal-value tests, but they can also be linked to age, sex, race and other forms of discrimination. The current Equality Act, designed to combine and harmonize all previously enacted discrimination laws, will prevent any imposition of secrecy clauses on pay rates. Employees will be free to disclose and discuss their pay. An added objective of the Equality Act is to reduce the gender pay gap.

2.5. UNITED STATES OF AMERICA

In the USA, most employees are considered to be employees-at-will and do not have a specific written individual agreement. The employer can terminate the employment at any time and the employee can also give notice to quit at any time. In practice, most employers provide at least two weeks notice and many have adopted employee

---

98. Eurofound, 2006.

handbooks that specify workplace rules and policies. Specific individual agreements are prevalent among highly paid professionals and executives, such as CEOs of companies, chief financial officers, and key sales personnel and other executives, as well as sports people, entertainers and scientists.

2.6.   CANADA

The collective bargaining regime is comprehensive and does not make provisions for individual agreements that override or exclude existing collective agreements. It would be illegal for employees who were covered by a collective agreement to be engaged under an individual agreement.

Individual employees are subject to the protections of employment law, notably with regard to broad provisions for non-discrimination under human rights legislation and charter obligations and for exercising statutory health and safety rights, compensation for occupational injuries, employment insurance and collective labour legislation.

2.7.   NEW ZEALAND

Before the Employment Contracts Act 1991, the main employment relations regulation focused on collective arrangements. Individual employment arrangements were dealt with under common law and employees covered by individual agreements had (besides statutory minima) only limited employment rights. This was changed in 1991 and since then, employees on individual agreements have had considerable protection through the personal grievance right, statutory minima and anti-discrimination rights.

The Employment Relations Act 2000 further bolstered such rights. The Act enhances the protection of individual choice, including the right to seek advice over an individual employment agreement and the prescription of default content items (such as, working time and place of work) in all individual employment agreements. The 2000 Act also aligns employee protections with the existing anti-discrimination legislation. The 'good faith' obligation also covers the negotiation and conclusion of individual employment agreements. While there are still concerns over compliance – informal agreements are still prevalent – legislation, has improved the protections for employees on individual employment agreements in the new millennium. It is still too early to tell whether the restriction on personal grievance rights for new employees will have any significant negative effect on protection for these employees.

2.8.   AUSTRALIA

An unusual feature of the Australian industrial system is that individual contracts, AWAs and ITEAs, could override awards and collective agreements.

AWAs cover only approximately 3% to 4% of all employees. Unregistered 'common-law' individual contracts cover about a third of employees. Generally, common-law contracts underpinned by an award operate to the extent that a common-law contract of employment will override the award to the extent of any inconsistency if it is more favourable. A contract of employment not underpinned by an award, but containing all relevant conditions of employment, may also operate and be subject to scrutiny by the courts in actions for breach of contract.

The Labor government elected in 2007 has sought to promote workplace flexibility through the use of individual flexibility arrangements. These arrangements allow for variations to modern awards or enterprise agreements to meet the needs of employers and individual employees, while at the same time ensuring that minimum entitlements and protections are maintained.

The FW Act 2009 requires that every modern award and enterprise agreement must include a 'flexibility term'. A flexibility term allows an employer and an individual employee to agree on an arrangement which varies the effect of the modern award or enterprise agreement to meet the genuine needs of the employer and the individual employee.

Flexibility agreements do not need to be approved by FWA. Instead, the employer is responsible for ensuring that each flexibility agreement:

- be genuinely agreed to by the employer and employee;
- result in the employee being 'better off overall' than the employee would have been if no flexibility arrangements were made; and
- be signed by both the employer and employee (or be signed by a parent or guardian if the employee is under 18 years old).

A copy of the flexibility agreement must be provided to the employee within 14 days of the agreement.

2.9.   JAPAN

Under the Trade Union Law, any portion of an individual employment contract contravening the standards in the collective agreement is void. The invalidated portion of the individual contract is governed by the standards in the collective agreement. If there are matters that an individual employment contract does not cover, the same rule applies. Collective agreements supersede individual contracts, and invalidate work rules that contravene the collective agreement.

Chapter 3
Non-standard Employment

This chapter covers various types of atypical work: fixed-term, part-time, casual, temporary agency as well as self-employment and independent contractors. In broad terms there is a common trend toward an increase in the use of non-standard forms of employment, but there does not seem to be a convergence when we consider the various forms of atypical work. Each country has its own mix. For example, the USA has the lowest proportion of temporary and part-time work of the countries examined here. The highest proportion of fixed-term contracts is found in Sweden. The United Kingdom and New Zealand have the highest proportion of part-timers.

The OECD[99] has analysed developments concerning temporary employment. It appears that the USA is the country where not only are there fewer temporary workers as a proportion of the workforce (less than 4%), but also where this percentage is declining (from 5% in 1995). The United Kingdom has had a relatively stable percentage since 1985 (around 6% to 7%). Canada and Japan each have a similar trend with an increase from 10% to 13% in fifteen years (1985–2000). Sweden is the country with the largest proportion (around 15%).

In most of the countries, earlier restrictions (for example, on the length of contracts) have been relaxed. As in the case of part-time workers in Europe (see below), fixed-term workers should receive similar benefits as workers who have an open-ended contract.

In all the countries (except New Zealand) the percentage of part-time workers has increased in recent years, following a trend that began in the 1990s. There remain, however, considerable differences between countries like the USA and Sweden (with less than 15%) and Japan, United Kingdom, New Zealand, Australia and Germany (with more than 20%).

---

99. OECD, 2004.

Table 3.1 Part-Time Workers as a Percentage of Total Employment

	EU	Germany	Sweden	UK	USA	Canada	New Zealand	Australia	Japan
2000	16.4	17.6	14.0	22.7	12.6	18.1	22.2	26.4	17.7[a]
2007	18.2	22.2	14.4	23.3	12.6	18.2	22.0	29.5[b]	18.9

Source: OECD (2009) Factbook.
a. 2002.
b. 2009.

Under European Union (EU) legislation, there should be 'equal treatment' with regard to pay and employment conditions between a part-time and/or fixed-term worker and one with a full-time, open-ended contract. This is unlike the situation in Canada (except in Quebec). Some protections are guaranteed in Japan. For very short part-time contracts and/or workers below a certain income threshold, there are lower levels of social security contribution/taxes in Germany and Japan.

With regard to casual work, there is a diverse picture. In some countries casual employees are covered by the part-time/fixed-term legislation; in others there are discussions about the appropriate regulations to adopt.

There is no comprehensive international quantitative comparison for temporary agency workers. An important difference is between countries where the temporary workers are paid at a rate agreed with the agency (for example, Sweden) or where they are paid or should receive the same rates as their colleagues in the place where they are employed (for example, Germany). Nevertheless, recent data shows that temporary employees are paid less than regular ones in Germany (because wage rates in collective agreements can be lower than the rates required by the principles of equal pay and equality of treatment).

There is no time limitation for the duration of temporary agency work in New Zealand, except that the employer must have a valid reason for the specified time limit. In Sweden the same rules apply for the duration of temporary agency work as for fixed-term contracts. In Germany, the use of agency work was previously restricted to a limited period; but since 2004 there has been no limit on the duration. For fixed-term contracts between the worker and the agency the same restrictions apply as for fixed-term contracts in general (fixed-term contracts can only be entered into for a total of up to twenty-four months). In Japan, agency workers are permitted across a wide range of occupations, except port transport services, construction work, security services and medical-related work in hospitals.

The proportion of the working population in self-employment tends to be reasonably stable in most of these countries, apart from Japan where there was a reduction from more than 22% in 1990 to less than 14% in 2004. The decreasing percentage in Japan can be explained by the rapid reduction in the number of small farmers. The lowest rate of self-employment is in the USA. This could reflect that country's very flexible employment regulation.

Table 3.2 Self-Employment as a Percentage of Total Employment

	EU15	Germany	Sweden	United Kingdom	USA	Canada	New Zealand	Australia	Japan
2000	16.7	11.0	10.3	12.8	7.4	10.6	20.7	14.1	16.6
2007	15.9	12.0	9.9	13.8	7.2	9.3	17.3	12.9	13.6

Source: OECD (2009) Factbook.

There is little difference between workers who are self-employed and those who are regarded as independent contractors. Debates about independent contractors are part of a broader discussion on work contracts. Italy has recognized a new category of employment relationship referred to as 'para-subordination'. Para-subordinate workers are self-employed, nominally independent, contractors. However, they are, in reality, economically-dependent workers because they work mainly or exclusively for only one client/enterprise.

3.1. EUROPEAN UNION

The EU has an important influence on atypical work regulations in Member States, following the adoption of two collective agreements, which were transformed into directives. The first covers part-time work and the second deals with fixed-term contracts.

A Framework Agreement on part-time work was concluded by BusinessEurope, CEEP and the ETUC in 1997. (This later became EU Directive 97/81.) The aim of the agreement is, on the one hand, to remove all forms of discrimination against part-time workers and thereby to improve the quality of part-time work. On the other hand, its aim is to facilitate the development of part-time work on a voluntary basis and to contribute to the flexible organization of working time. The main provision stipulates that, with regard to working conditions (including pay, holidays and superannuation by pension), part-time workers may not be treated less favourably, on a pro rata basis, than comparable full-time workers unless such unequal treatment is objectively justified. This means part-timers are entitled, for example, to the same hourly rate of pay, access to company superannuation schemes, annual leave and maternity/parental leave, sick pay and access to training as their full-time co-workers.

The directive contains provisions that allow for exceptions to the general principle of non-discrimination for part-time workers engaged on a casual basis. Member States can offer access to particular working conditions depending on a certain period of service, a certain amount of working time, and a certain level of earnings, but only if such restriction can be justified on objective grounds.

A Framework Agreement on fixed-term work was concluded by the social partners (ETUC, BusinessEurope and CEEP) in 1999. The social partners acknowledge that employment contracts based on an assumption of indefinite-duration employment are and will continue to represent the standard form of employment relationship. The purpose is to improve the quality of fixed-term work by ensuring that such employees' conditions of employment are protected by the principle of non-discrimination and that their employment relationship is protected from the abusive imposition of successive fixed-term contracts.

The principle of non-discrimination is based on a comparison with a worker who is employed to do similar work in the same establishment under an indefinite-duration contract. To avoid abuses, if there are no comparable workers with an indefinite-duration contract, the comparison must be based on the relevant collective agreement. If there is no relevant collective agreement, the comparison must be in accordance with national laws, collective agreements or accepted practices. Member States should introduce one or more of the following measures: objective reasons justifying the renewal of such fixed-term contracts; the maximum total duration of such contracts; and the number of renewals allowed. They should also determine the definition of 'successive' and 'indefinite duration'.

In 2001 the EU social partners initiated discussion on temporary agency workers but were unable to reach agreement. After the EU Commission proposed a draft directive, in November 2008 the European Parliament and Council adopted a directive on temporary agency work that must be implemented by all EU Member States by 2011. The directive provides that the basic employment conditions of temporary agency workers must be, for the duration of their assignment, the user undertaking, equal to those that would apply if the worker had been recruited directly by that employer to carry out the same job. However, under certain circumstances, unions and employers may agree on different arrangements, including a qualifying period that must be completed before equal treatment applies. For example:

- Member States may, after consulting the social partners, provide for an exemption from the principle of equal pay or remuneration in cases where temporary agency workers have a permanent employment contract with their agency and continue to be paid by their agency between assignments.
- Member States may, after consulting the social partners, give them the option of maintaining or concluding collective agreements that establish arrangements that differ from the directive's equal treatment requirements. However, these agreements must 'respect the overall protection' of temporary agency workers.
- Member States have to review existing restrictions or prohibitions on the use of temporary agency work, to verify if they are still justified.
- Temporary agency workers should have access to jobs, collective facilities (canteens, childcare and so on) and vocational training on the same basis as workers employed directly by the undertaking.

There is no specific EU legislation on self-employment and independent contractors.

Even if it is not a legal obligation, flexicurity – which seeks to combine a flexible labour market with employment security for workers – should also be mentioned. The Netherlands and Denmark are generally considered as having the best examples of policies that combine flexibility for enterprises and security for workers. According to the Commission,[100] flexicurity aims at ensuring that EU workers can enjoy a high level of employment security, that is, the opportunity of finding employment at every stage of their working life and having good prospects for career development in changing economic circumstances. It also aims at helping employees and employers to benefit fully from the opportunities presented by globalization, by creating the conditions in which security and flexibility can reinforce each other.

The flexicurity debate is also linked to the debate that is referred to previously in terms of the complementary aspects between institutions. Flexicurity is supposed to operate as a virtuous circle that encompasses a flexible labour market, a supportive welfare state that provides high unemployment benefits, and proactive policies to life-long learning.

At the EU level, ten general flexicurity principles have been adopted.[101] In the absence of a universal flexicurity model, the Commission's Communication proposes four pathways to enable Member States to define the strategy which best suits their individual circumstances. These pathways should address the following issues:

(a) reducing contractual segmentation;
(b) developing flexicurity within the enterprise and offering transitional security;
(c) remedying skills and opportunity gaps amongst the workforce; and
(d) improving job opportunities for unemployed and informally employed workers.

3.2. GERMANY

Labour law in Germany allows for fixed-term employment contracts of up to two years' duration. In principle, employees with fixed-term or part-time contracts should be treated equally with permanent employees. More than 8% of all employees are currently employed under fixed-term contracts. This percentage has been relatively stable, despite the easing of legal regulation on several occasions since the mid-1980s.[102]

There are two different forms of 'petty employment' (*geringfügige Beschäftigung*): 'mini-jobs' and 'midi-jobs'. Both forms refer to jobs with reduced social security contributions. A mini-job is a job with an income of up to EUR 400 a month. Employees do not have to pay social security contributions; the employer is obliged to pay a contribution of 25% of the wage (to cover health and superannuation insurance). Midi-jobs are those with an income of between EUR 401 and

---

100. Commission, 2007.
101. *Ibid.*
102. Percentages cited from Keller & Seifert, 2007.

EUR 800 a month. For these jobs, social security contributions have to be paid at higher rates, depending on the level of income – from zero contributions at EUR 401 up to full contributions at EUR 800. More than 6 million people are employed in mini-jobs and more than 700,000 in midi-jobs.

In 2008, almost 800,000 employees were temporary agency workers. This corresponded to more than 2% of all employees, the highest percentage ever reached but still a relatively low percentage when compared to other European countries. However, the number decreased to a considerable degree in the following economic crisis. However, there have been fairly high growth rates of temporary agency work for many years. Temporary agency work means a 'triangular' relationship involving a worker, a temporary work agency and a user company or host employer. The agency employs the workers and makes them available on a temporary basis to the host employer. Although in practice the temporary workers work for the host employer, from a legal perspective, the agency is their employer. Legal authorization is required to operate such an agency. Legislation enacted in 2003 abolished many legal restrictions on this specific kind of work. While temporary workers are granted, in principle, a right to equality of treatment with workers of the user company, in reality they are often paid less. Since 2004 there has been no restriction on the duration of assignments. The general regulation of fixed-term contracts applies to agency work as well as to other forms of employment. From a legal point of view, temporary agency workers have the same social security rights as permanent employees. The principles of equal treatment and equal pay apply. The basic terms and conditions of employment of temporary agency workers have to be at least on a par with those they would have if they had been directly recruited by the host employer for the same job. But deviations from the principle of equal treatment and equal pay are allowed on the basis of collective agreements.

In 2002, personnel service agencies were established (Personal-Service-Agentur (PSA)). These PSAs were meant to act as temporary work agencies with the aim of employing people who were hitherto unemployed and hiring them to employers on the basis of the terms and conditions provided under collective agreements. However, this new initiative was not successful in numerical terms, so it was soon abandoned.

There are two categories of self-employment: new, 'sole self-employed', without employees (own-account workers) and old 'self-employed with employees' (employers). Among the first group are those who are 'nominally self-employed' and who earn less than EUR 25,000 per year. Otherwise referred to 'bogus self-employment', these workers are actually in dependent employment relationships and are identified as self-employed only in a formal, rather than a substantive, sense. In 2004, these employment arrangements were institutionalized to decrease the high number of unemployed and to increase the number of self-employed. Such employment arrangements, then, were created for fiscal reasons and for avoiding social security contributions and employment protection laws. In 2007 this category was abolished and combined with other employment instruments. The notion of 'dependence' is the criterion that differentiates independent workers who are self-employed and employees who work for an employer. The indicators of 'dependence' include: the place, time and content of the work; whether the worker is integrated within the employer's company or uses the employer's tools and equipment. However, the main indicator is whether the self-employed worker works only for a single company. For such workers, the same employment conditions and protections enjoyed by regular employees must be applied. This means, for instance, that the enterprise employing such employees and the employees themselves have to pay social security contributions.

3.3.   SWEDEN

In Sweden, the normal type of employment is continuing or permanent employment. Several forms of atypical employment were introduced in the 1990s, such as temporary employment and trial employment.

The introduction of 'temporary employment without a cause' in 1997 is probably the most important flexibility measure devised to date. Before then, only permanent employment and seasonal work were allowed. The employer had to have a special need for temporary employees, such as the need to replace an employee absent on sick leave, or the need for seasonal agricultural workers at harvest time. The objectives of the new legislation were to benefit the labour force by increasing employment and to benefit businesses by enabling increased employment flexibility. An employee could be employed on a temporary basis for a maximum of twelve months in total during a three-year period. The minimum period of employment was a month. The number of fixed-term employees per employer was limited to five employees. In 2001, a new law on the re-hiring of people employed as temporary replacements was inaugurated. This law gave workers who had accrued more than three years' service with the same employer the right to a permanent position.

Discrimination against part-time employees in relation to pay or employment conditions is forbidden by Swedish law, in conformity with the relevant EU directive (see above EU section). There are no specific regulations to protect casual workers, but there is debate about what might be appropriate measures.

Until 1992, temporary agencies were not allowed, because private labour exchanges were prohibited. Temporary agency workers are covered by collective agreements and, therefore, their terms and conditions of employment are similar to those of permanent employees.

3.4.   UNITED KINGDOM

The rights of an employee depend on the type of employment contract that the individual worker has with an employer. Excluding the self-employed, all dependent workers are entitled to certain core rights. The self-employed are, however, covered by anti-discrimination legislation, occupational health and safety (OHS) laws, as well as standard entitlements such as the NMW and standard working hours, including paid annual leave. Employees who work under a contract of employment are also entitled to all minimum statutory rights, including unfair dismissal and redundancy rights, though some of these are only available subject to a qualifying period of continuous employment.

Regulations in force since 2002 have aimed to prevent fixed-term employees being treated less favourably than similar permanent employees, except in cases where the different treatment can be objectively justified on valid grounds. The regulations also limit the use of successive fixed-term contracts to no more than four years; a renewed contract after this period takes effect as a contract of permanent or continuing employment.

Regulations introduced in 2000 provide new rights for part-time workers. The regulations ensure that Britain's 6 million part-timers – around 80% of whom are women – are protected by the right not to be treated unfairly compared with their full-time counterparts. Any unequal treatment must be based on objectively justifiable reasons (see EU section discussed earlier).

Depending on the type of contract, casual workers may or may not have the legal status of employees. If, however, casual workers do have employee status then they are entitled to the same rights as other categories of employee.

The Employment Agencies Act 1973 and the associated 2003 Regulations govern the operation of employment agencies and employment businesses and are designed to protect people who seek employment through those intermediaries. One principle is that it is illegal directly or indirectly to charge work-seekers a fee for providing work-finding services. Agencies operating in the entertainment and modelling sectors are exempt from some requirements.

The 2004 Regulations include new protections for work-seekers such as:

(a) placing a restriction on transfer fees to help remove the barrier to individuals being offered permanent employment;

(b) requiring agencies and employment businesses to make enquiries on any health and safety risks known to the hirer and the steps taken to control those risks; and

(c) preventing employment businesses from withholding workers' pay merely because they do not have an authenticated timesheet.

Governmental institutions are responsible for enforcing the legislation. Figures for agency employment are not easily available, but the European Foundation estimates that agency workers comprised 2.6% of the total United Kingdom workforce in 2002. This is broadly in line with labour force survey estimates, though other estimates are considerably higher.

3.5.   UNITED STATES OF AMERICA

Labour and employment statutes provide benefits and protections to those workers that meet each statute's definition of 'employee'. In general, most of the statutes take into account the level of control that an employer exercises over a person's work in determining whether an individual engaged in a non-traditional form of employment is a 'covered employee'. In some cases, both the staffing agency (for example, a temporary employment agency) that provides the services of the individual to a client company and the client company may exercise enough control of the worker to allow that worker to qualify as an employee of both enterprises. Under current NLRA doctrine, temporary employees provided by an agency (jointly employed employee) may exercise collective bargaining rights only if both joint employers agree to permit it. This is a doctrine that is likely to change when the political composition of the NLRB changes.

Independent contractors are excluded from NLRA protection. Traditionally, a person providing services is considered to be an 'independent contractor' when the purchaser of those services pays for the result of a work activity, but does not control or influence how that result is accomplished. But this definition may be broadened in the future as employers attempt to declare additional 'workers' independent contractors. In 2005, the Bureau of Labor Statistics (BLS) reported that there were more than 10 million people working as independent contractors in the USA, accounting for 7.4% of the workforce.

3.6.   CANADA

Atypical forms of employment are a significant area of concern for public-policy analysis. This is related to a larger concern about the 'working poor' and the ramifications for child poverty and the health of workers. It has been established that many of the atypical forms of employment are not well protected by employment-standards legislation relating to a range of benefits. It is, however, likely that such legislative protections will be enacted in the coming years as the number of specific policy proposals has been growing in importance in the last decade. Following work by the Arthurs Commission and the publication of its 2006 report, the federal government is undertaking a major review of employment standards. The Quebec government has completed a review of the legislative provisions for non-standard work, but this has not yet given rise to any legislative change.

Although temporary workers have the benefit of minimum-standards legislation, they must satisfy applicable job-tenure thresholds if they are to have access to certain other employment rights.

Although most employment laws in Canada apply equally to full-time and part-time employees, in all jurisdictions except Quebec employers are free to treat part-time employees less favourably than full-time employees, provided the employers meet the minimum standards established by those laws. There is no requirement for equality of treatment between full-time and part-time employees. Part-time workers are often ineligible for non-statutory employment benefits, such as dental and health care plans and superannuation. In addition, they are excluded from the benefits of certain labour laws and policies, either directly or indirectly, through qualifying requirements based on total work time. In Quebec, an employer cannot rely on an employee's part-time status to provide inferior working conditions, compared with a full-time employee doing the same job in the same establishment. However, this protection applies only to those employees whose rate of pay is equivalent to less than double the standard minimum wage.

There are no particular provisions to protect casual workers, independent contractors and employees hired through employment agencies. A significant issue is the question of when an agency employee becomes subject to the employment regime of the host employer. In one major legal decision, the court declared that the client business rather than the employment agency should be treated as the employer for the purpose of labour relations legislation in Quebec.

Self-employment represents approximately 19% of the labour force. Approximately two-thirds of the self-employed are 'own-account' workers. Own-account self-employment is a growing percentage of the labour force and represents an increasingly important form of individual adaptation to economic downturns.

3.7.   NEW ZEALAND

The growth in atypical employment patterns was stimulated by the Employment Contracts Act 1991, which abolished the award system at a time of high unemployment. There is still a considerable overhang of sub-standard employment conditions from the 1990s and there has been increasing concern about the problems associated with fixed-term, casual and temporary employment. These sub-standard conditions tend to be found in sectors of the economy where greater regulation and compliance enforcement and expanded union activity could result in improved employment relationships for workers. There have been attempts to introduce more effective legislative controls over atypical employment. The Employment Relations Amendment Act 2004 provides specific protections to 'vulnerable workers' in situations where businesses are sold or transferred.

The practice of having employees on a series of fixed-term employment agreements has also been targeted under the Employment Relations Act. The Act makes explicit that there have to be particular reasons (such as temporary project work) to justify the use of fixed-term contracts.

Although recent legislation has tried to limit casualization and the use of fixed-term employment contracts, the area of self-employment is still relatively unregulated by the government and there are sectors where self-employment has become the norm.

Burgess, Connell & Rasmussen[103] found that agency employment was still 'wild west' territory with no regulation of agencies and with unclear employer-employee relationships. It is normal for agency workers to have an employment relationship with more than one employer, and many agency workers shift between

---

103.   Burgess, Connell & Rasmussen, 2005.

being an employee and a contractor. This lack of clarity surrounding self-employment has put the spotlight on the classic distinction at common law between a 'contract of service' (which establishes an employer-employee relationship) and a 'contract for services' (which establishes a principal-contractor relationship).

3.8.   AUSTRALIA

One of the major changes in the Australian labour market over recent years has been the decline of permanent full-time employment and the growth of non-standard forms of employment. Permanent full-time employment has dropped from around two-thirds of the labour force in the early 1980s to about half the workforce by 2006.

Compared to other OECD countries, Australia has a high proportion of part-time employment. Women comprise the majority of the part-time workforce, and 45% of all employed women work part time. In the male segment of the workforce, some 16% of employed men work on a part-time basis.

Temporary employment in Australia includes fixed-term contracts and casual employment. It is estimated that between 3% and 6% of the workforce are engaged under fixed-term contracts. Casual employment is a notable feature of the Australian labour market. One of the weaknesses of the industrial relations system has been the comparatively unregulated framework of casual employment, whereby casual workers are denied the entitlements that are normally available to permanent part-time and full-time employees. Employees can be engaged on a casual hourly or daily basis with no security of employment and no entitlement to annual leave, sick leave and other benefits. In exchange for these reduced benefits, casual employees are paid an hourly wage that comprises a 'loading' or increment of approximately 20% or more added to the standard rate. Casual employment has been growing in most industries and is particularly prevalent in the service sector. Approximately one-quarter of all Australian employees are engaged on a casual basis. Some two-thirds of casual employees work a similar number of hours to part-time workers, whereas a growing proportion of casual employees are working full-time hours.

Independent contractors are covered by separate legislation. The *Independent Contractors Act* 2006 and the FWA seek to prevent sham contracting arrangements whereby workers are engaged as independent contractors when, in reality, they are dependent employees. Independent contractors are excluded from basic employment entitlements such as sick leave, annual leave and statutory workers' compensation protection.

Private employment agencies are not regulated by FWA, the post-2009 regulatory authority; however, the 2009 federal industrial laws (FW Act) provide penalties for employers who misrepresent employment as an independent contracting arrangement.

Self-employed people comprise some 12% of the workforce. Approximately one-third of the workers who appear to be self-employed are dependent on a single employer or a small number of employers for employment. The size of the 'labour-hire' workforce is about 3% of the national workforce – a comparatively high level in international terms.

3.9.   JAPAN

Although the traditional system of employment relations has been predominantly characterized by permanency of employment, the prolonged recession after the early 1990s saw the rapid growth in atypical forms of employment. In 1994, the proportion of workers in the salaried workforce engaged in atypical forms of employment was around one-fifth of that segment of workforce; by 2007, that proportion had grown to more than one-third.[104]

The issue of the treatment of these workers under atypical forms of employment has attracted much public concern and is a subject of political debate because there is basically no legal requirement for equality of treatment between these workers and the regular, permanent employees. Temporary agency workers in particular were severely affected by the global financial crisis of 2008. According to figures released in May 2009 by the Ministry of Health, Labour and Welfare, among the 207,000 workers under atypical forms of employment whose contract had been cancelled or not renewed during the period from October 2008 to June 2009, more than 60% were temporary agency workers, mainly in the manufacturing sector. The newly elected DPJ government is contemplating to amend the existing law so as to restrict the use of temporary agency workers to 26 specialized jobs, and to go back to a regulation of the sector based on the 'positive listing' approach.

Under the current law, whereas temporary agencies must apply for an operating license from the government, the field of temporary employment is largely deregulated. For example, there is no statutory limitation on the reasons for which user companies may use temporary agency workers, which can be used in most business sectors without restrictions (with the exception of dock transport services, construction work and medical services, where use of temporary agency work is prohibited). The law covering employees hired through temporary employment agencies was initially enacted in 1985 and later revised in 1999 and 2003. Under the previous system, agency workers could be sent to a user company to perform only particular types of job specified on a prescribed list (positive listing). Later, this was converted to a system whereby agency workers could be hired to perform any job apart from those specified on a proscribed list (a negative listing). The length of time for which these workers could be employed was also extended from one year up to three years. An exception to this limit was permitted for jobs that required specialized knowledge or qualifications, jobs related to projects subject to specific timeframes, and jobs where the agency workers were needed as replacements for employees on leave.

---

104.   Ministry of Health, Labour and Welfare, 2003, 2007.

The Part-Time Work Law enacted in 1993 defines 'part-time workers' as 'workers whose prescribed weekly work hours are less than those of regular employees employed by the same establishment'. The law promotes the effective utilization of part-time workers' abilities and the improvement of their welfare by encouraging employers to provide appropriate working conditions and implementing education and training. The law, which was revised in 2008, required employers to improve the treatment of the so-called *seishain* part-time (part-time workers performing the same duties as permanent employees) by establishing mandatory arrangements to enable workers who want permanent full-time employment to make the transition from part-time to regular employment. Nevertheless, as this revised law applies only to those relatively few part-time workers working under the same conditions as regular employees, its impact is expected to remain limited.

A particular feature of part-time employment in Japan has been its relationship with the taxation, pension and health care systems. A large proportion of part-time employees are women who are also dependent family members. This has given part-time workers incentives to work within certain limits. Their annual salary is not taxed as long as it is less than 1,030,000 yen (JPY), and they are not required to join the employment-related health insurance and pension system if they work within defined limits (for example, by restricting their working hours to less than three-quarters of those of regular employees). However, there are moves to redefine these limits in order to extend the coverage of the health insurance and pension schemes to part-time workers.

There is no special legislation for casual workers. In general, they are covered by the same laws as other employees.

The number of self-employed people has been gradually decreasing. This segment accounted for approximately 10% of the total labour force in 2007.[105] The decrease is mainly due to the diminishing number of small farmers and small retail shops. However, there are concerns about 'disguised' self-employment (typically, truck drivers and construction industry sub-contractors). According to case law, therefore, people working under the control of another in a relationship of subordination will be deemed to be workers to whom the Labour Standard Law and Trade Union Act apply.

---

105. Statistic Bureau, 2008.

Chapter 4
Minimum Wage Levels

Of the European Union's (EU) twenty-seven members, only Austria, Cyprus, Denmark, Finland, Germany, Italy and Sweden have no National Minimum Wage (NMW).[106] In Germany, there has been a controversial debate about the introduction of minimum wages. The United Kingdom and Ireland introduced an NMW only recently, but the level has subsequently been increased significantly.

Table 4.1 indicates, in terms of purchasing power parity (PPP), the level of the NMW in various countries (expressed as an hourly rate). The PPP column is particularly interesting. It shows that among the countries analysed for this volume, the United Kingdom has the highest hourly minimum wage and Japan the lowest. In the USA, the minimum wage rate has not been increased for a decade after 1997. For comparison purposes, Table 4.1 includes several other countries that are not otherwise the focus of this volume. The International Labour Organisation (ILO) has a database covering more countries giving information about the minimum wage.[107]

4.1.   EUROPEAN UNION

A minimum wage applies in twenty of the twenty-seven Member States. They can be divided into three groups.[108] The first group includes the nine countries with minimum wages, between about EUR 100 and 350: Bulgaria, Romania, Latvia, Lithuania, Slovakia, Estonia, Hungary, Czech Republic and Poland. The second group comprises five Member States (Portugal, Slovenia, Malta, Greece and Spain) with an intermediate level of minimum wages, from EUR 500 to

---

106. For more information on the EU Member States, see <www.eurofound.europa.eu/eiro>.
107. See <www.ilo.org/public/english/protection/Condtrav/database/index.htm>; <www.ilo.org/travaildatabase/servlet/minimumwages>.
108. Eurostat, 2008.

Table 4.1 Comparison of Level of Minimum Wages across Selected Countries

Country	In UK £, using: Exchange Ratios	PPPs	Date of Review	Age Full Minimum Wage Usually Applies
Australia	6.14	6.20	October 2008	21
Canada	4.51	4.46	Date varies between provinces	16
Japan	4.73	3.45	October 2008	16
New Zealand	4.41	4.74	April 2008	16
United Kingdom	5.73	5.73	October 2008	22
United States	4.27	4.31	July 2008	20

Source: Low Pay Commission (2009).

EUR 700. The third group comprises six Member States (United Kingdom, France, Belgium, the Netherlands, Ireland and Luxembourg) in which the minimum wage is above EUR 1,100.[109] The EU treaty indicates that wages are not regulated at the EU level. However, following debates on this topic in Germany (see next), there are debates about the possibility of having a European minimum wage.

4.2.   GERMANY

Germany is one of a minority of EU Member States that does not have statutory minimum wages. Minimum wages, therefore, reflect the rates of pay of the lowest-paid groups under various collective agreements. An issue that has been gaining attention is that collective bargaining coverage has been diminishing since the early 1990s and has fallen to about 60%. A surprisingly high percentage of full-time employees (about 16% to 17%) earn less than 60% of the median income (the EU official poverty line).

There has been much political controversy over proposals for the introduction of minimum wages. The most critical issue is, of course, the appropriate level of pay, which could be regulated by legislation or collective bargaining. First, some unions were reluctant but did accept as a compromise an in-principle proposal for a legal solution, but all employer organizations rejected the concept. The then coalition government of Christian democrats and Social democrats could not agree on legislative action to introduce measures that would prescribe NMWs for all employees. Their lowest common denominator was a proposal to allow minimum wages at sector level, which would still permit wage differentials between sectors.

---

109.   *Ibid.*

In these cases, the lowest current wage could be declared to be a mandatory standard by amending certain legal provisions (*Allgemeinverbindlichkeitserklärung*). One disadvantage is that the political debate would be revived whenever new proposals are advanced to include previously excluded sectors.

The present government of Christian democrats and Free democrats has decided not to take some legislative action in the future to introduce provisions that would prescribe minimum wages at a national level for all employees. The government is also not in favour of collective action at sector level, which would allow for differences between sectors, but has agreed to some sector-specific exemptions. Another option would be utilize public funding to subsidize extremely low wages. A critical issue is, of course, the appropriate level of pay, which could be stipulated by legislation or collective bargaining.

There are legal provisions for minimal standards in relation to other terms and conditions of employment, such as paid holidays and maximum daily or weekly hours of work. In reality, however, these legally-prescribed standards are not important because collective bargaining has been the major instrument for the determination of minimum employment standards.

4.3.	SWEDEN

There are no statutory minimum wages in Sweden. Minimum wages are determined by collective agreements. The Labour Court has settled a few disputes, when wages decided by other kinds of agreements have been judged unreasonable and adjusted. This means that conditions in agreements can be adjusted if they are in relation to the content of the agreement, the creation of the agreement, or other circumstances. This was part of the above-mentioned dispute between the Swedish construction workers' union and the Latvian company, Laval. This dispute was referred to the ECJ. In short, the Swedish union demanded that the Latvian company should sign a Swedish collective agreement, which provided for wage rates on a par with those then current in the Stockholm region. The verdict of the EG court, while not wholly clear, seems to be that industrial action can only be used to achieve agreements concerning hard core issues, such as working environment, working hours, vacations and such. The verdict also means that industrial action has to be in proportion with the gain of the action, which is not presently the case in Sweden. In addition, the trade unions can only demand levels of conditions and payment equalling the minimum levels stated in the national agreements, not, as was the case here, in usual level in that particular field or region. According to the court, Sweden has to choose between introducing legal minimum wages or minimum wages in all collective agreements.

4.4.	UNITED KINGDOM

Almost all UK workers have a legal right to a minimum level of pay – the NMW. This applies even to 'atypical' workers such as those employed by a temporary-employment agency, home workers, part-time workers, casual workers, pieceworkers and those on fixed-term contracts. The NMW applies to all sectors, although certain agricultural workers must be paid more as there is a separate agricultural minimum wage, determined by the Agricultural Wages Board. The minimum hourly wage for adults was increased from GBP 4.85 in October 2004 to GBP 5.05 in October 2005, GBP 5.35 in October 2006 and GBP 5.80 from October 2009.

Each year, the level of the NMW is set by the government, based on the recommendations of the LPC, an independent statutory authority established in 1998. It makes its recommendations on the basis of research, consultation with employers and workers and their representatives, analysis of national statistics, surveys of enterprises in low-paying sectors and fact-finding visits. The terms of reference for the LPC are set each year by the government, and the LPC presents its recommendations to the government in the following year.

Individual employees can bring a claim before an employment tribunal to recover any money that they believe they are owed as a result of not receiving the NMW. Alternatively, workers can go to a civil court to recover the money. Employees may also bring a claim to an employment tribunal for unfair dismissal or victimization if their employer dismisses them or takes some other detrimental action against them for claiming the NMW. The number of NMW complaints to Employment Tribunals fell from 1,306 in 1999–2000 to 440 in 2005–2006.

The NMW Act allows for the appointment of enforcement officers to act on behalf of workers, where they identify that a business is failing in its obligations to remunerate employees. The UK tax authorities enforce the minimum wage and also provide information, inspection and enforcement services; in addition they respond to enquiries and complaints from workers, employers and third parties to help ensure that employers comply with the minimum wage legislation (see <www.hmrc.gov.uk>).

The relative value of the NMW has increased from around 45% of median hourly earnings to an estimated 50%. In spite of criticisms by some critics, there is no significant evidence of adverse consequences on levels of employment. Around 5% of employees each year have benefited from the increases in the NMW. In addition to those directly benefiting from the NMW, there is also evidence of low-paid workers on pay rates above the NMW benefiting indirectly from above-average increases.

4.5.   UNITED STATES OF AMERICA

In the USA, minimum wages are determined by federal and state laws. The FMW law is the Fair Labor Standards Act (FLSA). For employees covered by the FLSA, the minimum wage was increased to USD 7.25 per hour in July, 2009.[110]

---

110.   United States Department of Labor, Minimum Wage (2010).

Individual states can establish higher minimum wages than those provided by the FLSA for covered employees. Some states allow wage rates lower than the minimum, but in those cases the FMW standard applies. Minimum wage rates established by the FLSA may not be reduced by CBAs or individual agreements. The minimum wage is adjusted periodically by legislative action that includes consideration of interested parties' views as part of the legislative process. Enforcement of the minimum wage law is carried out by the Department of Labor's Wage and Hour Division (WHD) or by private legal action initiated by employees.

The WHD enforces the FLSA's minimum wage and overtime requirements. The WHD may recover back-wages, either administratively or through court action, for employees that have been underpaid in violation of the law. Violations may result in civil or criminal action. An employee may file a private suit for back-pay and an equal amount as liquidated damages, plus attorney's fees and court costs. An employee may not take legal action under the FLSA if he or she has been paid back-wages under the supervision of the WHD or if the government has already taken legal action to recover the wages. Most states have parallel enforcement agencies.

4.6.   CANADA

A legally-determined minimum wage is a basic labour standard which applies in all jurisdictions in Canada. Its main purpose is to protect workers in non-unionized workplaces, but it also influences the level of remuneration of some unionized employees. The rates for minimum wages in Ontario and Quebec, for example, are similar, but they are not identical from one jurisdiction to another.[111] The rate in each jurisdiction varies for a limited number of categories of employee, notably those people receiving gratuities and tips in hotels and catering. The federal jurisdiction applies the provincial minimum wage to employees within its jurisdiction in each province.

The minimum wage rates are reviewed and increased from time to time by minimum wage orders or regulations under a province's employment standards legislation, which are approved by Orders-in-Council. The final decision always rests with the government. Four provinces in Canada have multi-party minimum wage boards: Manitoba, Saskatchewan, New Brunswick and Nova Scotia. Two provinces (Prince Edward Island and Nova Scotia) are required to review the minimum wage annually; and two others (Saskatchewan and Newfoundland) every two years. Ontario did not increase its minimum wage for nine years, but since 2004 its government has committed to increasing the minimum wage on 1 February each year. Complaints about failure to respect minimum wage rates are

---

111. See <www.worksmartontario.gov.on.ca/scripts/default.asp?contentID=1-3-2&actionID= print#H3>; also <www.cnt.gouv.qc.ca/fr/normes/salaire.asp>.

generally overseen by administrative tribunals dealing with minimum labour standards.

Legislated general minimum wage rates can be supplemented by special orders, regulations or decrees that apply to particular industries, occupations or classes of employees. Such is the case in Quebec under the Act Respecting Collective Agreement Decrees, which extends the application of negotiated collective agreements to other workers in the same sector. Typical examples are cleaners, janitors and security guards. Other jurisdictions have special provisions for particular industries.

There has been considerable public-policy debate about the 'working poor', notably in relation to child poverty. Minimum wage legislation has not been seen as the major tool for addressing this problem. The primary mechanisms for dealing with low incomes have been through the federal and provincial tax systems and via direct transfers in the tax regime to individuals with low incomes and to families with children. Fiscal policy and direct transfers have been a moderating factor on otherwise rising levels of income inequality since the 1990s.

Complaints about non-compliance with statutory minimum wages are addressed to government agencies such as Ministries of Labour (as in Ontario) or Employment Standards Commissions (as in Quebec). In either case, individual complaints are investigated by an employment standards officer, who has discretion either to decline a complaint or to pursue it. Government agencies have access to a range of administrative and judicial powers to enforce compliance.

4.7.   NEW ZEALAND

The Conciliation and Arbitration System, instituted in 1894, provided minimum wages in the form of awards. Minimum wages for most workers were in terms of 'award wages' covering particular industries, occupations or designated jobs. Award wages were abolished in 1991. Those award wages, however, still influenced collective employment contracts in the post-1991 period, but there has not been a return to the award system since then.

Since 1994, the Minimum Wage Act has included statutory youth minimum wages. Generally, the Minimum Wage Act means that employers have to keep wages and time records for six years and employees and their unions have a right to access these. The Wages Protection Act 1983 also plays a role in recovering wages owed to employees.

The government reconsiders the statutory minimum wage in December every year, based on consultation with employers' associations, unions and other interest groups. There has been a significant rise in statutory minimum wages when the Labour-led governments were in power after 1999. The current adult (18 years and over) statutory minimum wage in New Zealand dollars (NZD) is 12.50 per hour; and this represents a 79% increase from 1999 to 2009. There is also a statutory minimum wage for young workers (those aged 16 and 17 years), which is currently

NZD 10.00. Recently, unions have been more active and a new union, Unite, has persuaded some of the major hospitality and retail employers to pay their young staff the adult statutory minimum wage.

The enforcement of statutory minima is normally through the Labour Inspectorate, which is part of the Department of Labour. After 1991, the Labour Inspectorate staff was expanded.

4.8.   AUSTRALIA

One of the prime functions of the industrial-relations regulator in Australia was long to set minimum wage levels. For a century, this function was the responsibility of the AIRC and its predecessors. But for a few years a new agency, the AFPC held the responsibility. FWA took over this responsibility from the AFPC in mid-2009. The regulator reviews minimum wages annually. Submissions are made by governments, unions, employers and other interested parties. The criteria to be used by the regulator for determining minimum wages are stipulated in industrial relations legislation. The criteria normally include a mixture of economic and social factors. Conservative governments tend to emphasise economic factors (such as the impact of wage increases on inflation, productivity and employment) over social criteria. In contrast, Labor Party governments are more likely to give some priority to social considerations (such as the needs of the low paid) in setting minimum wages. The FMW is currently AUD 14.31 per hour (AUD 543.78 per week). It was not increased during 2009, which was the first time there was no annual increase in the minimum wage since 1982. Lower rates of pay apply to some trainees, youth employees and disabled employees employed in special enterprises. The 2009–10 annual wage review is being conducted by the Minimum Wage Panel of FWA, to become operative on 1 July 2010.

4.9.   JAPAN

The Minimum Wage Law 1959 aimed to improve working conditions and guaranteed a minimum wage to low-paid workers. Minimum wages are determined in Japan through:

(a) Minimum Wages Councils. These set minimum wages following research and deliberation. Nearly all of the minimum wage levels are determined here (296 cases).

(b) Local-level or enterprise-level minimum wages in collective agreements. Only two cases have been set in accordance with such agreements.

Decisions of a Minimum Wage Council determine the level of the minimum wage and how widely it should be applied. Minimum Wages Councils are composed of members representing unions, employers, and the public interest. The council makes a decision after considering the local cost of living, starting wages, any collective agreements on minimum wages, and the distribution of workers along the pay scale. The Central Minimum Wages Council has been providing guidelines to prefectural[112] Minimum Wages Councils for minimum wage increases. The local councils use the guidelines to revise minimum wages to accord with the local situation.

Minimum Wages Councils rule on local- and industry-specific minimum wages. One local minimum wage is determined for each prefecture, regardless of the type of industry or occupation. Usually, the minimum wage in a given prefecture applies to all workers and to all employers who have one or more workers. The prefectural industry-specific wage may be determined by minimum wage councils for certain industries. In general, the industrial minimum wage is slightly higher (typically by 10% to 30%) than the local rate, whereas the industry-specific minimum wage applies nationwide.

The Minister of Health, Labour and Welfare or the Chief of the Prefectural Labour Bureau are required to publish their decisions. The minimum wage decision becomes effective on the 31st day after publication of the decision. Violations are punished by a fine.

Collective agreement provisions providing for wages that are lower than the legal minimum wages are void, and the legal minimum level is applied instead. Bonuses are an important component of annual wages in many Japanese enterprises, but these are not regulated by law.

An employer covered by the minimum wage legislation is required to inform workers of the minimum wages by posting them at conspicuous places in workplaces or by other means. To supervise employers' compliance, the labour standards inspector may enter establishments then inspect records and documents, and question the people concerned. The Ministry of Health, Labour and Welfare conducts annual information campaigns about minimum wage levels at the end of November each year. Such campaigns are aimed at enterprises and employers' organizations.

---

112. There are forty-seven prefectures in Japan.

Chapter 5
Working Time

This chapter discusses working time, overtime and overtime premiums, night work, shift work, holidays and flexible working time.

The European Union (EU) working time directive has had an important impact on three EU countries, and particularly on the United Kingdom. The directive set the maximum of a forty-eight-hour working week, with different standards able to be negotiated by the social partners. An individual 'opt-out' to the forty-eight hours per week limit was adopted to accommodate British preferences. This means that workers who have signed an individual opt-out can volunteer to work more than forty-eight hours per week.

Working time has various dimensions – for example, normal weekly hours of work, overtime, holidays and public holidays. By considering the average annual working time, we can take into account these different elements. These data are, however, difficult to compare, because they cover full-time and part-time workers and the size of the part-time workforce differs from one country to another. Figure 5.1 illustrates the changing trend of working hours.

Since the early 1990s, average working time has been reduced in Germany and Japan, albeit from different starting levels. However, there has been relatively little change in the USA, Australia, Canada and New Zealand – the countries with the longest average working hours among our sample. By 2005, the EU reported its average annual working hours at less than 1,700 per year; whereas all the other countries reported averages of more than 1,750.

With regard to overtime, the situation differs between countries and can be fully understood only by considering the national and more specific context. For example, overtime is mainly covered by statutory rules and collective bargaining in Germany and by collective bargaining in Sweden, whereas there is considerable flexibility in Japan. In many contexts, there is a premium for overtime work (generally at least 25% on top of normal pay). Overtime has three interrelated dimensions: the normal working hours per week; the period for the calculation of

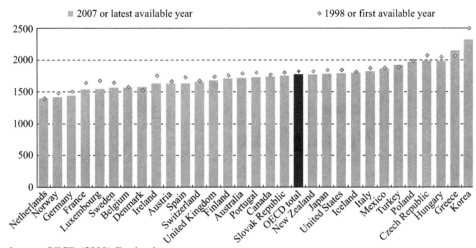

Figure 5.1   Average Annual Working Time (hours)

Source: OECD (2009) Factbook.

the working time average per week (it could be one week or a few months); and any maximum limit of overtime hours allowed per year. In many contexts, there is a trend towards an annualized working time standard, which generally results in reduced overtime premiums.

5.1.   EUROPEAN UNION

The directive on working time was adopted in 1995. This directive has two aspects: it defines minimum rest periods and it regulates specific aspects of night work and shift work. It prescribes minimum rest periods: eleven consecutive hours of rest per twenty-four-hour period, and thirty-five hours of rest in any week (which normally will include a Sunday). Weekly working hours, including overtime, may not exceed an average of forty-eight hours per week (averaged over a period of four to twelve months if negotiated with the unions). There must be a rest period permitted in any working day that exceeds six hours. The detailed arrangements for this are to be determined by the 'social partners' or, failing that, by national legislation. All workers must have at least four weeks of paid annual holiday, which may not be replaced by an allowance.

The directive prohibits night workers from working more than an average of eight hours in any twenty-four-hour period. This eight-hour limit is mandatory for occupations involving special hazards or heavy physical or mental strain. It also entitles night workers to regular health assessments and stipulates that anyone found to be suffering from health problems connected with their night work must be transferred as soon as possible to day work. Employers who regularly use night workers must inform the relevant authorities. Member States must adopt the necessary measures to ensure that night workers and rotating shift workers enjoy the appropriate health and safety protection according to the nature of their work. They must ensure that employers take account of general principles such as adapting the work to the individual and alleviating monotonous work.

Member States are free to introduce or maintain more favourable provisions and to encourage collective or other agreements that provide more favourable conditions to workers. The directive allows Member States to adopt alternative arrangements where the duration of working time is not measured and/or predetermined, or can be determined by the workers themselves. This applies particularly to managers, family workers and members of the clergy. Alternatives to the rules on daily, weekly on-call time, breaks, and night work limits, for example, may be established if there is an agreement between the social partners (at national, sector or enterprise level) but only if the workers concerned are granted an equivalent rest period. There are other alternatives; these are primarily the possibility for a voluntary, individual, opt-out from the forty-eight hours per week limit. This has been controversial and widely used in the United Kingdom. Suppression, prolongation or extension of the individual opt-out, as well as the definition of the rest period, are key issues as the directive is being reconsidered. There are also different sector working-time directives covering the transport sectors (for example, rail, road, air and shipping).

The two events that prompted the revision of the directive were the Court of Justice's reconsideration of on-call time as work time (within the health sector) and growing criticism of the individual opt-out provision.

The European Commission presented a new draft directive in September 2004. The main amendments were to restrict the opt-out and to specify new rules on the treatment of on-call time (particularly concerning healthcare professionals), with the Commission proposing that only the 'active' part of this time be classified as working time. Among the other proposed changes there was more flexibility for Member States in the definition of the 'reference period' over which the maximum forty-eight-hour week on average must be observed and clarification of the rules on when compensatory rest must be granted.

After the first reading of the draft directive by the European Parliament (EP) in 2005, the Council was unable to find a common position until 2008 because the national governments were profoundly divided on the future of the opt-out provision. The EP proposed further amendments, including the abolition of the opt-out within three years and the treatment of the entire period of on-call time, including any inactive part, as working time. The Conciliation Committee tried to find a common position, but no agreement was found between the representatives of the EP and the Council. Therefore, the working time directive was not revised.

5.2.   GERMANY

The parameters of working time are regulated by labour law, whereas actual working hours are mainly regulated by collective bargaining and, in some cases, by individual labour contracts. The Working Time Act (*Arbeitszeitgesetz*) is the most important statutory source of regulation. It defines standards in terms of maximum working hours, scheduling of working time and rest periods. Within its broad framework, working time issues are subject to collective bargaining, especially as regards the duration and distribution of daily and weekly working hours. The Working Time Act stipulates the maximum number of working hours per day, breaks and minimum rest periods. The general limit is eight hours daily, although there are exceptions: a ten-hour limit is admissible, subject to the provision that an average of eight hours is maintained over a six-month or twenty-four-week period. Saturdays are classed as regular working days. This means that, in general, a forty-eight-hour working week and, temporarily, a sixty-hour working week are acceptable from a legal point of view. A different reference period and an extension of working hours to ten hours (but on no more than sixty days per year) can be permitted by collective agreements. Work beyond the eight-hour limit is allowed in emergencies and extraordinary circumstances, where no other option is practicable (for example, when there is a risk of the deterioration of raw materials and food or tasks have not been completed correctly).

Collectively agreed average working time is 37.7 hours per week (in 2005). There are still differences between western (37.4 hours) and eastern Germany (39 hours). Actual working time is on average approximately 2.5 hours more than collectively agreed working time; 31% of employees work more than 40 hours.

In Germany, 87% of all establishments use overtime, a high percentage compared with other EU countries, whose average is 75%. Premium payment for overtime is not regulated by law, but by collective agreements. Due to the large number of collective agreements and differences between sector agreements, it is not possible to report an average overtime premium rate.

The law defines 'night work' as working time of more than two hours between 11.00 p.m. and 6.00 a.m. There are, however, broader definitions in collective agreements. The law does not specify a premium rate for night work. It states only that it has to be a 'reasonable' and/or 'appropriate' (*angemessene*) remuneration, in terms of paid days off or a premium. The typical premium rate varies between 15% and 25%. Sixteen percent of all employees work on a shift basis and/ or at night (Eurofound 2006). The premium rate varies according to the shift work arrangement. A typical premium is approximately 10%.

In principle, work on weekends and public holidays is forbidden by law. However, the Working Time Act allows for a broad range of exceptions from this general rule. Employees must have at least fifteen Sundays per year off work. Thirty-two percent of all employees work on Saturday once or twice a month, and 13% work on Sundays.[113] A typical premium rate is 50% to 60% for work on weekends (Sundays) and about 150% on public holidays.

Working time accounts are the most important mechanism for making working time more flexible. About 45% of male and 37% of female employees had such accounts in 2003. Approximately half of all employees can decide how to

---

113. Bauer et al., 2004.

organize their working time. Thirty-one percent of highly qualified white-collar employees reported a high degree of autonomy.

The use of flexible working accounts has increased, leading to a decrease in premium payments for overtime. In one survey, 27% of those interviewed reported that their employees are paid an overtime premium (compared to an average of 45% in the EU as a whole) and 65% indicated that overtime is compensated by time off (EU: 34%).[114] There is also a tendency to formulate definitions that exclude Saturdays.

5.3.   SWEDEN

In Sweden, maximum ordinary hours are established by law. Actual hours (below or above that level) are established by collective agreements. Usually, collective agreements determine working conditions such as working hours, overtime, on-duty hours and shift hours. The standard working week is forty hours. The standard week can be modified in collective agreements, but as an EU Member, Sweden has to follow the EU working time directive 2003/88, which states that working time cannot be amended in such a way that it violates the minimum level of employees' conditions according to the directive.

In addition to ordinary working hours, a maximum of fifty hours per month extra is allowed for certain occupations, such as doctors on duty. General overtime of 48 hours per four-week period is allowed, with a maximum of 200 hours per year. The Work Environment Authority can allow an additional 150 hours per year. For full-time employees, there is a maximum of forty-eight hours (including ordinary hours, overtime and on-duty hours) per seven days working time, based on a four-month period. Part-time employees are limited to 200 hours overtime per year. Regulations on overtime and on-duty time can be modified in collective agreements.

Shift work and shift premiums are also regulated in collective agreements. Conditions differ considerably between sectors. Proprietors with long opening hours have, therefore, attempted to negotiate collective agreements with unions from sectors where the standards for shift work and premiums are lower.

Generally, if working time is not regulated by collective agreements, it can be determined by employers.

5.4.   UNITED KINGDOM

The United Kingdom implemented the EU Working Time Directive via the Working Time Regulations of 1998. These provide for a limit of forty-eight hours a week (on average) on the time employers can require employees to work, though workers aged 18 and over can consent to exceed this limit. Consent to working more than forty-eight hours a week is demonstrated by the worker signing an opt-out agreement. Autonomous workers have certain derogations

---

114.   Riedmann et al., 2006: 24.

(possibilities to opt out) from the provisions of the directive – for example, limits on maximum weekly working hours and rest periods – but they are still covered by other provisions. For example, they are entitled to four weeks' paid annual leave.[115] The regulations also provide rights to paid holidays, rest breaks and limits on night work. Subject to certain exceptions, these basic rights and provisions are: a limit of an average of eight hours work in twenty-four that night workers can be required to work; a minimum of eleven hours rest a day; a day off each week; an in-work rest break if the working day is longer than six hours; and four weeks' paid leave per year.

There is no standard working week specified by law in the United Kingdom. Nevertheless there is a reference to a forty-eight-hour limit in the Regulations. The number of hours worked each week should be averaged over seventeen weeks. However, under a workforce or collective agreement, workers and the employer can agree to calculate the average hours over a period of up to fifty-two weeks. It is difficult to estimate accurately the number of workers who have signed the opt-out or who work excess hours without having chosen the opt-out. Research shows that not everyone who has signed the opt-out actually works excess hours; it may be that they have chosen the opt-out as a precautionary measure.[116]

The proportion of employees recorded as working more than forty-eight hours has fallen: from 23% of full-time employees in 1997 to 17% in 2006. Certain workers (mainly in the transport sector) are not subject to the regulations, because they are governed by sector-specific provisions. Enforcement of the regulations is split between different authorities. The forty-eight-hour limits and use of the opt-out are enforced by the Health and Safety Executive, local authority environmental health departments, the Civil Aviation Authority, the Vehicle and Operator Services Agency and the Office of Rail Regulation. The entitlements to rest and leave are enforced through Employment Tribunals.

There is no statutory right in the United Kingdom to pay for working extra hours (overtime), and there are no minimum statutory levels of overtime pay, though a worker's average pay rate must not fall below the NMW. The worker's contract of employment should include details of overtime pay rates and how these are calculated.

There are limits on night working. 'Night time' is defined as the period between 11.00 p.m. and 6.00 a.m. 'Night workers' are those who regularly work for at least three hours during this period. A night worker should not work more than an average of eight hours in each twenty-four-hour period (excluding overtime). It is not possible to opt out of the night working limit. Young workers (under 18) are generally not allowed to work at night. There is no statutory level of night time pay.

---

115. Initially, certain other workers were not subject to the regulations, because they are governed by sector-specific provisions. However, in 2003 the regulations were extended to sectors and activities previously excluded from the original regulations, including some sector-specific provisions.
116. This research was conducted by the former Department of Trade and Industry (DTI), UK.

Employees with children under 6 years of age or disabled children under 18 years of age have a 'right to request flexible working time'. Employers have a duty to consider these requests seriously, and may only refuse a request where there is a recognized business reason for doing so. Flexible working arrangements may include annualized hours, compressed hours, flexitime, home working, job-sharing, shift working, staggered hours and term-time working. The Work-Life Balance Employees' Survey[117] found that over a period of two years, 17% of employees had made a request for flexible work arrangements. (See also Chapter 1.)

5.5.   UNITED STATES OF AMERICA

If no union has been recognized, hours of work in the USA are determined by employer policy and/or individual agreement between employers and employees. If a union has been recognized, hours of work may be established by collective bargaining between employers and unions.

Generally, there is no ceiling on the number of hours that an employee may work. However, in some cases, hours of work may be regulated by safety considerations (for example, the government regulates the number of hours that truck drivers may work without an extended rest period). An employee covered by the FLSA's overtime provisions is generally entitled to pay of not less than 1.5 times the employee's regular rate of pay for all hours worked in excess of forty hours per week. Almost all employees who earn less than USD 455 per week (USD 23,660 per annum) are eligible for overtime pay. The rule applies whether the employee is blue-collar or white-collar. Most employees who earn between USD 23,660 and USD 100,000 per annum, and who are in executive, professional or administrative positions, are not eligible for overtime pay. However, salespeople are eligible for overtime pay.

According to the Department of Labor's BLS, almost 15% of full-time employees usually worked a non-standard shift (in 2004). On average, 4.7% worked evening shifts, 3.2% worked night shifts, 3.1% worked employer-arranged irregular schedules, and 2.5% worked rotating shifts. The proportion of full-time employees on non-standard schedules has fallen since 1991. More than half (55%) of those working an alternative shift did so because it was the nature of the job (for example, police officers, doctors and assembly-line workers).

Extra pay for working night shifts is a matter of agreement between the employer and the employee (or the employee's representative). The FLSA does not require extra pay for night work, but it does require that non-exempt workers be paid not less than 1.5 times the employee's regular rate for time worked over forty hours in a working week.

In 2004, the BLS estimated that more than 27 million full-time wage and salary workers had flexible work schedules, allowing them to vary the time

---

117.   DTI, 2006.

they began or ended work. Among the major occupational groups, flexible schedules were most common among management, professional, and related occupations (37%). Under some employers' policies, employees must work a prescribed number of hours per pay period and be present during a daily 'core time'. The FLSA does not address flexible work schedules. Alternative work arrangements, such as flexible work schedules, are a matter of agreement between the employer and the employee (or the employee's representative).

5.6.   CANADA

Jurisdictions in Canada generally specify maximum ordinary hours of work per week, but offer the option of increasing the number of hours with employee consent. The ordinary maximum in the federal and Ontario jurisdictions is forty-eight hours. A significant number of workers are excluded from the application of these federal and Ontario provisions, including managers, various professions, agricultural workers and students. The Quebec jurisdiction opts, instead, for a thirty-two-consecutive-hour rest period each week. In all three jurisdictions, individual employees can either consent to longer working hours or exceptional circumstances (with suitable justification) resulting in longer working hours.

The standard working week is eight hours per day and forty hours per week in the federal jurisdiction, forty-four hours per week in Ontario and forty hours per week in Quebec. Some workers, including most people in farming and horticulture, managers and superintendents, professionals and essential service workers are excluded from the hours of work provisions in the federal and Ontario jurisdictions. Some occupations and industries have varying provisions.

In the federal jurisdiction, the average hours of work over a two-week period must not exceed forty-eight hours. In Ontario, approval can be obtained for excess weekly hours (up to sixty hours per week and possibly even greater than sixty hours) subject to a set of provisions that include: an agreement with a union representing the employees concerned; approval from the Director of Labour Standards; compulsory posting of information about excess hours of work; and expiry dates (from one to three years depending on the regime).

In general, employees should not receive less than 1.5 times the regular rates of wages for hours worked in excess of the standard working week. Managerial and supervisory employees are excluded from overtime provisions. Quebec offers the possibility of an overtime equivalent in paid time-off, as long as it translates into 1.5 times equivalent the regular rates (seven hours overtime = 10.5 hours paid time off). There are some jobs where the overtime threshold is greater than the standard working week.

Shift work is subject to other provisions regarding the standard hours of work that offer averaging procedures over weekly or bi-weekly periods (for example, in the federal and Quebec jurisdictions). No particular provisions are made for shift premiums.

The premium for working on a public holiday is the overtime rate in the federal jurisdiction. The Ontario and Quebec jurisdictions also provide overtime premiums Special provisions are made for establishments with continuous hours of operation.

With regard to flexible working hours, employers covered by the federal jurisdiction can average the hours of work if the nature of the work requires an irregular distribution of hours. This allows hours of work to be averaged over a period of two or more weeks. The standard hours of work must be forty times the number of weeks being averaged. Similarly, the maximum hours of work must be forty-eight times the number of weeks being averaged. The averaging period can last only as long as the time in which fluctuations of work hours occur. Overtime rates apply after an average of forty hours a week. In Quebec, an employer can ask the Labour Standards Commission (*Commission des normes du travail*) for permission to change working hours to other than on a weekly basis, but the average working hours must equal the standards found in the relevant act or regulations. Ontario offers a range of options for exceeding standard working hours.

No particular provisions apply for employee choice, apart from the standards summarized previously.

5.7. NEW ZEALAND

New Zealand has only limited statutory restrictions on working hours. No maximum hours are prescribed; there is no prescribed break period between working periods and there is no legislative prescription on overtime payments, shift-work premiums or any other non-standard hours. There are specific working-time constraints on certain jobs (for example, rest periods for truck drivers), though these restrictions are relatively unusual. Awards used to prescribe restrictions, and such provisions are still in many collective employment agreements. However, numerous constraints and extra payments disappeared in the 1990s as employers replaced awards with new collective or individual employment contracts. More recently, skills shortages and collective employment agreements have forced some employers to re-institute extra payment for working non-standard hours or overtime, but extra payment premiums have not yet returned to the levels that sometimes prevailed before the 1990s.

The main general legislative constraints are health and safety obligations. Following high-profile cases on stress, the Health and Safety in Employment Amendment Act of 2002 explicitly covered stress and fatigue. Although this caused uproar amongst employers, there have been relatively few court cases. Employers, then, have considerable working time flexibility. This flexibility is further enhanced by the few constraints on atypical employment arrangements.

5.8. AUSTRALIA

Under the post-2009 National Employment Standard, standard hours comprise thirty-eight ordinary hours per week. Employees are obliged to work reasonable overtime if requested. What constitutes reasonable overtime will vary considerably between workplaces and industries. In determining reasonable hours, the employer must take into account relevant factors such as workplace health and safety considerations, fatigue management and work-life balance. Nevertheless, many employees, especially males, work long hours.

Until the 1980s, most industrial awards contained provisions for payment of overtime. With the shift to collective bargaining in recent years, overtime provisions have been traded-off in exchange for higher pay or improved benefits in many negotiated agreements.

There are few restrictions on the use of shift work in most industries. Nevertheless, unions have been reluctant to endorse 12-hour shifts in some industries. Under the award system, shift premiums were common for working shifts in the afternoon, at night or 'split shifts'. As with overtime payments, these premiums have been traded off in many collective and individual agreements.

Traditionally, employers paid overtime 'penalty rates' to employees for working unsocial hours at nights, weekends and during public holidays. As with overtime and shift premiums, many of these penalty rates have been traded-off for wage increases during enterprise agreement negotiations.

In recent years, there have been experiments with employees being allowed to work flexible hours. Many private sector employers use a time-off-in-lieu (TOIL) system whereby extra hours worked by employees are accumulated and taken off at a later date. Such arrangements can accompany the elimination of penalty and overtime payments. Some employers have experimented with annualized working hour arrangements. From 2010, as part of the new ten National Employment Standards, workers will have the right to request flexible working arrangements. However, the right to flexible working arrangements is not a guarantee to the employee that they will receive these arrangements.

Flexi-time systems are used extensively in the public sector. Workers have some flexibility in their starting and finishing times and can accumulate 'banked hours' to be taken at a later time.

5.9.   JAPAN

Japan's working hours legislation was established in 1947. Since 1988, statutory reform has gradually reduced the traditional forty-eight-hour working week. The standard working week across all industries and enterprise sizes fell to forty hours. Exceptions are the forty-four-hour weeks served by workers in: commerce; cinemas and theatres; health and hygiene; and service and entertainment workplaces with fewer than nine employees. Annual working hours declined by about 400 hours through the 1960s and the first half of the 1970s. After the post-1973 oil crisis working hours remained at about the same level, but they began falling again at the end of the 1980s. The effect of shortening the working hours set by law has played a large role in reducing actual hours worked since the late 1980s.

Overtime hours in Japan tend to vary in relation to the business cycle. Enterprises make use of overtime hours to adjust employment in the face of fluctuations in demand. Consequently, rather than recruiting people during times of prosperity, overtime hours for existing employees are increased. Furthermore, overtime is reduced as a means of avoiding lay-offs. This occurs because the cost of overtime allowances for current employees is generally less than labour costs related to hiring additional employees. The Labour Standards Law authorizes the Ministry of Health, Labour and Welfare to fix upper limits of overtime for fixed periods. There is an annual maximum of 360 overtime hours per worker. Further, the rate is 25% or more in ordinary cases and for late night work, but 35% or more for holidays.

A variable scheduling system allows monthly and annual variation systems, whereby weekly scheduled working hours will be increased to more than forty hours for a specified week(s) or specified month(s); all other weeks/months will be shorter. This system can be applied to manufacturing.

Under the annual variation system, it has been possible, since 1999, to plan scheduled working hours flexibly for a period greater than one month, although not exceeding ten hours per day and fifty-two hours per week. A flexible work hour system allows workers self-management over the starting and finishing times of their daily working hours over a one-month period. The free-style system of weekly variation was designed for enterprises in retailing, restaurants and hotels. This system provides for advance notice of changes. Approximately 15% of enterprises adopt the monthly variation system, 40% use the annual variation system, and 6% have accepted flexi-time.[118]

---

118. Ministry of Health, Labour and Welfare, 2006.

Chapter 6
Paid Leave Entitlements

This chapter discusses annual leave, public holidays and sick leave. (Parental leave schemes are discussed in Chapter 1.)

The minimum levels of paid annual leave can be increased by collective bargaining (on average paid leave is five weeks in Germany) or by seniority. In Canada, workers are entitled to three weeks paid leave after six years' service. In Japan, leave is twenty days for workers who have at least six and half years' service. However, there is a tendency in Japan for employees not to take all of the leave to which they are entitled. In Australia under certain circumstances, legislation allows for employees to agree to work and be paid for up to two weeks rather than take annual leave.

In Australia and Germany, public holidays are determined by governments but may differ slightly between the various States. In Sweden they are regulated by collective agreement. In the United Kingdom they are not a legal requirement, although they are widely observed. In the United States, although there is not a legal requirement, employees are entitled to take nine paid public holidays at a federal level. Employees are entitled to eight public holidays in Quebec and nine in Ontario. Workers in New Zealand can take eleven public holidays; those who work on such holidays are paid 1.5 times their normal pay. There are fifteen days of public holidays in Japan.

Sick leave, a complex topic, depends on various factors: the system of health care (universal, compulsory insurance or voluntary insurance); who is responsible (employers or employees); the possibility for collective agreements to modify the basic rules, and who is paying and in which proportion (employee, employer or the state). The broad division is between countries where employees have a general right to paid sick leave and those where there are no rights.

In the United States, there is no right to paid sick leave. Under certain circumstances, employees are entitled to unpaid leave as they are entitled to twelve weeks of unpaid family-medical leave that may be used for illness. Nine Canadian jurisdictions provide paid sick leave. Workers in the other countries have such a right, but differing rules apply. In the United Kingdom, all employees are entitled to statutory sick pay. In Japan, employees are covered by public health insurance, though they usually use their vacation leave for short periods of sickness. In Germany, employees are entitled to employer-funded leave for up to six weeks, after which they are covered by health insurance. In Sweden, sick leave arrangements can be modified by collective agreement. In New Zealand five paid sick days per year are allowed (with the possibility to accumulate them to the following year if they are not used).

6.1.   EUROPEAN UNION

According to the working time directive, the Member States must ensure that every employee is entitled to paid annual leave of at least four weeks. The minimum period of paid annual leave may not be replaced by an allowance in lieu, except where the employment relationship is terminated. Sick leave and paid holidays are not regulated at European Union (EU) level.

According to a study by Mercer Human Resource Consulting (2007) the average leave and public holiday entitlements (combined) across all twenty-seven EU states is thirty-four days,[119] with no significant difference between Eastern and Western Europe. The three countries with the most generous holiday entitlements are Finland (forty-four days), followed by France and Lithuania (both forty days). In contrast, employees in the United Kingdom, Netherlands and Romania have only twenty-eight days leave per year.

6.2.   GERMANY

Labour law (Federal Paid Leave Act, *Bundesurlaubsgesetz*) entitles all employees to a period of paid annual leave of at least twenty-four working days. This absolute entitlement cannot be reduced by individual contracts or collective agreements. Further days of paid leave have been added by collective agreements. Employees covered by collective agreements can claim an average of thirty days paid leave. Pay during public holidays is guaranteed by law. Employees are entitled to the equivalent of a normal working day's pay.[120]

In the case of absence from work due to sickness, employees are entitled to 100% pay from the first day of illness for a period of up to six weeks. After that time, sickness benefit is paid by the statutory health insurance. The level of absence from work due to sickness has declined in recent years to a considerable degree. In one recent year, the average absentee rate due to sickness was approximately 4%.

---

119.   The averages are based on statutory entitlements for an employee working five days a week, with ten years' service.
120.   Weiss & Schmidt, 2008, 103.

6.3.   SWEDEN

By law, the minimum amount of paid vacation is twenty-five days per year. The way in which payment for vacations is calculated may be amended in centralized collective agreements.

Paid work on public holidays is regulated in collective agreements. Employees have the right to keep their wages and other benefits when ill. The first day absent due to illness is unpaid. Thereafter, workers receive 80% of their wages. Such levels can be amended by collective agreements.

6.4.   UNITED KINGDOM

Most employees have a statutory right to paid annual leave. Employees begin to accrue these rights on commencement of their employment. On termination of an employment contract, employees are paid for unused accrued annual leave.

Employees are entitled to leave to deal with emergencies involving a dependent (a spouse, child or parent, or person who reasonably relies on the employee for assistance). This does not apply to long-term care arrangements such as childcare or caring for a sick relative.

Although public holidays are widely observed, they are not a statutory requirement, and any right to time-off or extra pay on public holidays depends on the terms of an employee's contract of employment. Payment for public holidays can be deducted from the minimum annual leave levels.

In its pre-election manifesto, the post-1997 government had proposed that it would extend the entitlements to a minimum of four weeks paid leave, in addition to public holiday leave. Consultation is underway on the implementation of this proposal.

6.5.   UNITED STATES OF AMERICA

Vacations and public holidays in the United States are established either by collective bargaining between employers and unions, or by employer policy or individual bargaining between employers and employees if no union has been recognized. There is no federal law requiring employers to provide paid time off for public holiday, vacation and sick leave.

If an employee works on a public holiday, there is no federal law requiring extra pay for working on that day, except that employees must be paid overtime if working on that holiday causes them to work more than forty hours per week. Nor is there a law requiring that employees get paid time-off for holidays. All those employees who work in the public service (federal or state) are afforded these federal holidays.

The FMLA 1993, which applies only to employers with at least fifty employees, provides such people with up to twelve weeks of unpaid leave for certain medical situations for either the employee or a member of the employee's immediate family. California and New Jersey are the only states that provide paid family leave to employees.

6.6.   CANADA

Vacation pay and annual leave are established in minimum standards legislation. Although details vary slightly from one jurisdiction to another, the principle is generally similar. According to the Canada Labour Code and Labour Standards Regulations, employees are entitled to two weeks annual paid vacation. After six consecutive years of service with the same employer, this entitlement increases to three weeks. After completing one year of employment, an employee is entitled to vacation pay equivalent to 4% of annual earnings. After six consecutive years of service with the same employer, the employee is entitled to vacation pay equivalent to 6% of annual earnings. Quebec follows a similar pattern, but the amount remains at 4% of annual earnings in Ontario, irrespective of the length of service.

All employees are entitled to take public holidays. For example, the federal jurisdiction and Ontario list nine paid public holidays, whereas Quebec lists eight paid public holidays. The premium for working on a public holiday is the overtime rate in the federal jurisdiction and one-twentieth of the wages earned in the four weeks prior to the public holiday in the Ontario and Quebec jurisdictions. Special provisions are made for establishments with continuous hours of operation.

Unpaid medical leave, including family-medical leave, varying from seventeen weeks (federal) to twenty-six weeks (Ontario and Quebec) is available to employees who have a continuous period of service (six months in most cases).

6.7.   NEW ZEALAND

There has been much change in terms of paid leave entitlements in the post-1999 period. The subsequent Labour-led governments instituted paid parental leave, extra pay for working public holidays, and increased paid sick leave. The paid parental leave entitlement was extended to the self-employed in 2006. These entitlements have also been underpinned by extensive legal precedents developed in the 1990s and the provisions are inspected by the Department of Labour. Entitlements are covered by a qualification period, which is normally six months paid employment with the same employer, and this can be a barrier for some employees in the current labour market with increasing numbers of employees on atypical employment arrangements. A fourth week of annual leave entitlement was introduced in 2007.

Normally, employees are entitled to eleven public holidays. If people work on public holidays they are, according to the Holidays Act 2003, entitled to be paid 1.5 times their normal level of remuneration.

Paid sick leave allows five sick days (after a six months qualifying period) each year; sick days can be accumulated from one year to the next only if there is an additional collectively-agreed entitlement.

6.8.	AUSTRALIA

Permanent employees are entitled to four weeks annual leave per year with an additional leave 'loading' (bonus) of 17.5% on top of their usual pay for annual leave taken. As a result of the Work Choices legislative changes retained under the Fair Work Act, some continuous permanent-shift workers are entitled to five weeks annual leave. Employees can trade off (cash out) two weeks annual leave for an equivalent increase in salary in some circumstances. The employee must still retain an entitlement to least four weeks paid annual leave before being able to do this. Part-time employees receive pro-rata holiday pay.

Employees have an entitlement of ten paid days of personal (sick)/carers leave to cover illness of themselves or their dependents, which accrues annually on a pro-rata basis. Employees also have access to two days paid compassionate leave per occasion and two days unpaid leave per occasion, once paid leave is exhausted.

6.9.	JAPAN

According to the Labour Standards Law 1947, ten days of paid holidays shall be granted to those workers with an 80% or greater attendance rate and at least six months of continuous service with an enterprise, whereas twenty days shall be given upon reaching six years and six months of service. Nevertheless, the average number of vacation days taken throughout Japan in 2006 was only 8.4 days. Interestingly, only half of the vacation entitlements were actually consumed. The number of legal public holidays in Japan was fifteen days in 2006.

All workers are covered by public health-insurance schemes and, are entitled, therefore, to sick leave (with income maintenance through insurance funds). For minor sickness of one or two days, Japanese workers tend to use their paid annual leave.

Chapter 7

Employment Protection

This chapter covers the topics of employment protection and job security, including the regulation of individual dismissals and collective redundancies, as well as anti-discrimination and equality between men and women. At first sight, such topics might seem unrelated; however, anti-discrimination regulation is becoming an important part of employment protection in many countries. In the case of Canada, for example, key initiatives have resulted from continuing developments in human rights legislation. There have been court cases dealing with the interface between collective agreements, human rights legislation and arbitrators. Those dealing with disputes during the life of the collective agreement have increasingly sought to apply provisions of human rights charters and collective agreements in their determinations about appropriate workplace conduct. In a comparative perspective, the European Union (EU) Member States, especially Germany and Sweden, still have relatively strong employment protection laws.

The courts and tribunals play a key role in interpreting employment protection and anti-discrimination measures. The information summarized here should be interpreted with caution and put into context. Specific cases could be treated in different ways if they were litigated, depending on the national or enterprise context.

There are various facets of EU legislation dealing with employment protection. In the 1970s, two directives introduced an obligation to inform and consult workers in relation to redundancies and transfers of undertakings. Another directive defines the procedures in case of employer insolvency. The three directives were revised in the 1990s. Directive 98/59 relates to redundancies that consolidate Directive 75/129 (see also Chapter 8). Directive 2001/23 defines employees' rights in transfers of undertakings, or parts of enterprises. As a result of enterprises becoming more fragmented by outsourcing certain functions (e.g., transport, cleaning, security or catering), there has been increased litigation and many EU court cases. Directive 2002/74 defines the protection of employees if their employers are insolvent.

7.1. WHAT ARE FAIR AND UNFAIR INDIVIDUAL DISMISSALS?

This segment summarizes what are considered as fair and unfair individual dismissals.

7.1.1. EUROPEAN UNION

At EU level, there is no regulation of unfair dismissal or individual dismissal.

7.1.2. GERMANY

Fair: Factors include personal characteristics and/or behaviour (such as insufficient skill), and enterprise needs and compelling operational reasons.

Unfair: Where the employee can be retained in another capacity, for redundancy dismissals where due account has not been taken of 'social considerations' (e.g., seniority, age, family situation). Rehabilitation must already have been attempted before the dismissal.

7.1.3. SWEDEN

Fair: 'Objective grounds' – economic redundancy and personal circumstances, including lack of competence. A past incident may constitute part of a legitimate reason for termination if the employee was given a warning for the incident. In cases of redundancy, the selection of workers to be made redundant has to be justified (mainly based on a last-in, first-out basis).

Unfair: If an employee could reasonably have been transferred to other work, or if dismissal is based on events that happened more than two months previously. Unfair dismissal cases can be taken to the Labour Court, which is composed of seven members: three neutral, two employer representatives and two employees.

7.1.4. UNITED KINGDOM

Potentially Fair: Relating to the capability, qualifications, conduct or retirement of the employee; because a statutory restriction prevents the employment continuing, due to economic redundancy or some other substantial reason. The employer must have acted reasonably in carrying out the dismissal (this reasonable test is replaced by a procedural test for retirement dismissals). A one-year qualifying period is necessary to be able to file for unfair dismissal.

Automatically Unfair: Related to a range of reasons including union activity, health and safety, whistle blowing, pregnancy or maternity, the NMW, and all matters related to discrimination. No qualifying period is required for automatically unfair dismissals.

7.1.5. UNITED STATES OF AMERICA

Fair: No justification or explanation is necessary (there is an employment-at-will principle) unless the parties have placed specific restrictions on terminations or unless the judiciary in a state has created exceptions. Court decisions in approximately forty states have placed some restrictions on the right of employers to dismiss employees-at-will. Generally, these restrictions apply where the court finds an implied contractual term that permits discharge only for 'cause'. Other states also restrict discharge for an employee refusal to act in violation of the law or to avoid payments of money owed, such as commissions for a salesperson.

Unfair: The employment-at-will doctrine is superseded by statutes that prohibit certain forms of discrimination in employment or require advance notice of mass layoffs. For example, laws prohibit discrimination based on concerted (collective) activity (including union organizing), race, colour, sex, age, national origin, religion and disability. In some cases, State statutes or court decisions have created a 'just cause' standard for dismissing employees, and employers are prohibited from discharging an employee for reporting illegal activity to public authorities.

Only Montana has a state law regulating unjust dismissal.

7.1.6. CANADA

Fair: Where there is just cause, dismissal is permitted, but the burden of proof generally is with the employer. Judicial interpretations of common-law employment obligations also establish tests for adequate or reasonable notice for termination of employment.

Unfair: According to statutory and charter obligations, dismissal is unfair if it is on the basis of discrimination (sex, race, disability, religion, sexual orientation), pregnancy, garnishment proceedings, or the exercise of a right under human rights or labour statutes (employment standards, occupational safety and health and labour-relations legislation). There are also common law employment obligations with regard to adequate notice. The notion of constructive dismissal, entailing a unilateral change in the conditions of employment without prior notice or consent is present in employment standards legislation, court interpretations of common law contracts and civil law in Quebec. Employees with varying levels of service, for instance, in the federal jurisdiction (twelve months) and in Quebec (two years) can file complaints for unfair dismissal under employment-standards legislation.

7.1.7. NEW ZEALAND

Fair: If there is a good substantive reason (misconduct, lack of competence, redundancy) to dismiss and the employer carries out the dismissal fairly and reasonably in those circumstances.

Unfair: Emphasis by the authorities and the Court is put on employees being given reasonable notice of the specific allegation against them and a reasonable opportunity to respond to those allegations. An employer must also give unbiased consideration to an employee's explanation.

7.1.8. AUSTRALIA

Fair: If there is a good substantive reason (misconduct, lack of competence, redundancy) to dismiss, and the employer carries out the dismissal fairly and reasonably in those circumstances.

Unfair: As a preliminary observation, in Australia there is a legal distinction between the meaning of the terms 'unfair dismissal' and 'unlawful termination'. Unfair dismissal refers to a dismissal at the employer's initiative where there is no valid or substantive reason for the dismissal (such as misconduct, lack of competence or redundancy). It also refers to circumstances where the employer may have a valid reason for the dismissal but implements it in a procedurally unfair manner (e.g., the employee is not advised of the reasons for dismissal and is denied an opportunity to respond to adverse allegations). The right to pursue an unfair dismissal claim is a statutory right, which normally is available only to permanent employees. It is not available to certain categories of employee such as casual workers, workers on fixed-term contracts whose contract has expired or workers who have been employed by the employer for less than six months or one year (if less than 15 employees within the organization). There are other restrictions such as limits on the pay level of the employee dismissed. The employer must give the relevant government agency (Centrelink) written notice if the proposed dismissal is of 15 or more employees.

FWA may determine that an unfair dismissal (a dismissal that is harsh, unjust or unreasonable in the particular circumstances) has occurred when all of the following conditions have been met:

(a) an employee has been terminated at the employer's initiative;
(b) the dismissal was not consistent with the Small Business Fair Dismissal Code; and
(c) the dismissal was not a genuine redundancy.

Under certain circumstances an alternative claim of unlawful dismissal can be made by an employee, if they have not lodged already lodged an unfair dismissal claim or a discrimination claim under the state anti-discrimination acts. It reflects an employee's employment being terminated for one or more of the unlawful prohibited reasons prescribed by the FW Act. For example, an unlawful termination of employment is one based an attribute of the employee such as race, sex, pregnancy, age, disability, union membership, criminal record, medical record or family responsibilities.

There is emphasis by the authorities and the courts on employees being given reasonable notice of the specific allegations of misconduct or incompetence made against them and a reasonable opportunity to respond to those allegations. An employer must also give unbiased consideration to an employee's explanation.

7.1.9.   JAPAN

Fair: For 'reasonable cause' – incompetence of the employee or non-compliance with disciplinary rules. Redundancies require urgent business reasons to justify the enterprise's reduction of staff; reasonableness of selection criteria and reasonableness of procedures.

Unfair: For reason of nationality, gender, belief or social status, of workers on sick leave, childbirth and maternity leave, and when conditions on fair dismissal have not been satisfied.

7.2.   COLLECTIVE REDUNDANCIES[121]

With regard to collective redundancies, what are the thresholds and the notification processes to the workers, unions and the public authorities?

7.2.1.   EUROPEAN UNION

For the European countries, the EU has adopted a directive on collective redundancies (98/59) defining minimum standards concerning the definition of a collective redundancy and the information/consultation obligations.

7.2.2.   GERMANY

The definition of collective redundancies is that within thirty days an employer is dismissing five or more employees (in enterprises with 21–59 employees); 10% of the workforce or twenty-five or more workers (in enterprises with 60–499 employees); or thirty or more employees (in enterprises with 500 or more employees). In all such cases there has to be consultation with the relevant works council and notification to the local employment office.

---

121. Redundancies may also be known as layoffs or retrenchments.
    For more information, see OECD, 2004.

7.2.3.   SWEDEN

Collective redundancies are governed by governmental regulations. Employers have a duty to inform and consult with relevant unions and to notify the County Labour Board.

7.2.4.   UNITED KINGDOM

The definition of collective redundancies is that within ninety days, an employer is dismissing twenty or more employees. Employers have a duty to inform and consult with union or employee representatives and a requirement to notify the national government's BIS.

7.2.5.   UNITED STATES OF AMERICA

The definition of collective redundancies is that within sixty days an employer is dismissing a hundred or more employees or within a period of thirty days an employer is dismissing fifty or more employees or there is a plant closure. Employers have a duty to inform affected employees or unions (where they are relevant) and to notify state and local authorities.

7.2.6.   CANADA

The national-level definition of collective redundancies is that within a period of four weeks an employer is dismissing fifty or more employees who are in the federal jurisdiction. This definition also applies in Ontario, albeit with some exceptions. The definition of collective redundancies in Quebec is that an employer is dismissing ten or more employees. Notice must be given to the bargaining agent of each affected employee in the federal jurisdiction and Quebec. An employer is required (federal jurisdiction) or may be required (Quebec) to establish a joint committee with employee representatives to discuss alternatives to redundancies and measures to assist those affected in finding other employment. In all jurisdictions, the employer must notify the relevant authorities (such as the Minister of Labour).

7.2.7.   NEW ZEALAND

There is no definition of collective redundancies but there are particular protections for so-called vulnerable workers (see section 7.3.7). There are no special regulations for notifying employee representatives and notification of public authorities is not required.

7.2.8.   AUSTRALIA

Special regulations apply when an employer decides to dismiss fifteen or more employees for economic, technological, structural or similar reasons. The employer must give written notice about the proposed dismissals to the Commonwealth Services Delivery Agency (Centrelink).

7.2.9.   JAPAN

No special statute applies. If thirty or more employees are being dismissed, they should receive at least thirty days' notification. Information and consultation with union or employee representatives is required. Also notification should be given to public employment service.

7.3.   ANTI-DISCRIMINATION

With regard to anti-discrimination legislation, the three European countries have been influenced by the EU legislation and the numerous judgments of the ECJ, which has forbidden direct and indirect discrimination. In Germany (by law) and Sweden (by collective agreement), the rights are mainly collectively protected. In the other cases (such as United States) anti-discrimination legislation at an individual level has played a dominant role; sometimes the effects of an individual case also have a collective impact.

7.3.1.   EUROPEAN UNION

EU legislation is important in terms of anti-discrimination policies and regulations. The Racial Equality Directive 2000/43 implements the principle of equal treatment between people irrespective of racial or ethnic origin. It gives protection against discrimination in employment and training, education, social protection (including social security and healthcare), membership and involvement in unions and employers' associations and access to goods and services, including housing. The directive prohibits direct and indirect discrimination, harassment and victimization and allows for positive action measures, to ensure equality in practice. Each Member State should have an agency to promote equal treatment and provide independent assistance to victims of racial discrimination.

The Employment Equality Directive 2000/78 implements the principle of equal treatment irrespective of religion or belief, disability, age or sexual orientation. The principle applies in employment, training as well as membership and involvement in unions and employers' associations. It includes identical provisions to the Racial Equality Directive on the prohibition of harassment, discrimination and victimization, on positive action, rights of legal redress and the sharing of the burden of proof. Employers are required to make reasonable accommodation to enable a person with a disability to participate in training or advance in employment. The directive allows for exceptions to the principle of equal treatment, for example, where the ethos of a religious organization needs to be preserved. This legislation is complemented by a program to deter discrimination.

Since the 1970s the EU has developed the principle of equal pay into a general principle of equal treatment for men and women. The first Directive 1975 deals with equal pay and clarifies the scope of the treaty provision. The directive on equal treatment in employment followed in 1976. Directive 79/7 encompasses the statutory social security schemes. Directive 86/613 introduced the principle of equal treatment for self-employed men and women. Directive 86/378 introduced the principle of equal treatment for men and women in occupational social security schemes. This directive was amended (Directive 96/97) after a landmark court decision in the 'Barber Case', in which the court held that benefits under occupational social security schemes, and in principle all contributions, had to be defined as pay (except for voluntary contributions and employer's contributions in defined-benefit schemes and defined-contribution schemes) if they were paid into an occupational social security scheme. A directive on the protection of pregnant workers was adopted in 1992 as a health and safety measure. In 1995, the framework agreement on parental leave was concluded between the European social partners BusinessEurope, CEEP and the ETUC. This was revised in 2009.

In 1997, the Burden of Proof Directive was adopted. The complainant was required to establish before a court or other competent authority, only the facts about discrimination, whereas the respondent was required to prove that there was no breach of the principle of equal treatment.

The Equal Treatment in Employment Directive was amended by Directive 2002/73. The scope of the principle of anti-discrimination is enlarged by including harassment and sexual harassment as well as instructions not to discriminate. Less favourable treatment of a woman relating to pregnancy or maternity leave is defined as discrimination. There is protection against victimization, with a right for other entities to support complainants with their approval in any judicial or administrative procedure. The Member States are obliged to promote 'social dialogue' with a view to fostering equal treatment.

7.3.2.   GERMANY

Important provisions for employment protection have been developed by labour courts (e.g., the necessity to give dismissal notice in writing, minimum terms of notice, justified reasons, special provisions for members of specific groups, ordinary versus extraordinary dismissals, consideration of 'social aspects', consultation of works councils, reinstatement versus financial compensation). Justified reasons for individual dismissals may be the employees' personality, the employees' behaviour or economic circumstances. Additional rules can be included in collective agreements. Protection against unfair dismissals has been curtailed in recent years. For example, the opportunities to conclude fixed-term contracts have been extended and thresholds of dismissal protection in small enterprises have been increased.

In times of high rates of employment and demands for further deregulation of the labour market there have been discussions about whether employment protection provisions prevent new job opportunities and, therefore, should be relaxed or even abolished. Research (by the OECD as well as national studies) indicates that there is at least no clear statistical effect, or most likely, even no effect of employment protection regimes on job creation. Their impact is not on the overall level of employment but, if at all, only on its structure and composition (between 'insiders' and 'outsiders'). Critics of employment protection seem to underestimate the positive implications (e.g., development and protection of specific human capital, stabilization of internal labour markets, higher level of social peace, less negative external effects). Job security is granted only after a specific period of employment; the period has been extended several times since the mid-1980s. Currently, limited contracts can be concluded for a period up to two years. The proportion of these contracts has not significantly increased.

The issue of 'equal pay for equal work' is more relevant with regard to gender than to race. In spite of the legislation, there are still considerable pay discrepancies.

The national law on anti-discrimination implementing the EU Directive was enacted only in mid-2006. It covers more issues than the directive indicates and has been heavily criticized for this reason. It is too early to evaluate its precise impact.

7.3.3.   SWEDEN

The Employment Protection Law (*Lagen om anställningsskydd*) states that, usually, employment is permanent. Any dismissal should be due to factual grounds, such as shortage of work. Employers have the right to give notice before the actual shortage of work, if they expect that there will be a shortage of work when the period of notice ends. Also, dismissals may follow grave misconduct. One of the most debated rules is the seniority rule (the last-in-first-out rule). In times of shortage of work, the person most recently employed is dismissed first. There may be exceptions from such rules in companies with ten or less employees. Employees dismissed due to shortage of work have the right to be reinstated in a new position for a period of nine months after their dismissal, should the shortage of work cease. The right to be reinstated is dependent on whether the employee is qualified for the new job. Lay-off compensation is in collective agreements. Redundancy pay levels are regulated by law.

Discrimination between women and men at work has been forbidden since 1979. In contrast to other labour laws, this law includes job applicants and trainees. Direct and indirect discrimination are both forbidden. In 1999, three new laws relating to discrimination were added: sexual orientation, ethnic or religious origin, and people with disabilities. Employers (with more than nine employees) are required to adopt two plans, one promoting equality issues at work and the other on equal wages.

127

7.3.4. UNITED KINGDOM

With the exception of the collective redundancy and unfair dismissal provisions, legislation does not make specific provision for job security. Collective agreements, negotiated by the employer and the union may, however, make provision for various forms of job security.

All employers should have minimum procedures for the administration of dismissal, disciplinary action and grievances in the workplace. They should inform employees about the procedures and, subsequently, follow them when considering dismissal or disciplinary action. Similarly, employees must follow the required procedures. These usually consist of three steps:

(a) the employee sets out his/her grievance in writing to the employer;
(b) there is a meeting between the parties to discuss the matter; and
(c) there is an appeal meeting, if the matter has still not been resolved.

In a case of dismissal, if the employer fails to follow the above recommended procedures, the employment tribunal will be likely to find the dismissal unfair. For a brief period between 2004 and April 2009 the government experimented with statutory minimum procedures, but these now no longer apply.

Employers are under a statutory obligation to consult employee representatives about proposed collective redundancies (see EU Directives). The consultation must start in 'good time'. In addition, consultation must be completed before any notices of dismissal are issued to employees (following a ECJ judgment 2005). Redundant employees are entitled to a lump-sum payment from their employer. This provides a 'safety net' of protection. Many employers have more generous schemes. There is a two-year qualifying period before employees are eligible to claim a statutory redundancy payment, and a limit on the level of weekly pay.

There is specific legislation to prevent discrimination on the basis of gender, race (including colour, ethnic background or nationality), or disability (including long-term illness). In addition (more recently) there is specific legislation to prevent discrimination on the basis of religion or belief, and sexual orientation. Legislation to prohibit age discrimination at work was implemented in 2006. Equality legislation protects employees from direct and indirect discrimination, as well as harassment and victimization.

Since 2000, the Human Rights Act has included provisions to protect workers' rights and freedoms, including a right to privacy. Employees can lodge claims of discrimination with an Employment Tribunal if endeavours to resolve their complaint directly with their employer are unsuccessful.

The EHRC was established in 2007. It brought together the Disability Rights Commission and the Equal Opportunities Commission to promote equality and tackle discrimination in relation to sexual orientation, age, and religion or belief – areas that were not covered by the former commissions. The Commission for Race Equality joined the EHRC in 2009. The EHRC focuses on advising individuals of their rights under discrimination law and how to secure them, including how to initiate proceedings.

The EHRC has statutory powers to promote changes and improvements in respect of equality and diversity, human rights and good relations. It can conduct inquiries, either thematic or specific, into named organizations. It is able to initiate these inquiries independently or at the request of the government.

The Equal Pay Act (EPA) came into effect in 1975. It gives an individual a right to the same contractual pay and benefits as a person of the opposite sex for work that is proved to be of equal value. The employer will not be required to provide the same pay and benefits if it can prove that the difference in pay or benefits is genuinely due to a reason other than one related to sex. The EPA covers indirect sex discrimination as well as direct discrimination.

7.3.5.   UNITED STATES OF AMERICA

Generally, employment can be terminated without cause ('employment-at -will'). However, there are some exceptions. Courts in approximately forty states have established some protection from unjust dismissal, but only one state (Montana) has enacted legislation modifying the employment-at-will doctrine.

The Worker Adjustment and Retraining Notification Act (WARN) requires private-sector employers to give sixty-days' notice of large-scale lay-offs and plant closures; it allows exceptions for unforeseen emergencies and other cases. Several states have independently adopted more stringent requirements.

The employment-at-will doctrine is superseded by statutes that prohibit certain forms of discrimination in employment or require advance notice of mass lay-offs. For example, US laws prohibit discrimination based on concerted activity (including union organizing and concerted protected activity), race, colour, sex, age, national origin, religion and disability.

The employment discrimination laws include federal and state statutes. The US Constitution and some state constitutions provide additional protection (where the employer is a government agency or the government has taken significant steps to foster the discriminatory practice of the employer). The Fifth and Fourteenth Amendments of the US Constitution limit the power of the federal and state governments to discriminate. Discrimination in the private sector is not directly constrained by the Constitution but may be constrained by state constitutions and is subject to federal and state statutes.

The EPA amended the FLSA in 1963. The EPA prohibits determining pay levels based on sex. It does not prohibit other discriminatory practices (e.g., bias in hiring). It provides that where workers perform equal work in jobs requiring 'equal skill, effort, and responsibility and performed under similar working conditions', they should be afforded equal pay. The FLSA applies to employees engaged in an aspect of interstate commerce.

The Civil Rights Act 1964 prohibits discrimination based on race, colour, religion, sex or national origin. Sex includes pregnancy, childbirth or related medical conditions. It makes it illegal for employers to discriminate in hiring, discharging, remuneration, or terms, conditions, and privileges of employment.

Likewise, employment agencies may not discriminate when hiring or referring applicants.

The Age Discrimination in Employment Act (ADEA) prohibits employers from discriminating on the basis of age. The ADEA contains explicit guidelines for benefit, superannuation and retirement plans. The purpose of the Act is to 'promote and expand employment opportunities in the public and private sectors for handicapped individuals', through affirmative action programs and the elimination of discrimination. The Americans with Disabilities Act (ADA) aims to eliminate discrimination against those with disabilities.

The Equal Employment Opportunity Commission (EEOC) interprets and enforces parts of the Equal Payment Act, ADEA, ADA, and the Rehabilitation Act (see <www/eeoc/gov> and <www.law.cornell.edu/wex/index.php/Employment_discrimination>).

The Immigration Reform and Control Act 1986 also provides narrow prohibitions against certain types of employment discrimination based on immigration status. It encourages states to pass their own anti-discrimination laws; most states have done so. Certain states and local governments have also enacted statutes that expand on the rights that federal law offers, either by offering greater remedies or broader protections, or have legislated in areas that federal law does not cover, such as discrimination based on sexual orientation or marital status.

7.3.6.   CANADA

With the exception of many forms of discrimination in relation to dismissals, legislation does not make provisions for job security. Collective agreements may, however, make provision for job security.

Employees are protected from termination of employment because they exercise their legal rights, including complaints about discrimination as well as more general considerations regarding minimum standards legislation and the rights to freedom of association and engaging in union activities.

Employees who are dismissed in some jurisdictions (e.g., the federal jurisdiction) may request a written statement from their employer outlining reasons for their dismissal; in Quebec the employer must provide such a statement. In this latter case, the period of written advance notice will vary from one to eight weeks according to the length of service. Furthermore, in Quebec, employees with a minimum length of service may appeal against unjust dismissal. Economic reasons can justify dismissal, but non-unionized employees are protected against arbitrary treatment. Most unionized employees are subject to a distinct labour-relations regime, set out in their collective agreement, as regards the principles that apply in the case of discipline and dismissals as well as lay-offs and other forms of enterprise restructuring.

There are redundancy-pay provisions in most jurisdictions, although there are significant variations as to when terminated employees can access such payments. The federal jurisdiction grants access after twelve months of continuous employment.

Ontario requires that an employee has five years service and applies this requirement only to enterprises with an annual payroll in Canadian dollars of more than CAD 2.5 million. The amounts paid can also vary, but tend to be equivalent to one week's pay for each year of continuous service.

Employees in all Canadian jurisdictions are protected by discrimination-at-work codes. In Ontario, the Human Rights Code (the 'Code') gives everybody equal rights and opportunities without discrimination in specific areas such as jobs, housing and services. Employment decisions should be based on the applicant's ability to do the job and not on factors that are unrelated to the job. The Code prohibits discrimination in employment on the grounds of race, ancestry, place of origin, colour, ethnic origin, citizenship, creed, sex, sexual orientation, age, record of offences, marital status, same-sex partnership status, family status and disability. Any person in Ontario who wishes to make a code-related complaint to the Commission is entitled to do so (<www.ohrc.on.ca/english/guides/hiring.shtml>). As specified in the Québec Charter of Human Rights and Freedoms, discrimination need not necessarily be direct. It may also arise out of an apparently neutral, generally applicable rule that has a prejudicial effect on a specific person due to a 'personal characteristic' defined as a ground for discrimination.

The federal jurisdiction seeks to measure the equality of pay according to the principle of work based on equal work of equal value. It uses a composite of skill, effort, responsibility and working conditions to determine if work is equal. Different performance ratings, seniority, 'red-circling', rehabilitation assignments, demotion, phased-in wage reductions, temporary training position, internal labour shortage, salary protection for downward reclassification and regional rates of wages are considered acceptable reasons for differences in pay. A complaint may be initiated by an individual or a group of people, or the Canadian Human Rights Commission, or an inspector under the Canada Labour Code. A Human Rights Tribunal may be appointed to decide the matter.

Ontario has three laws that address equal pay: the Employment Standards Act addresses pay rates and is based on the principle of substantially the same kind of work and the same kind of skill; the Human Rights Code addresses equal treatment with respect to employment and is not bound by a particular set of criteria; and the Pay Equity Act addresses total economic rewards for work (all payments and benefits) on the basis of work of comparable value. The pay-equity legislation generally has a threshold point (minimum number of employees or total payroll cost) at which it is applicable, whereas the charter rights are applicable to all workplaces.

7.3.7.   NEW ZEALAND

New Zealand's Employment Relations Act has attempted to support job security through the protection of employees when work was contracted out or in the case of transfers of undertakings (section 54). However, the protection was originally discussed during the debates over the Employment Bill in 1999–2000. Subsequent to the Employment Relations Act there was also inconclusive tripartite consultation about possible solutions. Stronger measures were introduced in the Employment Relations Amendment Act 2004. The Amendment Act provides two kinds of protection – a specific protection of so-called vulnerable employees (e.g., in cleaning and residential care) and a general protection of employees. The protection of vulnerable employees provides three alternate employee responses:

(a) they could choose to transfer to the new employer on their existing terms and conditions, in which case their service would be continuous;

(b) they could negotiate an alternative arrangement, for example, redeployment within the enterprise; or

(c) they could decide not to transfer to the new employer, which may result in their current employer declaring them redundant.

In the case of redundancy during or shortly after the transfer of an undertaking, the redundancy entitlement can be determined by the Employment Relations Authority. This development is a change from the practice of legislative abstention in the area of redundancies.

The general protection of employees is by a default clause in all employment agreements on 'employee-protection provision'. This should stipulate the processes, matters to be negotiated, and possible financial entitlements. It is not yet clear what the effects have been of these 'employee-protection provisions'. It is also not yet clear whether the legislative changes have had any impact on transfer of undertakings; particularly in industries which are covered by the specific obligations.

Redundancies are often dealt with in collective employment agreements, which stipulate the required payments and processes. Several precedent-setting court cases in the 1990s considered redundancy entitlements.

Anti-discrimination covers, for example, sex, ethnicity, religious and political beliefs, and so on. Disability and age often feature in discrimination complaints. Drug abuse and drug testing have featured prominently, as have privacy concerns over electronic surveillance and employer control of the content of computer files (see Rasmussen 2009, Chapter 8).

New Zealand has had equal-pay legislation since 1972, but this legislation appears to have lost some of its relevance in the contemporary labour market. Pay equity, however, is a public-policy issue in the new millennium. The Pay Equity Taskforce between 2003 and 2009 was abolished by the incoming National-led government in early 2009. The taskforce had prepared research for several pay equity cases, which were curtailed when it was abolished. The decision by the National-led government prompted critical media reports, which pointed to a similar abolishment of the Employment Equity Act by the National government in 1991 (Rasmussen 2009, 207).

7.3.8.   AUSTRALIA

Allegations of unlawful discrimination commonly include: sex; relationship status; pregnancy; parental status; breastfeeding; age; race; impairment (disability);

religious belief or religious activity; political belief or activity; union activity; lawful sexual activity; gender identity; sexuality; family and carers' responsibilities; association with, or in relation to a person identified on the basis of any of the above. Employees who have been terminated for an unlawful reason can bring an action of discrimination to FWA, the Australian Human Rights Commission (AHRC) (formerly the Human Rights and Equal Opportunity Commission (HREOC)) or the State Anti-Discrimination Commissions.

All genders and races are entitled to be paid at the same rate for work of similar value. An employer may not discriminate on these grounds. However, there is much debate about what 'similar work' actually includes and the fact that minorities often tend to work in jobs that offer low wages and conditions.

Claims for unlawful discrimination in employment may include the use of any one of the following federal Acts: FW Act, Australian Human Rights Commission Act 1986 (formally called the *Human Rights and Equal Opportunity Commission (HREOC) Act* 1986, *Race Discrimination Act* 1975; *Sex Discrimination Act* 1984; *Disability Discrimination Act* 1992, *Equal Opportunity for Women in the Workplace Act* 1999; and the *Age Discrimination Act* 2004 or State/Territory Anti-Discrimination Acts. The new federal *Fair Work Act* also includes a general protections provision against adverse action for unlawful discrimination in the workplace. This means that the employer is prohibited from treating an employee in a discriminatory manner, or altering or injuring an employee's employment. Furthermore, this section now also covers prospective and current employees and not just dismissed employees.

This section has not yet been tested but may be a challenge for employers as it appears broader than the discrimination provision under the former legislation.

7.3.9. JAPAN

There are several statutory restrictions on dismissal. First, the Labor Standards Law (LSL) prohibits dismissal during periods of medical treatment of work-related injuries, and thirty days thereafter, as well as periods of leave before and after childbirth. Second, workers must be given thirty days' advance notice for dismissals. Third, discriminatory dismissal is illegal and invalid.

In Japan, there has been no legal provision specifically requiring the employer to have just cause for termination. Under the Civil Code, an indefinite-term labour contract may be terminated by either party at any time if two weeks' notice is given. The LSL has modified this principle by stipulating an obligation to give thirty days' notice, if the contract is being terminated by the employer. The 2003 amendment to the law required valid reason for dismissals. This amendment has been transferred and consolidated into the Law of Employment Contract of 2007.

Though Japan has no system of severance pay for workers who are made redundant, there is a distinction between voluntary retirement on the part of the employee and redundancy imposed by the employer. The benefits payable to employees whose employment comes to an end in these circumstances is greater in the case of redundancy. Some clauses may precipitate a reduction or forfeit of the retirement allowance, depending on such things as the worker's job-performance ratings, moving to another enterprise engaged in the same business, or 'disciplinary dismissal', which undermines the employer's interests.

Two approaches have been taken to equal employment opportunity (EEO) between men and women: a prohibition of and redress for discrimination based on sex, and legal assistance to facilitate workers' harmonization of work and family life. They are mainly regulated by the LSL, the Equal Employment Opportunity Law (EEOL) and case law.

A 1997 amendment abolished LSL provisions concerning special protection for women. The EEOL generally prohibits preferential treatment of women, but promotes 'positive actions' to mitigate gender-based employment disparities.

The LSL prohibits discriminatory treatment of employees on the grounds of employees' nationality, creed or social status with respect to terms and conditions of employment. 'Social status' refers to a social classification from which one cannot escape of one's own volition. Thus, class differentiation on the basis of being a part-time worker, a status created by mutual assent of the parties, does not fall within this category of 'social status'.

Chapter 8
Dispute Settlement Procedures

This chapter discusses dispute settlement procedures. These are still important in all of the jurisdictions examined, even though there have generally been fewer industrial disputes in most jurisdictions in recent years. Dispute settlement procedures include negotiation, conciliation, mediation, arbitration and other forms of governmental or judicial intervention. In some jurisdictions (e.g., Germany and New Zealand), there is a legal distinction between conflicts of rights (*Rechtsstreitigkeiten*) and conflicts of interest (*Interessenstreitigkeiten*). The former are differences in the interpretation of existing collective agreements or contracts; the latter are differences about the making of new agreements or contracts. In other jurisdictions (e.g., the United Kingdom), there is no such distinction. Canada and the United States represent two different approaches to dispute settlement in the private sector. Such procedures are generally voluntary in the United States but mandatory in Canada.

8.1.   EUROPEAN UNION

In 2001 there was a debate within the European Union (EU) in relation to proposals to establish a supra-national panel of conciliators and mediators who would be deployed to deal with employment conflicts of a transnational character. This proposal was not adopted; however, a report was produced (<http://europa.eu.int/eur-lex/lex/LexUriServ/site/en/com/2005/com2005_0033en01.pdf>).

8.2. GERMANY

In a comparative perspective, the German system of employment relations has often been described as being highly legalized.[122] One institutional consequence is that there is a differentiated system of labour courts (*Arbeitsgerichte*) at local, state and national levels. These are specialized agencies, independent from the general court system with the power to make binding and final decisions. Conflicts of rights are always settled by binding decisions of the labour courts, whereas collective bargaining, which includes the option of industrial disputes, constitutes the only means for settling conflicts of interest.

Furthermore, in this system of employment relations, there is no statutory system of arbitration and/or mediation; there are no binding cooling-off periods, and there are no official mediation agencies. Mediation agreements (*Schlichtungsabkommen*), as procedural arrangements, can be concluded between the bargaining parties (social partners), but these are not compulsory. There are voluntary provisions for conflict management and, if possible, conflict prevention in most sectors (e.g., engineering, chemicals, construction and the public sector). In practice these provisions are often invoked. From time to time there is intervention in disputes by neutral, 'third parties', but the recommendations are not binding on the parties.

8.3. SWEDEN

Disputes are usually settled in negotiations between the union and the employer. If there is no local shop steward, a regional shop steward (ombudsman) will act for the employees if they are union members. If the dispute remains unsettled, negotiations will follow between the employers' association (if the employer is a member) and the union at the national or sector level. If the dispute continues and the social partners cannot find a settlement, the case can be taken to the Labour Court. Before the court considers the case, negotiations or arbitration are held, with or without external help. There are no formal rules on how arbitration should be conducted. Many cases are settled at this stage; this may include an undisclosed sum of money being paid to the worker(s) bringing the case or their union. The Labour Court is the last resort for settling disputes.

8.4. UNITED KINGDOM

The ACAS is an independent public agency whose roles include offering mediation, conciliation and arbitration services, and helping disputing parties to reach agreement without recourse to legal proceedings. ACAS arbitrators are independent, part-time and may, for example, be academics, retired public servants, employment

---

122. Keller, 2008.

lawyers or someone with suitable expertise who is impartial. ACAS' advisory and research work has increased in importance. This includes conducting investigations and advising the parties on how to prevent disputes and, more generally, how to foster 'good employment relations'. Where there is collective bargaining, agreed disputes procedures often include some form of access to ACAS. ACAS is increasingly promoting individual mediation procedures (see <www.acas.org.uk>).

8.5.   UNITED STATES OF AMERICA

The NLRA 1935, as amended in 1947 by the Taft- Hartley Act, created the Federal Mediation and Conciliation Service (FMCS) to assist in settling disputes that impact on inter-state commerce. The FMCS facilitates the settlement of disputes by providing mediators to assist the parties in resolving disputes over the terms of a CBA. Almost all collective agreements provide for final and binding arbitration as an alternative to a strike or lockout to settle disputes that arise during the term of an agreement. The FMCS facilities this process by maintaining lists of qualified arbitrators and procedures for selecting arbitrators. The private American Arbitration Association also maintains such lists and rules, as do some states. Parties may also establish their own private systems of arbitration and/or arbitrator selection.

In the railroad and airline industries, the Railway Labor Act provides for arbitration for minor disputes or grievances, and settlement of major disputes through mediation and the appointment of a presidential emergency board in certain situations.

For disputes in the federal jurisdiction, the FMCS supplies mediation, after which the parties can invoke the Federal Labor Relations Authority's Federal Service Impasse Panel for a variety of settlement procedures, including fact-finding and arbitration (either final-offer or regular arbitration). Non-unionized employers are not required to enter into arbitration agreements with employees, although some employers require an arbitration agreement to settle disputes as a condition of employment. This trend seems to have accelerated since the mid-1990s with US Supreme Court decisions making such arbitration agreements enforceable in court.[123]

Most state jurisdictions also provide for mediation and sometimes arbitration of disputes. (See the Association of Labor Relations Agencies (ALRA; <www.alra.org>). For information about the NLRB and FMCS and the Federal Labor Relations Authority (FLRA), see <www.nlrb.gov>; <www.fmcs.gov>; <www.flra.gov>. With regard to disputes concerning statutory rights and discrimination, information can also be gathered from the EEOC: <www.eeoc.gov>.)

---

123.   Wheeler, Klaas & Mahony, 2004.

8.6.   CANADA

Ministry of Labour mediation and conciliation services seek to assist employers and unions in settling employment relations disputes and in improving their labour-management relations. These include conciliation, mediation, preventive mediation and grievance mediation. When unions or employers are negotiating, either party may request a conciliation officer. The minister may also appoint a mediation officer in the case of an impasse in bargaining. Ministers may limit the right to strike or lockout during mediation procedures. Labour relations boards also adjudicate issues such as the failure to 'bargain in good faith' or other forms of breach of procedure. In the case of negotiations over a first collective agreement, the Minister of Labour in seven provinces (including Ontario and Quebec) and the federal jurisdiction may, on the request of either party, impose binding interest arbitration to settle the first-contract dispute. This provision seeks to enhance the access of newly unionized employees to the right of association.

A number of Ministries of Labour have sought to develop their capacity to intervene in preventive mediation to help the parties develop more constructive working relationships over contentious and developing issues. The federal government also contributes to financing capacity-building and innovation-building initiatives in labour-management cooperation.

Disputes procedures in the public sector can include compulsory interest arbitration (Ontario) and specific administrative bodies (Quebec) to regulate recourse to strikes and lockouts through the designation of 'essential services' after a compulsory mediation process.

In addition to these forms of dispute resolution procedures in collective labour relations, most government human rights agencies offer forms of mediation to resolve disputes involving fundamental human rights. The Labour Standards Commission in Quebec also intervenes in the case of disputes relating to labour standards, unfair dismissal, psychological harassment and bankruptcy.

8.7.   NEW ZEALAND

Dispute settlement has been part of the legislative framework since the Industrial Conciliation and Arbitration Act 1894. Since then, the original institutions – Conciliation Boards and the Arbitration Court – have faced many changes. In particular, the distinction between disputes of interest and disputes of rights made by the Industrial Relations Act 1973 has been important. The provisions for dealing with personal grievances were also introduced in the 1973 Act. These provisions have become a major employment relations issue since the Employment Contracts Act 1991 extended these provisions to all employees. Compulsory arbitration was abolished in 1984 and the award system was abolished in 1991. Despite its rejection of the award system and union membership rights, the Employment Contracts Act retained the main institutions and some dispute-settlement mechanisms.

The Employment Relations Act 2000 changed the institutions and their roles. The main institutions are: the Mediation Service, the Employment Authority and the Employment Court. The Court of Appeal has also played a major role, especially in the 1990s when it often overturned decisions made by the Employment Court. Personal grievance cases overwhelmed the capacity of the institutions in the 1990s, which led to a considerable backlog and long delays. The current Mediation Service has been crucial in expediting dispute settlements. Most personal grievance cases are referred to mediation before the parties can access the more formal legal process in the Employment Authority.

The traditional collective disputes of strikes and lockouts are either settled by the parties or the Employment Authority and the Employment Court can intervene. Strikes and lockouts are lawful if:

(a) they are in support of a collective agreement;
(b) the employees concerned are not bound by a current collective agreement;
(c) the parties involved have already negotiated for at least forty days; and
(d) in the case of the 'essential services' listed in the Employment Relations Act, the notice requirement has been met.

Although some opponents of the Employment Relations Act 2000 expected that strikes and lockouts would increase significantly under the Act, the low level of collective industrial disputes from the early 1990s has continued. In particular, there have been relatively few legal arguments over good-faith and multi-employer collective employment agreements.[124]

8.8.   AUSTRALIA

Before 2009, government had significantly reduced the role of the former AIRC. In 2009 FWA reintroduced a greater emphasis on dispute-settlement procedures in employment relations. FWA also prescribes a model dispute-settlement procedure for agreements negotiated after 1 July 2009 that fail to make adequate provision for the minimum steps required by the FW Act. The industrial relations parties are expected to settle their disputes at workplace level wherever practicable. All agreements must contain a dispute settlement procedure. Where a dispute cannot be settled at the workplace level, the parties may seek to engage FWA or a mutually acceptable third party to conciliate or conduct arbitration. An industrial relations agreement may, in its dispute-settlement procedure clause, expressly provide FWA with additional powers, including whether an appeal from a hearing may be conducted. The emphasis under the FW Act is for parties to attempt to settle disputes voluntarily or by conciliation before they resort to a formal hearing (arbitration).

---

124.   Rasmussen, 2009.

8.9.   JAPAN

The Labour Relations Adjustment Law provides for The Labour Relations Commission in each prefecture to settle disputes through conciliation, mediation and arbitration. The role of the commission is important, because Japan does not have active private dispute-settlement systems.

The basic principle is voluntary settlement. Thus, the commission defers to the parties' own volition to settle disputes in the process of conciliation, mediation and arbitration. In conciliation and mediation, the commission may propose a settlement plan. In arbitration, the commission's final award is binding. There is no compulsory arbitration.

The Labour Tribunal Law was implemented in 2006 to expedite settlement of individual labour disputes. It has the following features: first, the labour tribunal is composed of one career judge and two nominated part-time arbiters who are experts in labour relations. The arbiters have the same dispute-settlement rights as a judge; second, the labour tribunals mediate and make decisions to settle the case. These decisions are not binding and if either party objects, the case is transferred to ordinary civil procedures. Apart from this new individual dispute settlement procedure, all labour and employment-related lawsuits must be filed in ordinary civil courts.

Chapter 9
Freedom of Association and Representative Organizations

This chapter covers three topics: recognition of unions and employers' associations; unions' rights of entry to members' workplaces; and forms of employee representation (works councils).

In relation to recognition of unions, there are two groups of countries. The first group includes Germany and New Zealand, where recognition has not been a major issue, as well as Sweden, which has no specific provision for recognition. For the second group (Canada, the United Kingdom, Australia and the United States), there are various processes for recognition of unions by the employer when a majority of the employees endorse union representation. Japan has only a certification process. The difference between the countries reflects the different level at which collective bargaining is conducted: primarily at the sector (industry) level for the first group, but primarily at the enterprise level for the second group.

Unions' rights to workplace entry differ from one country to another. The practices could be more or less flexible according to the power and the relationship between the employers and the unions. In Sweden, union officials have the right to enter workplaces to execute their duty. In general, UK union officials do not have this right, but there are a few exceptions. In Canada, they have no right to enter non-unionized workplaces, but generally in these workplaces the employer has an interest to settle pending issues with the union. In New Zealand, union officials have access and the right to hold two meetings a year. In Japan, they cannot enter without prior permission, but the issue remains controversial.

There is a cleavage between countries having collective forms of representation (works councils) and those not having such institutions. There are works councils in most of the European Union (EU) countries and at the EU level (European Works Councils (EWCs) for multinational companies). There are works councils with statutory rights only in Germany. Information/consultation is conducted through the local union in Sweden. Following the EU Directive on Informing and Consulting Employees, British and Swedish employees gained new legal rights to be informed and consulted on a regular basis about developments in their workplace. The rights are being extended to cover more enterprises. The EU Directive will not change the situation in Sweden. In Japan, most of the unionized enterprises have some form of consultative representation. In New Zealand, the Health and Safety in Employment Amendment Act 2003 (HSE Act) introduced health and safety committees in medium-sized and larger organizations. In the United States and Canada, there is no similar legislation which requires employers to establish such committees.

9.1.   EUROPEAN UNION

To be recognized as representative at EU level, union and employers' associations have to fulfil three criteria:

    (a) include cross-industry membership, or relate to specific sectors or categories and be organized at a European level;

    (b) consist of organizations which are themselves an integral and recognized part of Member States' social-partner structures and have the capacity to negotiate agreements, and which are representative of all Member States; and

    (c) have adequate structures to ensure the effective participation in the consultation process.

On this basis the cross-industry social partners were recognized.

At sector level, thirty-six sectors have been recognized and have social dialogue committees.[125] The European Foundation for the Improvement of Living and Working Conditions (Eurofound) – a tripartite EU agency, coordinates representativeness studies for the sector social partners (see <www.eurofound.europa.eu>).

Three pieces of EU legislation have established consultative bodies at national and EU level.

The main legislation for the establishment of a EWC and consultative mechanisms within enterprises that operate across EU borders is Directive 94/45, which provides for information sharing and consultation with employees.

It is possible to create an EWC in each undertaking of more than 1,000 workers that have at least two subsidiaries in two EU countries with more than 150 workers. The directive encourages negotiations between employees and managers. The negotiations could lead to agreements which are below the minimum standards. The directive states that EWCs must cover (as a minimum) the following topics:

    (a) structure, economic and financial situation of the company;

    (b) probable developments of the business, and production and sales;

---

125.   Dufresne, Degryse & Pochet, 2006.

(c) number of jobs and future prospects;
(d) investment;
(e) substantial changes in organization, new working methods or processes;
(f) transfers of production;
(g) mergers, cutbacks or closures; and
(h) collective redundancies.

By 2009, around 910 multinational companies had created an EWC from a potential total of 2,400 companies, which fit the criteria for establishing EWCs. The functioning of the EWCs is different from one company to another. It is mainly limited to an exchange of information. Few EWCs have begun to negotiate binding collective agreements.

In May 2009, the European Parliament and the Council reached an agreement on a recast directive, which is expected to be implemented in all the Member States no later than 2011.

The second piece of legislation concerns the establishment of a *Societas Europaea* (SE) European Company statute. The main purpose of the SE statute (EC 2157/2001) is to enable companies to operate their businesses on a cross-border basis in Europe under the same corporate regime. An important feature of this new company form is that – by means of the associated SE Directive (2001/86/EC) – obligatory negotiations on worker involvement in SEs were introduced, which include the question of representation of the workforce at board level. By mid-2009, ninety-nine companies had adopted the European company statute (see <www.workerparticipation.eu>).

The third piece of legislation addresses the national level. Following the closure of the Renault car plant in Belgium, the EU adopted a directive on information and consultation at national level. The purpose of the Directive 2002/14 is to establish a general framework specifying minimum requirements. Member States can choose whether to apply the directive to establishments of at least fifty employees or establishments with at least 20 employees. Information and consultation shall cover:

(a) information on the recent and probable development of the undertaking's or the establishment's activities and economic situation;
(b) formation and consultation on the situation, structure and probable development of employment within the undertaking and on any anticipatory measures envisaged, in particular where there is a threat to employment; and
(c) information and consultation, with a view to reaching an agreement on decisions likely to lead to substantial changes in work organization or in contractual relations.

Information has to be given at such time so as to enable employees' representatives to conduct an adequate study and, where necessary, prepare for consultation. Employers may require employee representatives to treat information as confidential.

Information and consultation arrangements defined by agreements between national social partners may differ from those set out by the directive. Sanctions for non-compliance with the provisions of the directive must be effective, proportionate and dissuasive.

9.2.   GERMANY

The right of freedom of association is legally guaranteed in the constitution, the Basic Law, in two variants. In its negative form, it means that no employee can be forced to join any interest organization (e.g., a union); in its positive form, it implies that no individual can be prevented from joining. There are certain legal procedures to declare agreements generally binding. However, these procedures are rarely applied and the number of cases has decreased since the mid-1990s.

In contrast to certain other countries, certification and recognition have never been of major importance in the German context. The most important general legal prerequisites for a union are: it must promote its members' working and economic interests and conditions; membership has to be on a voluntary basis; unions have to be independent from the 'other side of industry' as well as from all state authorities and political parties; unions have to be organized on a supra-enterprise (or sector) base; they must have democratic structures; they must be able to exert pressure on their opponent, and they must recognize the law on collective bargaining.

Within a so-called dual system of employment relations, there is a clear legal distinction between interest representation at enterprise and sector levels. The former has as its legal base the Works Constitution Act (*Betriebsverfassungsgesetz*). It allows, but does not enforce, the institutionalization of works councils (*Betriebsräte*) and is valid for all companies in the private sector with at least five permanent employees, whether or not they are union members. Membership in unions is voluntary. More recently there has been a growing non-union sector. In contrast to unions, works councils are not allowed to initiate a strike.

Membership numbers as well as union density ratios have been deteriorating since the early 1990s. Between the mid-1990s and the early 2000s several mergers also decreased the number of affiliates to the German Trade Union Federation (*Deutscher Gewerkschaftsbund*) from sixteen to eight. This is a remarkable development because union structures had not changed hitherto in the post-1945 period.

Since the mid-1990s, coverage rates of works councils, in contrast to those at sector level, have been relatively stable at about 55%. There are obvious differences relating, among others, to the number of employees per company, to the age of the company, to specific sectors as well as to regions. For example, there are fewer works councils in the eastern than in the western part of Germany.

9.3.   SWEDEN

The Co-determination Act includes the right to unionize and the right for unions and employees to negotiate on issues concerning employees, hiring and firing, and reorganizations. The right to information in negotiations is also included, as is the right to strike and to bargain collectively. According to Swedish labour law, unions are legal entities. The right to unionize and to belong to an employers' association is unconditional. All people, or employees, have the right to belong to an organization, to create such an organization or to work for it, and that right is not in any way to be violated. Each union and employer has the right to negotiate. There is no provision for certification/recognition of bargaining agents.

The right for union officials to conduct their duties in their workplace is protected. Employers should not interfere and the official has the right to paid leave from employment for union work and also to have an office in which to do this work. Employees in companies and public-sector organizations employing more than twenty-five people can have two representatives (and two deputies) on the board. The decision to initiate such representation is with the local unions that have a collective agreement with the employer. The representatives should already be employees of the enterprise. They are prohibited from making decisions on collective agreements and strikes.

Employee representation in Sweden is organized via the unions without independent channels. Whereas works councils represent all employees, the local union branches represent only union members. The local branches are an important part of the union structure as they are the face of the union to the individual members. An exception is EWCs. These were inaugurated with the implementation of EU Directive by-law in 1996. The unions have actively promoted the EWCs, but oppose using works councils for collective bargaining of core areas such as pay, but other issues (e.g., equality) may be negotiated.

Sweden implemented the EU directive on information/consultation at the national level by amending its law so that employers not bound by collective agreements are required to keep unions (which have members in that workplace) informed on output, finance and personnel policy. Information should be given to the local union. All employers covered by the co-determination act are obliged to comply, irrespective of the number of employees. Union representatives have the right to time-off from work to receive such information.

9.4.   UNITED KINGDOM

The certification officer maintains a list of unions and employers' associations. For unions, listing is an essential preliminary to any application for a certificate of independence, which in turn is needed to apply for statutory recognition under the Employment Relations Act 1999. It also brings taxation concessions, although this requires the union to submit to financial and other regulatory supervision. The certification officer does not have general powers to investigate the affairs of a union. The powers are limited to adjudicating on specific complaints of alleged breaches of statute or certain union rules. The certification officer can also appoint an inspector to investigate the financial affairs of a union but only in restricted circumstances and if there is evidence to suggest financial irregularities.

The 1999 Act established a statutory procedure that enables a union to obtain recognition by the employer for collective bargaining purposes where at least 40% of the relevant workforce vote for this and constitute a majority in the ballot. The Act also established a similar procedure regarding the de-recognition of such a union after three years of statutory recognition. Employers' associations can also apply to the certification officer to be listed, but there are fewer advantages associated with doing so.

The CAC adjudicates on applications relating to the statutory recognition and de-recognition of unions for collective bargaining purposes, where such decisions cannot be agreed voluntarily. In addition, the CAC has a role in settling disputes between unions and employers over the disclosure of information for collective bargaining purposes.

The European Convention on Human Rights guarantees freedom of assembly and association, including the right to form and join unions for the protection of employees' interests. This was implemented in the United Kingdom in 1998. Employers or employment agencies are not allowed to discriminate against potential or current employees because they belong (or do not belong) to a union, or because they refuse to join or decide to leave.

Unions do not have a general right of workplace entry. Under the Employment Act 2002 Regulations, employees are entitled to be accompanied to disciplinary or grievance hearings by a companion who may be a union official. In this case, union officials have the right to enter the workplace. There is also provision to allow union officials to attend a workplace as part of a lawful picket (in contemplation or furtherance of a dispute), if they are accompanying and representing an employee for the purpose of peacefully obtaining or communicating information, or they are peacefully persuading any person to work or abstain from working.

Joint Consultative Committees (JCCs) constitute the most common form of representative voice in workplaces where there are no union members. They are present in 14% of workplaces, with higher levels of presence in large workplaces and in the public sector. Elections are held for employee representatives on almost 60% of these committees.

Large enterprises are required, under the EWC Directive, to inform and consult employees at the European level. In 2008 employees in enterprises with 150 or more employees gained new legal rights to be informed and consulted on a regular basis about developments in their workplace, as the United Kingdom implemented the EU Regulations on Informing and Consulting Employees. These rights are based on an agreement with the CBI and the TUC. The rights are being extended to cover more enterprises over a three-year period.

The requirements in the legislation do not apply automatically. Employers can initiate the process, or an employee can submit a request if it is supported by at least 10% of workers in the enterprise (subject to a minimum of 15 employees and a maximum of 2,500 employees). Existing agreements may continue where they enjoy the support of the workforce. This new law is designed to encourage employers, employees and their representatives to agree on information and consultation arrangements that suit their particular circumstances. It does not specify the subjects, method, timing or frequency of the arrangements that are allowed. Agreed arrangements may cover more than one enterprise, or establish different processes in different parts of an enterprise.

Standard provisions based on the directive apply as a fallback in situations where no agreement is reached. These require the employer to inform employee representatives about the enterprise's activities and economic situation, and consult them on employment issues, major changes in work organization and employees' contractual matters. A failure to comply with the regulations resulted in the imposition of a penalty of GBP 55,000 by the Employment Appeal Tribunal on Macmillan publishers in 2007.

9.5.   UNITED STATES OF AMERICA

The NLRA (for private sector), the Railway Labor Act (railroads and airlines), and the Civil Service Reform Act (federal-sector employees), and various state statutes covering state and local employees, regulate collective employment relations in the United States. The Labor-Management Reporting and Disclosure Act of 1959 (also known as the Landrum-Griffin Act), deals primarily with the relationship between a union and its members. It protects union funds and promotes union democracy by requiring unions to file annual financial reports, by requiring union officials, employers, and labour consultants to file reports regarding certain employment relations practices, and by establishing standards for the election of union officers. In general, supervisory or managerial employees are not eligible to have union representation.

The United States does not have works-councils legislation, but the unions and management may form labour-management committees (LMCs) and under the Taft-Hartley Act, employers can fund these committees. These LMCs deal with workplace issues as well as productivity and include representatives from the union and the employer. A non-union employer may not legally establish employee committees if the committee addresses terms and conditions of employment and engages in bilateral dealing with the employer.

9.6.   CANADA

Unions and employers' associations are regulated by industrial relations commissions. All non-supervisory salaried workers are free to join a union according to the various labour codes and also according to the increasing reference to international labour norms in legal decisions. These rights are administered in the first instance by labour-relations boards and, therefore, in the case of disputes about rights, by various courts. The Supreme Court has made landmark decisions protecting freedom of association. It made a decision in 2007 pertaining to British Columbia Health Services, which enlarged its interpretation of the meaning of freedom of association to include collective bargaining. There are public debates about the effective exclusion from access to the freedom of association of a wide range of workers from freedom of association rights, especially in the growing numbers of people involved in new forms of work arrangements.

Unions must be certified for the purposes of collective bargaining. A union gains exclusive bargaining rights when it demonstrates that it has majority support from the employees in the particular unit that it seeks to organize. The predominant method for determining union recognition is through certification elections. These are often expedited to ensure effective access to the right of association. Quebec remains the jurisdiction that relies on the detailed verification of the signatures on union membership cards. The certification process is generally overseen by an administrative tribunal, the Labour Relations Commission, or its equivalent. Where it can be demonstrated that employers have interfered with the formation of a union, industrial relations commissions are empowered to impose union representation on the employer. Once a union is designated as the monopoly bargaining agent, it is the exclusive agent for all employees in a bargaining unit. Generally, all employees pay union dues, whether they are a member of the union or not. Employers are obliged to deduct the union dues at source. Such a 'union-shop' provision is a legal requirement in most jurisdictions in Canada.

Unions usually do not have initial access to the workplace to recruit union members. Once a union is certified, however, it can hold meetings on the premises. As bargaining relations mature, employers generally wish to have access to union officials to settle pending issues expeditiously.

There are not legally designated alternate forms of collective representation (e.g., works councils) that provide alternatives to collective agreements in the workplace. Many non-unionized employers do, however, seek to promote some form of employee representation or consultation procedure.

9.7. NEW ZEALAND

Freedom of association rights are prescribed by legislation. The Employment Relations Act 2000 re-introduced the registration of unions; unions can play their formal role in collective bargaining only if they have been accepted by the registrar. Unions have to adhere to the rules about accountability and internal democracy and they need to have at least fifteen members. There are few limits on union formation. This has prompted a proliferation of new, small unions, though these unions have not contributed to resurgence in union density as they have relatively few members.

With regard to employers' associations, the 2000 Act is silent, but such associations (e.g., Business New Zealand, EMA) are often incorporated societies and are governed by the regulations covering these societies.

The unions' bargaining role is underpinned by access and information rights. Unions have access to workplaces to consult with their members; there is an entitlement to hold at least two union meetings a year (with employees being paid) and employees have the opportunity to participate in paid union-education leave.

In comparison with the pre-1999 period of National-led governments, the representation of employees, employers and the self-employed had a higher profile under the Labour-led governments after 1999. Although employers' associations – particularly the Business Roundtable (a lobby group for big business) – held more sway before 1999, there was no formalized tripartite consultation and negotiation. Since 1999 the Council of Trade Unions (CTU) and Business New Zealand are often consulted by the government and they have had considerable input on current legislative changes, as well as influencing government initiatives in areas such as workplace partnerships, work-life balance, and the protection of vulnerable workers in the case of transfers of undertakings. After 1999, such tripartite consultations were part of the government's strategy to build a more inclusive society; they also aligned with the government's policy to promote self-regulation and workplace partnerships.

Besides promoting collective bargaining, traditionally unions and the Labour Party displayed relatively little interest in promoting employee influence and participation in workplace decision-making. This has changed, however, since the 1990s (though there is still no legislation prescribing works councils). The focus on bargaining in 'good faith' has meant that in employer-employee dealings, there is more emphasis on information and consultation, as well as due process. There was a major break-through in formalized workplace decision-making rights with a 2002 Act, which stipulated that safety and health committees should be instituted in all workplaces with more than thirty employees. Unions have allocated resources to try to make these committees effective, in terms both of health and safety as well as employee participation. Although formalized employee participation has been limited, after 1999, there has been a growth in the extent of informal information and consultation at workplace level.[126] In the 1990s, many enterprises tried to increase the degree of information disclosure and job-related involvement of employees. This was further encouraged by the legislative changes after 1999.

9.8.   AUSTRALIA

Employees and employers may be represented by bargaining representatives. For employees, this is likely to be a union, though bargaining representatives such as lawyers or family members may be also play such roles. A bargaining representative may represent an employee to negotiate an enterprise agreement. The negotiations during a bargaining period may result in a protected industrial-action ballot being requested. Industrial action is lawful if there is a successful protected action ballot. Under the former legislation, in the pre-2009 period, the obligation for an employer to bargain in good faith was removed. The post-2007 federal Labor government reintroduced the obligation to bargain in good faith under the FWA. Should an employer resist meeting, or frustrate the course of

---

126. Haynes, Boxall & Macky, 2005.

meetings conducted for the purpose of negotiating an agreement, employees, or their bargaining representative, may seek a good-faith bargaining order. In that event, FWA will consider all the circumstances and determine whether a good-faith bargaining order should be issued compelling the employer to return to the negotiating table and demonstrate the criteria for bargaining in good faith.

At a federal level, unions and employer associations must have fifty or more members to be a recognized registered organization. Additionally there may also be enterprise employee associations that consist of a group of twenty or more employees, employed in a particular enterprise.

Organizations must be registered to be a party to awards and agreements, and to be permitted to submit industrial disputes to FWA for conciliation or appear in a termination claim on behalf of their members. There is provision for general protection orders that adverse action should cease and for other matters to be heard either in the Federal Court of Australia or the Federal Magistrates Court. Unions may appear in these jurisdictions as a party.

The registration of unions also assists in setting union boundaries by requiring that each union have an eligibility rule that sets out who may be members of the union, and restricting registration if there is another union to which such person could 'more conveniently belong'. In return for these advantages, registered unions are subjected to extensive control of their internal affairs and of inter-union structure. The provisions regarding unions in the remaining State industrial relations statutes have a similar framework.

Legislation regulates the rights of employees, employers or independent contractors in reference to freedom of association, allowing individuals to be, or not to be part of unions or other industrial associations. Those who believe their right to freedom of association has been breached are able to request assistance from the statutory FWO, who has the power to investigate complaints and enforce the law. Penalties of up to 33,000 Australian dollars are provided for non-compliance with the law.

Unions are permitted to enter workplaces to hold discussions with potential members, to represent their members and to investigate suspected breaches of employment laws or industrial instruments, including workplace health and safety. However, strict criteria must first be met, which includes the union official holding a right of entry permit after being deemed a fit and proper person. Before entering the premises the official must have a current right-of-entry permit issued by FWA, which may impose certain conditions on the use of the permit. The permit can be revoked or suspended at anytime. While on the premises, the permit holder can inspect work and equipment, interview people, inspect records, and copy employee records during working hours, including the records of non-members who give their consent.

There are 'peak organizations'. From an employer perspective, most of these are industry-based associations (for instance Australian Chamber of Commerce and Industry, and Australian Industry Group), whereas for unions it is the ACTU. This reflects in part the centralized tradition of the arbitration system, as well as the requirements for formal organizations to be registered under the relevant legislation.

150

9.9.   JAPAN

The law defines 'unions' as autonomous organizations for the purpose of maintaining and improving the conditions of work and for raising the status of workers. Unions can be formed without any formal recognition procedure. However, to enjoy legal protection provided for by the law, they have to be registered as unions by the Labour Commissions. Most unions are organized at the enterprise level where most collective bargaining takes place. In general, employers' associations are not parties to collective bargaining.

Unions cannot claim the right of entry or the use of employers' facilities without prior permission. However, numerous cases have been brought to the Labour Commission as constituting unfair labour practices where the employer opposes union meetings and refuses to permit a union to use the employers' facilities to hold such meetings.

There is no formal collective representation (e.g., European-style works councils) apart from in the specific industrial relations arena. However, there is joint-consultation machinery in most unionized enterprises. Joint consultation (often involving exchange of information between the parties) may take place before formal collective bargaining sessions or bargaining for specific purposes such as job security or welfare matters. A majority of collective agreements are concluded through joint consultation before there is formal collective bargaining. As joint consultations and collective bargaining are performed by the same people from both sides, the demarcation line between consultation and collective bargaining is often blurred. The statutory protections accorded to collective bargaining are also applicable to labour-management consultation procedures.

Chapter 10

Collective Bargaining and Collective Industrial Action: Coverage and Legal Framework

After considering the recognition of unions and employers' associations in the preceding chapter, this chapter discusses how collective bargaining is regulated. What are the main bargaining levels? Who do the collective agreements cover and what do they generally contain? The relationship between agreement provisions and legislated minimum standards, and the circumstances in which collective agreements can override minimum standards are summarized.

In all the countries discussed, there is a balance between minimum legislative standards and collective-bargaining autonomy. In general, collective bargaining cannot undermine legal minimum standards, but can only improve them. Collective bargaining is most important in Sweden, where the coverage is also the highest: more than 90%. In certain countries there is an obligation to bargain in good faith (e.g., United Kingdom, United States, Canada, Australia and Japan). In the Anglophone countries and in Japan, minimum standards cover workers in non-unionized places. In Germany and Australia, collective agreements cover not only union members, but also all other employees, even though it is not a legal requirement. Much of the public sector is generally governed by different rules.

In all the countries, unions have experienced difficulties in recruiting young employees to unionize in small enterprises and in the private-services-sector. There is an increasing difference in union density between the public sector and the private sector. The public sector usually has a higher union density. Some segments typically have a low level of unionization (e.g., retail, hospitality and information technology). This has a significant impact for the countries that do not have a mechanism to expand the agreements to all workers at the sector or national level (United Kingdom, United States, Canada and New Zealand). For example, in recent years, New Zealand and Germany had a similar rate of union density, but a greater proportion of workers are covered by collective agreements in Germany compared with New Zealand.

Table 10.1 Union Density and Bargaining Coverage (%)[a]

	Germany	Sweden	UK	USA	Canada	NZ	Australia	Japan
Union density (1997)	27	82	31	14	32	24[b]	30	23
Union density (2007)	20	74	28[e]	11	31	21[c]	19[c]	18
Collective bargaining coverage (2007)	48[f]	92[d]	35[e]	13	29	18	38[c]	23[g]

Sources: Adapted from Visser (2006); ILO (2009).
a. Proportion of wage and salaried earners, rounded to nearest whole number.
b. 1996.
c. 2008.
d. Approximate 2009, since no exact figures are available.
e. Reported proportion (ILO 2009). See also 4.3 above.
f. 2006.
g. 2003.

There is relatively little change concerning the main level of bargaining, at least since the early 1990s.[127] The sector level is still dominant in Sweden and Germany and the enterprise is usually the main level in the other countries.

There are constraints on industrial action in all of the countries mentioned. The constraints are generally linked to the duration of the collective agreement. In practice, the incidence of industrial action is very low only in Germany and Japan. The high level in Canada (and the medium level in the United States) reflects strikes of long duration in specific sectors.

Table 10.2. Labour Disputes: Working Days Not Worked per 1,000 Employees in All Industries and Services (Average)

	Germany	Sweden	United Kingdom	USA	Canada	New Zealand	Australia	Japan
1997–2001	1	6	14	54	192	17	65	1
2002–2006	6	34	28	15	180	15	30	(0)*
1997–2006	4	20	21	34	186	16	46	(1)

Source: Hale, 2008.
* ( ) Brackets indicate averages based on incomplete data.

---

127. Peetz, Preston & Doherty, 1992; Bamber & Sheldon, 2007.

10.1.   EUROPEAN UNION

European-level cross-industry social dialogue started in the mid-1980s and has been developed considerably since. The Maastricht and Amsterdam Treaties gave the European Union's (EU) social partners a de facto role as legislators by enabling them to conclude contractual agreements, which can subsequently be transformed into directives by the EU Council of Ministers. Social dialogue is different from traditional collective bargaining at national level, for it does not cover pay bargaining.[128] (On the procedures and the actors, see this volume's Introduction.)

In the second half of the 1990s, BusinessEurope, the ETUC and the CEEP embarked on several rounds of negotiations with a view to reaching framework agreements. The first collective agreement was on parental leave in 1995 (revised in 2009); the second, in 1997, on part-time work; the third, in 1999, on fixed-term contracts. All of these agreements were transformed into Community directives. The next attempt to reach a 'legislative' framework agreement, on temporary work, initially failed. After the failure there was a move towards 'autonomous' agreements. Autonomous agreements between the social partners are a legal instrument based on the Maastricht Treaty (see Introduction). Implementation is left to the national organizations that have signed the agreement at the EU level through their peak organizations: the ETUC and BusinessEurope. An autonomous agreement on telework was signed in 2002; another, on stress at work, was signed in 2004; and yet another, on harassment and violence at work, in 2007.

At a national level, the implementation of the three autonomous agreements involved a great deal of variation, with the use of law (in some of the new EU members), national collective agreements, sector collective agreements, enterprise agreements, or common guidelines. Autonomous agreements will, therefore, be implemented very differently in each country because of national differences in industrial relations traditions, structures and the differing involvement of the social partners.

Since 2000, the social partners have also adopted various frameworks of action that contain best-practice examples and guidelines for initiatives to be implemented at a national level. For example, in 2009 a framework of action in relation to employment was being negotiated.

Because of diverging interpretations, the social partners decided in their 2005–2008 joint work programme to assess and evaluate the implementation of EU social-dialogue framework agreements and tools. This evaluation will continue in 2009–2010. They will determine their impact on the various levels of social dialogue. Another important development is the will to better coordinate the various levels of social dialogue and negotiations.

Next on their agenda is the adoption of an autonomous framework agreement on inclusive labour markets.

---

128. Dufresne, Degryse & Pochet, 2006.

Other future initiatives include:

(a) joint recommendation aimed at contributing to the definition of the post-2010 Lisbon agenda in the context of the global financial crisis;
(b) the development of a joint approach to the social and employment aspects and consequences of climate change policies;
(c) jointly monitoring the implementation of the common principles of flexicurity, to draw joint lessons; and
(d) jointly addressing mobility and economic migration issues and promoting the integration of migrant workers in the labour market and at the workplace.

They will also finalize the national studies on economic and social change in the EU-27 to effectively manage change and restructuring and continue the work on capacity-building for social partners in an enlarged EU, and in candidate countries.

The sector-level social dialogue is becoming increasingly important. In 1998, an EU decision formally established the sector Dialogue Committees to promote the dialogue between the Social Partners at European Level. At the sector level, there are currently thirty-six active committees that conduct meetings and seminars and produce joint texts, though these may differ from 'traditional' collective agreements that may apply at a national level. Certain nationally-important sectors have obtained recognition only in recent years. Sector committees were established for the chemicals industry and the local and regional government sector in 2004; for the steel industry and hospitals in 2006; for gas and catering in 2007; and for football in 2008. Three other sectors (non-ferrous metals, the automotive industry and cycling) have submitted a formal request to create a committee. The growing number of committees is in itself an indication of increasing interest. Another interesting indicator is the number of the documents adopted by the social partners, with almost 300 joint texts adopted by the social partners over the period 1999–2007. These committees negotiate agreements (less than 2% of the texts adopted) and recommendations, or adopt common positions aimed to influence the EU sectoral legislation, which counts for more than 60% of texts adopted.[129]

10.2.   GERMANY

The legal base for collective bargaining is the Collective Agreement Act (*Tarifvertragsgesetz*, enacted in 1949; it has subsequently had several amendments), which includes the principle of bargaining autonomy (*Tarifautonomie*) and excludes all kinds of governmental interference.

Collective contracts concluded at regional and sector level between employers' associations and unions are dominant. National sector agreements, which were typical for the public and other sectors, have lost importance. In times of flexibilization

---

129. Dufresne, Degryse & Pochet, 2006.

and decentralization, enterprise bargaining has grown in importance since the mid-1980s. However, enterprise bargaining still covers less than 10% of all employees; its coverage is higher in the east than in the west and more important in large companies. The present extent of 'pattern bargaining' is difficult to detect because variation between sectors has increased to a considerable degree. Until the 1990s, engineering was the dominant sector or 'pattern setter' for the rest of private industry and frequently also for the public sector.

Collective bargaining should not be confused with negotiations at the company level. The latter can only take place between management and the works council (*Betriebsrat*). The legal base is not the above-mentioned Collective Agreement Act but the Works Constitution Act (*Betriebsverfassungsgesetz*). In contrast to unions, works councils have no legal right to lead industrial disputes, but are obliged to engage in peaceful cooperation with management. From a legal point of view, works councils represent all, not only unionized employees.

Collective agreements cover all issues related to working conditions. Wages and working hours are the most important. Agreements could, however, also include issues such as overtime premiums, length of holidays, training, re-training or even measures to cope with rationalization. They cover all employees. Until recently, the historical distinction between blue-collar (*Arbeiter*) and white-collar employees (*Angestellte*) was important. Managers (*leitende Angestellte*) are typically not covered but have individual contracts. In the public-sector, civil servants (*Beamte*) are excluded from collective bargaining, but blue-collar and white-collar employees are included.

It is difficult to generalize about the relationship between provisions in agreements and legislated minimum standards. There is no legislated minimum wage. As far as other working conditions are concerned, the general pattern is that minimum standards are set by legislation but frequently supplemented and improved by collective agreements. A typical example is the length of holidays; another is the maximum number of daily or weekly working hours. Agreements cannot undercut the minimum standards. The only option is provided by so-called opening clauses (*Öffnungsklauseln*), which have to be agreed on in collective agreements. If these procedural arrangements are applied, management and works councils – the parties at the enterprise level – are allowed to deviate from regulations in collective agreements concluded at the sector level. The first generation of these clauses referred only to working time issues; subsequently, they have been extended to wages and salaries. The number of opening clauses as well as the instances of their application has increased considerably since the mid-1980s. About 13% of all companies are bound to sector collective agreements containing opening clauses; in only half of these companies are opening clauses used.[130]

In contrast to all other major ingredients of Germany's highly legalized system of employment relations, there is no legalization on industrial action. All of the rules have been established by major decisions of the Federal Labour Court and the

---

130. Kohaut, 2007.

Constitutional Court. Industrial conflict includes lockouts, as well as strikes. In comparative perspective (with other OECD or EU Member States) Germany has generally had a low level of industrial disputes.

10.3.   SWEDEN

Collective agreements are signed by two parties: a union and an employers' association or an individual employer. In the latter case it is seen as a substitute agreement. Collective agreements have to be in writing. Collective agreements have to include certain stipulated subjects, mainly employment conditions.

Although bargaining had become increasingly decentralized in the 1980s, the 1997 Industrial Agreement (*Industriavtalet*) heralded a new close cooperation at sector level. It has been a role model for other sectors of the labour market. The Industrial Agreement includes a common view on economic and industrial policy. It is a new way of negotiating and indicates a return towards centralization, although at a sector level. Such agreements are considered main agreements. Central agreements are signed by an employers' association and a union. In addition, a local union can sign a local agreement with an employer as a complement to a main agreement. Actual pay levels are usually set locally, with the levels and increases usually elaborated in the agreement.

The collective agreements cover pay, working hours and overtime, while additional benefits may be legislated, such as insurance and holidays. Usually the agreements are valid for the whole of Sweden, for a particular sector. A collective or substitute agreement signed in a workplace is valid for all employees, not only for union members. An agreement will be signed if at least one employee demands it, but, unlike the situation in many other countries, there is no extension of the collective agreement to other enterprises. As there are no legislated minimum standards concerning pay levels, collective agreements could set any levels of pay or conditions.

Throughout the duration of a collective agreement the parties are bound not to initiate or engage in industrial disputes. If, on the other hand, the parties are not bound by a collective agreement, they are free to initiate strikes and lockouts. The right to strike is protected by the Constitution. The initiator has to give advance notice to the other party and the National Mediation Office. Approval for strikes and lockouts is determined by the appropriate board. Disputes that might be potentially dangerous to society can be referred to a special board, whose decision is not binding, but in certain circumstances, it might precipitate the enactment of a special law.

10.4.   UNITED KINGDOM

Collective bargaining in the United Kingdom has traditionally been characterized as 'voluntary'. The Employment Relations Act 1999 does, however, provide statutory recognition for unions in certain circumstances and under specific conditions. The CAC can enforce statutory recognition on a recalcitrant employer. This, however, is rare. Since the passing of the Act, most new union recognition agreements have been made on a voluntary basis.

The Trade Union Recognition Order 2000 sets out a method for collective bargaining which the CAC must take into account when using its powers to impose a legally-binding method of conducting collective bargaining on an employer and a union. Most collective agreements provide for workplace bargaining or enterprise bargaining. There is very limited scope for pattern bargaining. The statutory recognition procedure provides for recognition for the purposes of negotiating pay, hours and holidays. However, voluntary collective agreements may provide wider scope for bargaining and may include other topics such as training, redundancy, sick pay, equal opportunities and superannuation.

Legislated minimum standards apply to all employees or workers. Although collective agreements can enhance minimum standards, they cannot reduce the standards below those defined by legislation. Industrial action is protected by law as long as:

(a) the dispute is between workers and their employer;
(b) a secret postal ballot has been held and the majority of members voting have supported the action; and
(c) detailed notice about the proposed action has been given to the employer at least seven days before it commences.

There is no protection for 'unofficial' industrial action, which is, for example, action called when it is not supported by a ballot; secondary industrial action (in support of workers of another employer); action promoting 'union-labour only' practices; and action in support of anyone dismissed for taking 'unofficial action'.

10.5.   UNITED STATES OF AMERICA

Collective bargaining conduct is covered by the NLRA, which sets forth procedures for holding union representation elections and protecting employers, employees and unions against 'unfair labour practices'. There is no official source of data on the contents of bargaining in the United States. However, in the past few years the single most important issue has been health insurance. Spiralling healthcare costs have influenced the general tone of collective bargaining.

Generally, CBAs may not be used to undermine minimum labour and employment protections established by federal labour laws. In some cases, the statutes themselves provide for exemption from coverage based on the presence of similar protections in labour contracts (CBAs). For example, the FLSA states that an employer does not need to pay overtime for an employee's performance of work in excess of the statutory maximum (forty hours a week), if the employee is employed under a CBA containing alternative maximum hours provisions.

The NLRA requires that, for a strike to be protected or for a lockout to be legal, the parties must have bargained in 'good faith' before arriving at a legal impasse, which must be solely over legal terms and conditions of employment. Until an impasse is reached, the status quo in existing terms and conditions of employment must be adhered to. Once an impasse is reached, an employer may implement its final pre-impasse proposal with the exception of a proposal that contains complete employer discretion over wage adjustments. No law mandates requirements or conditions for workers to begin, sustain or end an industrial dispute. The NLRA also mandates that unions and employers provide certain types of notice, allows for no-strike clauses to be included in collective agreements, and allows for injunctions against strikes in 'national emergencies'. The Labor Management Relations Act (LMRA), permits labour injunctions where a strike or lockout creates a 'national emergency'. Under these provisions, if the president believes that an actual or threatened strike or lockout will imperil 'the national health or safety', he or she may appoint a board of inquiry to investigate the issues in dispute and report publicly on them. Upon receiving this report, the president may direct the attorney general to seek a court injunction against the strike or lockout.

There are differences in the procedures and regulations for strikes in the airline and railway sectors. The most notable difference is provision for an eighty-day 'cooling off' period.

10.6. CANADA

The framework for the conduct of collective bargaining is established by the labour code or labour relations act in each jurisdiction. Although this framework legislation applies to the private sector, the general legislation sometimes includes special provisions for particular groups of workers in the public sector, where specific legislation otherwise governs, for example, the conduct of collective bargaining and the right to strike.

Agreements must define a beginning and end of the agreement and specify the parties to the agreement. They cover all workers in the bargaining unit for the life of the agreement. They must also establish a procedure for settling disputes, ultimately leading to binding arbitration by a third-party neutral, since strikes or lockouts are not permitted during the life of the agreement. These provisions tend to be the only legal stipulations covering the content of collective agreements. In practice, collective agreements in Canada, because they are legally binding on both parties, tend to cover most issues pertaining to the operation of the workplace. These include: pay, a wide range of benefits, the definition of jobs, internal mobility between jobs, union security disciplinary procedures and the often extensive application of seniority rights for different aspects of life at work. They have become progressively more complex – running to hundreds of pages in some cases – and have assumed an unexpected status as a relatively autonomous workplace regime, subject only to some public order provisions in other legislation. In essence, a matter that is not within the terms of a collective agreement cannot be the subject of independent arbitration. Matters that are within the terms of an agreement can be the subject of third-party determination once internal dispute resolution procedures have been exhausted. In general, management prerogatives apply if they are not specifically limited by the terms of the collective agreement; hence the unions try to get coverage for as many matters as possible in the collective agreement. Nevertheless, there has been a tendency to simplify the contents of some collective agreements, often by seeking to introduce more comprehensive parity mechanisms for settling disputes during the life of the agreement.

Bargaining units are typically decentralized – a single establishment being the norm – unless it can be demonstrated that many separate units of a larger enterprise are effectively managed as a single unit or that there is a sufficiently overlapping community of interest. The parties may ultimately agree to conduct bargaining at a higher level. This is the case in car assembly plants and several other sectors. The public sector is likely to have more centralized forms of bargaining, though this varies markedly from one segment to another.

Legislated minimum standards apply to all workers, subject to the provisions of these acts. Collective agreements can enhance minimum standards, but they cannot reduce the standards below those defined by legislation. Maximum hour provisions are specified in the relevant acts and sometimes an agreement to exceed the standard working week can be negotiated (subject to the relevant statutory provisions). This would be the only situation in which the overriding of normal labour standards is allowed, and the applicable criteria are detailed in the relevant legislation.

Employers are further obliged to deal with the union 'in good faith'. This does not mean, however, that they are obliged to conclude agreements with their employees' unions. The only exception would be in the case of an imposed interest arbitration pursuant to an existing legally-imposed collective agreement. Administrative tribunals in most jurisdictions are also permitted to impose first collective agreements to try to 'regularize' collective bargaining relationships.

Strikes and lockouts may occur only at the end of a collective agreement. Strikes during the term of an agreement are illegal. Instead, the parties have recourse to a several-stage process of grievance settlement within the workplace, before any such 'rights' disputes are put to binding third-party arbitration. Even at the end of the agreement, strikes or lockouts may be delayed until a process of conciliation has been completed. The state maintains the power to limit the right to strike or lockout during periods of conciliation.

Parties are normally subject to advance notice, and in most jurisdictions the Minister of Labour has the right to subject the parties to a compulsory period of conciliation, before a strike or lockout is permitted. Before a strike, the bargaining agent (usually a union) must conduct a secret ballot authorizing strike action, either during a specified period prior to the expiry of the collective agreement or after the collective agreement has expired. Before undertaking any such action, a union must obtain majority support from those participating in the vote.

10.7.   NEW ZEALAND

The Employment Relations Act 2000 seeks to build productive employment relationships 'by promoting collective bargaining'. It also seeks to promote the key ILO conventions (Conventions 87 Freedom of Association; and 98 Right to Organise and to Bargain Collectively).

The 2000 Act instituted two important changes. First, the concept of 'good faith' was emphasized. This concept raised awareness of bargaining behaviour and processes and increased the amount of information and communication made available to unions and employees. Nevertheless, issues of good faith seldom surface in collective bargaining or in media reports. Besides further refinement of the good faith concept in 2004 legislation, there were surprisingly few legal developments in the following few years. Second, unions are allowed to strike in pursuit of multi-employer collective employment agreements. There have been important multi-employer collective employment agreements (e.g., nurses in public hospitals), but most collective agreements are still enterprise or workplace based.

Although there have been some successful union campaigns (e.g., the '5% in 2005' wage campaign by the Engineering Union and the minimum wage campaign by Unite), unions appear to have had little impact on influencing employment conditions across the private sector. Instead, they were successful in their collaboration with the Labour-led governments and union campaigns involving work-life balance, stress, 'up-skilling' and employment protection, which became 'hot' topics of employment relations. A key question in current New Zealand collective bargaining is whether unions can build on these achievements and overcome the individual nature of statutory minima.

Overall, collective bargaining has suffered a substantial decline under the Employment Relations Act 2000. 'Our data for the year to June 2003 show collective bargaining levels declining to the lowest level seen over the last twenty-five years' (Thickett, Walsh & Harbridge 2004, 39). There are several explanations for this, but it seems that giving unions the exclusive right of concluding collective agreements under the Employment Relations Act 2000 has facilitated a paradoxical outcome. Under the 1991 Act, many employees were part of so-called collective contracting, where collective contracts were concluded without the involvement of unions (and often without much negotiation or discussion with the covered employees). These employees were usually employed on individual agreements under the 2000 Act as collective contracting was no longer an option since (registered) unions had to be party to collective employment agreements.

There is currently a stark difference between collective bargaining coverage in the public and private sectors. In the public sector (health, education, local and central government) collective bargaining coverage is widespread and has grown in several areas. In the public sector it is a trend-setter and, in several high-profile cases, is associated with closer employer-union relationships. The concept of workplace partnerships has developed. In the private sector, however, unions have had difficulty gaining traction beyond their traditional strongholds and in many workplaces collective coverage tends to have declined to lower levels than it was in the 1990s.

10.8.   AUSTRALIA

Similar to all previous industrial legislation since 1904, the FW Act 2009 provides for collective bargaining and industrial action. Employees are allowed to lawfully bargain collectively if their current agreement has expired, although pattern bargaining is unlawful. The new legislation reinforces the role of collective bargaining in Australia. It re-introduces the obligation for both parties in the federal system to collectively bargain 'in good faith' to reach agreement. This principle was removed by the previous Howard Coalition government in 1996. The FW Act removes individual statutory agreements from the industrial landscape, which was the primary focus of the previous 1996 legislation. The new legislation focuses on collective bargaining for enterprise agreements at the workplace level.

The ten minimum National Employment Standards introduced under the new legislation provide for a national statutory floor of rights. These minimum standards must be included in either an enterprise agreement or contract of employment. With collective agreements and contracts of employment, employees and their representatives must make an agreement that does not fall below the statutory minima. This replaces the previous system that allowed workers to trade off conditions of employment and entitlements in return for pay and other forms of reward.

New industry-based modern awards began operation in the federal system from 1 January 2010. The new award covers most workers in Australia and is relevant as a safety net for most workers not covered by a collective agreement. Approximately 39% of all Australian workers remain covered by enterprise agreements. Approximately the same numbers of workers are covered by individual common law contracts of employment.

10.9.   JAPAN

Japan's Constitution guarantees the right of employees to bargain collectively. This constitutional right is reinforced by the 'unfair labour practice' concept established in the Trade Union Law of 1949. An employer's refusal to bargain collectively with the representative of the employees without proper reason is an unfair labour practice. The Labour Relations Commission will issue a remedial order and insist that the employer bargain with the union.

The Trade Union Law does not adopt an exclusive representation system. Collective agreements do not have universal application even within a single enterprise union. The legislation does not impose on unions a duty to bargain.

Most collective bargaining takes place at the enterprise level and most CBAs are at the enterprise level.

A collective agreement applies to union members but case law establishes the possibility of extending the coverage of the collective agreement to workers who are not members of the union that concluded the collective agreement. When at least three-quarters of the workers of the same classification come under the application of a particular collective agreement, the agreement will then be applied to the remaining workers. When a majority of the workers of the same classification are covered by a particular collective agreement, the authorities may decide that the collective agreement should apply to the remaining workers in the same locality and to their employers.

References

General

Aglietta, M. & L. Berrebi. *Désordres dans le Capitalisme Mondial*. Paris: Odile Jacob Économie, 2006.

Albert, M. *Capitalisme Contre Capitalisme*. Paris: Edition du Seuil, Collection Point, 1991.

Amable, B. *The Diversity of Modern Capitalism*. Oxford: Oxford University Press, 2003.

Bamber, G.J. 'How Is the Asia-Pacific Economic Cooperation (APEC) Forum Developing? Comparative Comments on APEC and Employment Relations'. *Comparative Labour Law & Policy Journal* 26, no. 3 (2005): 423–444.

Bamber, G.J., R. Lansbury & N. Wailes (eds). *International and Comparative Employment Relations*. London/Sydney: Sage/Allen & Unwin, 2010.

Bamber, G.J. & C.J. Leggett. 'Changing Employment Relations in the Asia-Pacific Region'. *International Journal of Manpower* 22, no. 4 (2001): 300–317.

Bamber, G.J., et al. (eds). *Employment Relations in the Asia Pacific: Changing Approaches*. Sydney/London: Allen & Unwin/Thomson, 2000.

Bamber, G.J. & P. Sheldon. 'Collective Bargaining: An International Analysis?'. In *Comparative Labour Law and Industrial Relations in Industrialized Market Economies*, edited by R. Blanpain. The Netherlands: Wolters Kluwer, 2007: 585–632.

Begg, I., et al. *Social Exclusion and Social Protection in the European Union: Policy Issues and Proposals for the Future Role of the EU*. London: South Bank University, European Institute, 2001.

Begg, I. & D. Mayes (with M. Levitt & A. Shipman). 'A Strategy for Economic and Social Cohesion in Europe after 1992'. European Parliament Research Paper 19, 1991.

Berger, S. 'Introduction'. In *National Diversity and Global Capitalism*, edited by S. Berger & R. Dore. Ithaca, NY: Cornell University Press, 1996.

Blanpain R. (ed.). *Comparative Labour Law and Industrial Relations in Industrialized Market Economies*. 9th edn. The Netherlands: Wolters Kluwer, 2007.

Blumenfeld, S. 'Collective Bargaining'. In *Employment Relationships: Workers, Unions and Employers in New Zealand*, edited by E. Rasmussen. Auckland: Auckland University Press, 2010, forthcoming.

Boyer, R. & M. Freyssenet. *Les modèles productifs*. Paris: Repères, La Découverte, 2000, 128.

Burchill, F. *Labour Relations*. London: Palgrave, 2008.

Cartapanis, A., A. Koulinsky & N. Richez. 'L'hétérogénéité sociale de l'union Européenne après l'élargissement et la question des délocalisations; communication au colloque international les nouvelles frontières de l'europe, Marrakech'. 16–17 March 2005.

Crouch, C. *Capitalism Diversity and Change, Recombinant Governance and Institutional Entrepreneurs*. Oxford: Oxford University Press, 2005.

Crouch, C., et al. 'Dialogue on Institutional Complementarity and Political Economy'. *Socio-Economic Review* 3, no. 2 (2005): 359–382.

Davoine, L. & C. Erhel. 'Monitoring Employment Quality in Europe: European Employment Strategy and Beyond'. Working Paper CEE no. 66. Noisy-Le-Grand: Centre d'Etudes de l'Emploi, 2006.

Deeg, R. & G. Jackson. 'Towards a More Dynamic Theory of Capitalist Variety'. Research Paper no. 40. King's College, London: Department of Management Research Papers, 2006.

De la Graza, M. 'Converging Divergences or Converging Through Four Patterns?'. *Industrial and Labor Relations Review* 54, no. 3 (2001): 694–697.

Dore, R. *Stock Market Capitalism: Welfare Capitalism: Japan and Germany versus the Anglo-Saxons*. Oxford: Oxford University Press, 2000.

Dufresne, A., C. Degryse & P. Pochet (eds). 'The European Sectoral Social Dialogue: Actors, Developments and Challenges'. Joint Programme for Working Life Research in Europe, The National Institute for Working Life and The Swedish Trade Unions in Co-operation. PIE Peter Lang, 2006.

Esping-Andersen, G. *The Three Worlds of Welfare Capitalism*. Cambridge: Polity Press, 1990.

Ferrera, M. 'The "Southern Model" of Welfare in Social Europe'. *Journal of European Social Policy* 6, no. 1 (1996): 17–37.

Freeman, R.B. 'On the Divergence in Unionism among Developed Countries'. Discussion Paper no. 2817. National Bureau of Economic Research, 1989.

Freeman, R.B. 'Single Peaked vs. Diversified Capitalism: The Relation between Economic Institutions and Outcomes'. National Bureau of Economic Research, Inc. (NBER) Working Paper no.7556, 2000. <www.nber.org/papers/w7556>.

Galbraith, J.K. *The New Industrial State*. Boston: Houghton Mifflin, 1967.

Giles, A. 'Globalisation and Industrial Relations Theory'. *Journal of Industrial Relations* 42, no. 2 (2000): 173–194.

Goldthorpe, J.H. 'The End of Convergence: Corporatist and Dualist Tendencies in Modern Western Societies'. In *Order and Conflict in Contemporary Capitalism: Studies in the Political Economy of Western European Nations*, edited by J.H. Goldthorpe. Oxford: Clarendon Press, 1984.

Gospel, H. & A. Pendleton. *Corporate Governance and Labour Management*. Oxford: Oxford University Press, 2005.

Hale, D. 'International Comparisons of Labour Disputes in 2006'. *Economic and Labour Market Review* 2, no. 4 (2008).

Hall, P.A. & D.W. Gingerich. 'Varieties of Capitalism and Institutional Complementarities in the Macroeconomy'. MPIfG Discussion Paper 04/5. Cologne: Max Planck Institute for the Study of Societies, 2004.

Hall, P. & D. Soskice. *Varieties of Capitalism: The Institutional Foundations of Comparative Advantage*. Oxford: Oxford University Press, 2001.

Hall, P.A. & K. Thelen. 'The Politics of Change in Varieties of Capitalism'. Conference paper given at the American Political Science Association Annual Meeting, 1–4 September, Washington, D.C., 2005.

Hancke, B. 'Review of Katz and Darbishire Converging Divergences'. *British Journal of Industrial Relations* 39, no. 2 (2001): 305–307.

Hollingsworth, J.R. & R. Boyer. *Contemporary Capitalism: The Embeddedness of Institutions*. Cambridge: Cambridge University Press, 1997.

Howell, C. 'Varieties of Capitalism: And Then There Was One?'. *Comparative Politics* 36 (2003): 103–124.

Industrial Labor Organisation (ILO). <www.ilo.org/public/english/bureau/inf/download/ecosoc/decentwork.pdf>.

International Labour Office (ILO). 'International Statistical Inquiry on Trade Union Density and Collective Bargaining Coverage 2008–09'. ILO Industrial and Employment Relations Department (no date).

Jacoby, S.M. *The Embedded Corporation: Corporate Governance and Employment Relations in Japan and the United States*. Princeton, NJ: Princeton University Press, 2005.

Katz, H. & O. Darbishire. *Converging Divergence: Worldwide Changes in Employment Systems*. Ithaca, NY: Cornell University Press, 2000.

Kenworthy, L. 'Institutional Coherence and Macroeconomic Performance'. *Socio-Economic Review* 4 (2006): 69–91.

Kerr, C. *The Future of Industrial Societies: Convergence or Continuing Diversity?*. Cambridge, MA: Harvard University Press, 1983.

Kerr, C., et al. *Industrialism and Industrial Man: The Problems of Labour and Management in Economic Growth*. London: Penguin, 1960.

Kochan, T., H. Katz & R. Cappelli. *The Transformation of American Industrial Relations*. New York: Basic Books, 1986.

Kochan, T.A. *Restoring the American Dream: A Working Families Agenda for America*. Boston: MIT Press, 2005.

Lansbury, R. & N. Wailes. 'Employment Relations in Australia'. In *International and Comparative Industrial Relations*, edited by G. Bamber, R. Lansbury & N. Wailes. Sydney/London: Allen & Unwin/Sage, 2010.

167

Lorenz, E. & A. Valeyre. 'Organisational Innovation, Human Resource Management and Labour Market Structure: A Comparison of the EU-15'. *The Journal of Industrial Relations* 47 (2005): 424–442.

Low Pay Commission. 'National Minimum Wage'. Low Pay Commission Report 2009. <www.lowpay.gov.uk/lowpay/report/pdf/7997-BERR-LowPayCommission-WED.pdf>, 9 March 2010.

Madsen, J.S., J. Due & S.K. Andersen. 'Employment Relations in Denmark'. In *International and Comparative Industrial Relations*, edited by G. Bamber, R. Lansbury & N. Wailes. Sydney/London: Allen & Unwin/Sage, 2010.

Martin, R. & G.J. Bamber. 'International Comparative Employment Relations Theory: Developing the Political Economy Perspective'. In *Theoretical Perspectives on Work and the Employment Relationship*, edited by B.E. Kaufman. Annual Research Volume. Champaign, IL: Industrial Relations Research Association, 2004: 293–320.

Millward, N., A. Bryson & J. Forth. *All Change at Work? British Employment Relations 1980–1998*. Workplace Industrial Relations Survey Series. London: Routledge, 2000.

Molina, O. & M. Rhodes. 'Conflict, Complementarities and Institutional Change in Mixed Market Economies'. In *Beyond Varieties of Capitalism: Contradictions, Complementarities & Change*, edited by B. Hancké, M. Rhode & M. Thatcher. Oxford: Oxford University Press, 2007.

Monger, J. 'Labour Market Trends'. *Office for National Statistics*. London: Palgrave-Macmillan, 2005, 160.

Morgan, G. & I. Kubo. 'Beyond Path Dependency? Constructing New Models for Institutional Change: The Case of Capital Market in Japan'. *Socio-economic Review* 3 (2005): 55–82.

OECD. *Employment Outlook*. Paris: Organisation for Economic Cooperation and Development, 2000.

OECD. 'A Detailed Description of the Employment Regulation in Force in 2003'. *Background Material for the 2004 Edition of the OECD Employment Outlook*. Paris: Organisation for Economic Cooperation and Development, 2004.

OECD. *Factbook: Economic, Environmental and Social Statistics*. Paris: Organisation for Economic Cooperation and Development, 2006a.

OECD. *Employment Outlook*. Paris: Organisation for Economic Cooperation and Development, 2006b.

OECD. *Factbook, Economic, Environmental and Social Statistics*. Paris: Organisation for Economic Cooperation and Development, 2009.

Peetz, D. 'Assessing the Impact of "WorkChoices" One Year On'. Report in conjunction with Industrial Relations Victoria in the Department of Innovation, Industry and Regional Development, March 2007. <www.business.vic.gov.au/busvicwr/_assets/main/lib60104/4827wcanniversaryreportweb.pdf>, 7 April 2007.

Piore, M.J. 'Convergence in Industrial Relations? The Case of France and the United States'. Working Paper no. 286. Cambridge: Massachusetts Institute of Technology Department of Economics, 1981.

Piore, M. 'The Reconfiguration of Work and Employment Relations in the United States at the Turn of the 21st Century'. <www.ilo.org/public/english/bureau/inst/download/piore.pdf>, 7 April 2007.

Pontusson, J. 'Between Neo-Liberalism and the German Model: Swedish Capitalism in Transition'. In *Political Economy of Modern Capitalism: Mapping Convergence and Diversity*, edited by C. Crouch & W. Streeck. London: Sage, 1997, 55–70.

Pontusson, J. *Inequality and Prosperity, Social Europe vs. Liberal America*. Ithaca, NY, and London: Cornell University Press, 2005.

Poole, M. *Industrial Relations: Origins and Patterns of National Diversity*. London: Routledge, 1986.

Poole, M., R. Mansfield & P. Mendes. *Two Decades of Management*. London: Chartered Institute of Management, 2001.

Schmidt, V.A. *The Futures of European Capitalism*. Oxford: Oxford University Press, 2002.

Shonfield, A. *Modern Capitalism. The Changing Balance of Public and Private Power*. Oxford: Oxford University Press, 1965.

Sopart, D. 'A State-of-Art Literature Report on Varieties of Capitalism Approach'. Working Paper, Münster: Westfälische Wilhelms-Universität Münster, 2005. <http://nez.unimuenster.de/download/Literaturbericht_Dominik%20mit%20Deckblatt.pdf>, 17 March 2007.

Streeck, W. 'High Equality, Low Activity: The Contribution of the Social Welfare System to the Stability of the German Collective Bargaining Regime'. *Industrial and Labor Relations Review* 54, no. 3 (2001): 698–704.

Streeck, W. & K. Thelen. *Beyond Continuity, Institutional Change in Advanced Political Economy*. Oxford: Oxford University Press, 2005.

Tangian A.S. 'Monitoring Flexicurity Policies in the EU with Dedicated Composite Indicators'. WSI Diskussionspapier 137. Dusseldorf: Hans Böckler Stiftung, 2005.

Taylor, M. Z. 'Empirical Evidence against Varieties of Capitalism's Theory of Technical Innovation'. *International Organization* 58 (2004): 601–631.

Thelen, K. & I. Kume. 'Coordination as a Political Problem in Coordinated Market Economy'. *Governance* 19, no. 1 (2006): 11–42.

Visser, J. 'Union Membership in 24 Countries'. *Monthly Labour Review* 129 (January 2006): 38–49.

Visser, J., S. Martin & P. Tergeist. 'Trade Union Density (%) in OECD Countries'. 1960–2007 (spreadsheet), 2009. <www.oecd.org/dataoecd/25/42/39891561.xls>, 15 December 2009.

Visser, J., S. Martin & P. Tergeist. Trade Union Members and Union Density in OECD Countries. <www.oecd.org/dataoecd/37/2/35695665.pdf>, 15 December 2009.

Wailes, N. 'Review of Katz and Darbishire, Converging Divergences'. *Relations Industrielles/Industrial Relations* 55, no. 3 (2000): 540–543.

Weber, M. *The Methodology of the Social Sciences*, edited and translated by E.A. Shills & H.A. Finch. Glencoe, IL: The Free Press, 1949.

Whitley, R. *Divergent Capitalisms: The Social Structuring and Change of Business Systems.* Oxford: Oxford University Press, 1999.

Whitley, R. 'How National Are the Business Systems? The Role of Different State Types and Complementary Institutions in Constructing Homogenous Systems of Economic Coordination and Control'. Working Paper no. 450, 2003.

Womack, J. P., D.T. Jones & D. Roos. *The Machine That Changed The World.* New York: Rawson Associates, 1990.

Yamamura, K. & W. Streeck. *The End of Diversity? Prospects of German and Japanese Capitalism.* Ithaca, NY: Cornell University Press, 2003.

Websites

International Labour Organisation (ILO). Database of Conditions of Work and Employment: Maternity Protection, Minimum Wages, Working Time. <www.ilo.org/public/english/protection/condtrav/database/index.htm>.

International Labour Organisation (ILO). Database of Conditions of Work and ILO <www.ilo.org/public/english/bureau/inf/download/ecosoc/decentwork.pdf>.

Low Pay Commission (LPC). <www.lowpay.gov.uk/lowpay/lowpay2005/appendix4.shtml>.

Employment: Working Time Database (2006). <www.ilo.org/travaildatabase/servlet/workingtime?pageClass=org.ilo.legislation.work.web>.

Office for National Statistics. <www.statistics.gov.uk/downloads/theme_labour/Index_2005.pdf>.

Organisation for Economic Co-operation and Development (OECD). <www.oecd.org/home/>.

European Union

Commission of the European Community (Commission) (1998). Commission Decision 98/500/EC of 20 May 1998 on the Establishment of Sectoral Dialogue Committees Promoting the Dialogue between the Social Partners at European Level. OJ L 225, 12 August 1998, 27–28.

Commission (2007). Communication from the Commission: Towards Common Principles of Flexicurity: More and Better Jobs through Flexibility and Security, COM (2007) 359, Brussels 27 June 2007.

Commission (2008). Report from the Commission on the Implementation of the Barcelona Objectives Concerning Childcare Facilities for Pre-school-age Children; COM (2008) 638, Brussels, 3 October 2008.

Dufresne, A., C. Degryse & P. Pochet (eds). *The European Sectoral Social Dialogue: Actors, Developments and Challenges.* Brussels: PIE-Peter Lang, 2006.

Eurostat (2008). Minimum wages 2008, Statistics in focus, 105/2008.

Keller, B. & H.W. Platzer (eds). *Industrial Relations and European Integration.* Ashgate: Aldershot-Burlington, 2003.

Riedmann, A. et al. 'Working Time and Work-Life Balance in European Countries'. Establishment Survey on Working Time 2004–2005. Dublin: European Foundation, 2006.

Wolfson, C. & J. Sommers. 'Labour Dispute in Construction: European Implication of the Laval un Parneri Dispute with Swedish Labour'. *European Journal of Industrial Relations* 12, no. 1 (2006): 49–68.

Zeitlin, J. & P. Pochet (eds). *The OMC in Action*. Brussels: PIE-Peter Lang, 2005.

Websites

Europa: A Constitution for Europe (2010). <http://europa.eu/scadplus/constitution/competences_en.htm>.

European Commission Directorate General Employment, Social Affairs and Equal Opportunities. <ec.europa.eu/employment_social/index_en.html>.

European Commission Labour Law and Work Organisation. <ec.europa.eu/employment_social/labour_law/index_en.htm>.

European Employment Observatory (EEO). <www.eu-employment-observatory.net>.

European Foundation for the Improvement of Living and Working Conditions (Eurofound). <www.eurofound.europa.eu>.

European Industrial Relations Observatory (EIRO). <www.eurofound.europa.eu/eiro/>.

European Union Social Agenda 2005–2010. Communication from the Commission on the Social Agenda, COM (2005) 33 final of 9 February 2005. <europa.eu.int/eur-lex/lex/LexUriServ/site/en/com/2005/com2005_0033en01.pdf>.

European Union Treaties. <eur-lex.europa.eu/en/treaties/index.htm>.

European Working Conditions Observatory (EWCO). <www.eurofound.europa.eu/ewco/>.

Germany

Artus, I., S. Böhm, S. Lücking & R. Trinczek (eds). *Betriebe ohne Betriebsrat. Informelle Interessenvertretung in Unternehmen*. Frankfurt, New York: Campus, 2006.

Bauer, F., H. Gross, K. Lehmann & E. Munz. *Arbeitszeit 2003: Arbeitszeitgestaltung, Arbeitsorganisation und Tätigkeitsprofile. Bundesweite repräsentative Beschäftigtenbefragung im Auftrag des Ministeriums für Wirtschaft und Arbeit*. Köln: ISO, 2004.

Endruweit, G., E. Gaugler, W.H. Staehle & B. Wilpert (eds). *Handbuch der Arbeitsbeziehungen. Deutschland-Österreich-Schweiz*. Berlin: de Gruyter, 1985.

Keller, B. & H. Seifert. 'Atypical Employment and Flexicurity'. *Management-Review* 16, no. 3 (2005): 304–323.

Keller, B. *Einführung in die Arbeitspolitik. Arbeitsbeziehungen und Arbeitsmarkt in sozialwissenschaftlicher Perspektive*. 7th edn. München-Wien: Oldenbourg, 2008.

Keller, B. & A. Kirsch. 'Employment Relations in Germany'. In *International and Comparative Employment Relations*, edited by G.J. Bamber, R. Lansbury & N. Wailes. London/Sydney: Sage/Allen & Unwin, 2010.

Keller, B. & H. Seifert (eds). *Atypische Beschäftigung – Flexibilisierung und soziale Risiken*. Berlin: Edition Sigma, 2007.

Klenner, C. *Erwartungen an einen familienfreundlichen Betrieb*. Berlin: HBS, 2004.

Kohaut, S. 'Tarifbindung und tarifliche Öffnungsklauseln. Ergebnisse aus dem IAB-Betriebspanel 2005'. *WSI-Mitteilungen* 60, no. 2 (2007): 94–97.

Müller-Jentsch, W. *Soziologie der industriellen Beziehungen*. 2nd edn. Frankfurt, New York: Campus, 1997.

Müller-Jentsch, W. (ed.). *Konfliktpartnerschaft. Akteure und Institutionen der industriellen Beziehungen*. 3rd edn. München-Mering: Hampp, 1999.

Müller-Jentsch, W. & P. Ittermann. *Industrielle Beziehungen. Daten, Zeitreihen, Trend 1950–1999*. Frankfurt: Campus, 2000.

Müller-Jentsch, W. & H. Weitbrecht (eds). *The Changing Contours of German Industrial Relations*. Mering: Hampp, 2003.

Schnabel, C. *Tarifpolitik unter Reformdruck: Benchmarking Deutschland aktuell*. Gütersloh: Bertelsmann-Stiftung, 2003.

Schröder, W. & B. Wessels (eds). *Die Gewerkschaften in Politik und Gesellschaft der Bundesrepublik Deutschland. Ein Handbuch*. Wiesbaden: Westdeutscher Verlag. 2003.

Schröder, W. & B. Wessels (eds). *Die Arbeitgeber- und Wirtschaftsverbände in Deutschland*. Wiesbaden: Verlag für Sozialwissenschaften, 2010.

Weiss, M. & M. Schmidt. *Labour Law and Industrial Relations in Germany*. 4th rev. edn. The Netherlands: Wolters Kluwer, 2008.

Journals/Periodicals

Industrielle Beziehungen. The German Journal of Industrial Relations. WSI-Mitteilungen (monthly journal).

Bispinck, R. WSI, WSI-Tarifhandbuch. Frankfurt (annual volumes).

Websites

European Foundation for the Improvement of Living and Working Conditions, 2004, Working Time in Germany. <www.eurofound.eu.int/ewco/2004/12/DE0412NU01.htm>.

European Foundation for the Improvement of Living and Working Conditions 2006, Contract of Employment – Germany. <www.eurofound.eu.int/emire/GERMANY/CONTRACTOFEMPLOYMENT-DE.html>.

Ministry of Labour and Social Affairs. <www.bmas.de/portal/16702/startseite.htmlEnglisch/Navigation/root.html>.

Confederation of German Employers' Associations (BDA). <www.bda-online.de>.

Confederation of German Trade Unions (DGB). <www.dgb.de>.

Information on collective bargaining and contracts. <www.tarifvertrag.de> (<www.boeckler.de/cps/rde/xchg/hbs/hs.xsl/275.html>).

Revue WSI Collective Agreement Archive (2005). <www.boeckler.de/pdf/ p_ta_jb_2005.pdf>.

Sweden

Murhem, S. 'Flexicurity in Sweden'. In *How Secure Is Flexicurity?*, edited by M. Jepsen. Brussels: ETUI-REHS, forthcoming.

De Geer, H. *Arbetsgivarna: SAF i tio decennier.* Stockholm: Svenska Arbetsgivareföreningen, 1992.

Elvander, N. 'The New Swedish Regime of Collective Bargaining and Conflict Resolution: A Comparative Perspective'. *European Journal of Industrial Relations* 8, no. 2 (2002): 197–216.

Elvander N. & B. Holmlund. 'The Swedish Bargaining System in the Melting Pot. Institutions, Norms and Outcomes in the 1990s'. Solna: The National Institute for Working Life, 1997.

Kjellberg, A. 'Sweden: Restoring the Model?'. In *Changing Industrial Relations in Europe*, edited by A. Ferner & R. Hyman. Oxford: Blackwell Business, 1998.

Kjellberg, A. *Fackliga organisationer och medlemmar i dagens Sverige.* Lund: Arkiv, 2001.

Kjellberg, A. 'Sweden: Mergers in a Class-Segmented Trade Union System'. In *Restructuring Representation: The Merger Process and Trade Union Structural Development in Ten Countries*, edited by J. Waddington. Brussels, New York: PIE-Peter Lang, 2005.

Lundh, C. *Wage Formation, Labour Market Institutions and Economic Transformation in Sweden 1860–2000.* Stockholm: Almqvist & Wiksell International, 2004.

Murhem, S. *Turning to Europe. A New Swedish Industrial Relations Regime in the 1990s.* Uppsala: Acta Universitatis Upsaliensis, 2003.

Nycander, S. *Makten över arbetsmarknaden. Ett perspektiv på Sveriges 1990-tal.* Stockholm: Studieförbundet Näringsliv och Samhälle, 2002.

Öberg, P. & T. Svensson 'Power, Trust and Deliberation in Swedish Labour Market Policies'. *Economic & Industrial Democracy* 23, no. 4 (2002): 451–490.

Visser, J. 'Corporatism beyond Repair? Industrial Relations in Sweden'. In *Industrial Relations in Europe. Traditions and Transitions*, edited by J. Van Ruijsseveldt & J. Visser. London: Sage Publications, 1996.

Journals/Periodicals

Arbetsmarknad & Arbetsliv.
Economic and Industrial Democracy.

Websites

The Industrial Committee. <www.industrikommitten.se/>.
LO. <www.lo.se/>.

Ministry of Employment. <www.sweden.gov.se/sb/d/8270>.
National Mediation Office. <www.mi.se/>.
Statistics Sweden. <www.scb.se/default_2154.aspx>.
Svenskt Näringsliv. <www.svensktnaringsliv.se/>.
The Swedish Labour Court (*Arbetsdomstolen*). <www.arbetsdomstolen.se>.
The Swedish Work Environment Authority (*Arbetsmiljöverket*). <www.av.se>.
TCO. <www.tco.se/>.

United Kingdom

Beynon, H. *Working for Ford*. 2nd edn. London: Penguin, 1985.
Brown W., A. Bryson, J. Forth, et al. (eds). *The Evolution of the Modern Workplace*. Cambridge: Cambridge University Press, 2009.
Brown, W. & B. Towers. *Employment Relations in Britain: 25 Years of the Advisory, Conciliation and Arbitration Service*. Oxford: Blackwell, 2000.
Cully, M., S. Woodland, A. O'Reilly, et al. *Britain at Work: As Depicted by the 1998 Workplace Employee Relations Survey*. London: Routledge, 1999.
Department of Trade and Industry. *Fairness at Work*, HMSO, Cm 3968. London: Department of Trade and Industry, 1998.
Department of Trade and Industry. *Success at Work: Protecting Vulnerable Workers, Supporting Good Employers*. URN 06/1024. London: Department of Trade and Industry, 2006.
Dickens, L., M. Hall & S. Wood. 'Review of Research into the Impact of Employment Relations Legislation'. *Employment Relations Research Series*, 45, URN 05/1257. London: Department of Trade and Industry 2005.
Dickens, R., P. Gregg & J. Wadsworth (eds). *The Labour Market under New Labour: The State of Working Britain*. London: Palgrave Macmillan, 2004.
Flanders, A. *Management and Unions: Theory and Reform of Industrial Relations*. London: Faber, 1975.
Grainger, H. & M. Crowther. *Trade Union Membership 2006*, URN 07/899. London: Department of Trade and Industry, 2007.
Hyman, R. *The Political Economy of Industrial Relations: Theory and Practice in a Cold Climate*. London: Macmillan, 1989.
Kersley, B., C. Alpin, J. Forth, et al. *Inside the Workplace: Findings from the 2004 Workplace Employment Relations Survey*. London: Routledge, 2006.
Millward, N., J. Forth & A. Byson. *All Change at Work? British Employee Relations 1980–98*. London: Routledge, 2000.
Neal, A. & L. Dickens. *The Changing Institutional Face of British Employment Relations*. The Netherlands: Wolters Kluwer, 2006.
Smeaton, D. & A. Marsh. 'Maternity and Paternity Rights and Benefits: Survey of Parents 2005', *Employment Relations Research Series*, 50. London: Department of Trade and Industry (DTI), 2006, <www.dti.gov.uk/files/file27446.pdf?pubpdfdload>.
Wood, S.J. *The Transformation of Work?*. London: Unwin Hyman, 1989.

Journals

British Journal of Industrial Relations.
Industrial Relations Journal.
People Management (CIPD).

Websites

Advisory, Conciliation and Arbitration Service (ACAS). <www.acas.org.uk/>.
Business Info. <www.businesslink.gov.uk>.
Confederation of British Industry (CBI). <www.cbi.org.uk>.
Department for Business, Innovation and Skills (BIS). <http://www.bis.gov.uk/policies/employment-matters>.
Employee Info. <www.direct.gov.uk/Employment/fs/en>.
Equality and Human Rights Commission (EHRC). <www.equalityhumanrights.com>.
Low Pay Commission (LPC). <www.lowpay.gov.uk/>.
Trades Union Congress (TUC). <www.tuc.org.uk>.
Tribunals Service – Employment. <www.employmenttribunals.gov.uk>.

United States of America

Bernstein, I. *Turbulent Years: A History of the American Worker 1933–1941.* Boston, MA: Houghton-Mifflin, 1971.

Block, R.N. (ed.). *Bargaining for Competitiveness: Law, Research, and Case Studies.* Kalamazoo, MI: WE Upjohn Institute for Employment Research, 2003.

Block, R.N. 'Industrial Relations in the United States and Canada'. In *Global Industrial Relations*, edited by M. Morley, P. Gunnigle & D.G. Collings. London: Routledge, 2006, 25–52.

Block, R.N., J. Beck & D.H. Kruger. *Labor Law, Industrial Relations, and Employee Choice.* Kalamazoo, MI: WE Upjohn Institute for Employment Research, 1996.

Block, R.N. & D. Belman. 'Competitiveness and Employment Protection and Creation: An Overview of Collective Bargaining in the United States'. In *Bargaining for Competitiveness: Law, Research, and Case Studies*, edited by R.N. Block. Kalamazoo, MI: WE Upjohn Institute for Employment Research, 2003, 13–44.

Block, R.N., P. Berg & D. Belman. 'The Economic Dimension of the Employment Relationship'. In *The Employment Relationship: Examining Psychological and Contextual Perspectives*, edited by J.A.-M Coyle-Shapiro, L.M. Shore, M.S. Taylor & L.E. Tetrick. Oxford: Oxford University Press, 2004.

Block, R.N. et al. (eds). *Justice on the Job: Perspectives on the Erosion of Collective Bargaining in the United States.* Kalamazoo, MI: WE Upjohn Institute for Employment Research, 2006.

Bronfrenbrenner, K. 'The Role of Union Strategies in NLRB Certification Elections'. *Industrial and Labor Relations Review* 50, no. 2 (1997): 195–221.

Clark, P.F., J.T. Delaney & A.C. Frost (eds). *Collective Bargaining in the Private Sector*. Champaign, IL: Industrial Relations Research Association Series, 2002.

Dresser L. & A. Bernhardt. 'Bad Service Jobs: Can Unions Save Them: Can They Save Unions?' In *Justice on the Job: Perspectives on the Erosion of Collective Bargaining in the United States*, edited by R. Block et al. Kalamazoo, MI: WE Upjohn Institute for Employment Research, 2006, 115–138.

Dubuque Packing Co. (1991), 303 NLRB 386.

Hecksher, C.C. *The New Unionism: Employee Involvement in the Changing Corporation*. New York: Basic Books, 1988.

Higgins, Jr, J.E., (Editor-in-Chief). *The Developing Labor Law*. 5th edn. Washington, DC: BNA Books, 2006.

Katz, H. *Shifting Gears: Changing Labor Relations in the U.S. Automobile Industry*. Cambridge, MA and London: MIT Press, 1987.

Katz, H. & T. Kochan. *An Introduction to Collective Bargaining and Industrial Relations*. 3rd edn. New York: McGraw-Hill, 2003.

Katz, H. & A. Colvin, 'Employment Relations in the United States' In *International and Comparative Employment Relations*, edited by G.J. Bamber, R. Lansbury & N. Wailes. 5th edn. London/Sydney: Sage/Allen & Unwin, 2010.

Kochan, T.A., H.C. Katz & R.B. McKersie. *The Transformation of Industrial Relations*. Ithaca, NY: ILR Press, 1994.

Ruben, A.M. National Right-to-Work Committee. <www.right-to-work.org/>.

Rubinstein, S. & T. Kochan. *Learning from Saturn: Possibilities for Corporate Governance and Employee Relations*. Ithaca, NY: ILR Press, 2001.

Sutton v. United Air Lines (1999). 527 U.S. 471.

Toyota Motor Mfg., Ky., Inc. v. Williams (2002). 534 U.S.184.

United States Bureau of Labor Statistics. 'Labor Force Statistics from the Current Population Survey: Access to Historical Data for the Tables of the Union Membership'. *News Release* (2009).

United States Department of Labor. Minimum Wage. <www.dol.gov/dol/topic/wages/minimumwage.htm>, 11 March 2010.

Wheeler, H.N., B.S. Klaas & D.M. Mahony. *Workplace Justice without Unions*. Kalamazoo, MI: WE Upjohn Institute for Employment Research, 2004.

Journals/Periodicals

Bailey, S. 'Stock Bonuses at Airlines Anger Pilots'. *New York Times*, 27 March 2007.

Hirsch B.T. & D. Macpherson. 'Earnings, Rents, and Competition in the Airline Labor Market'. *Journal of Labor Economics* 18, no. 1 (2000): 125–155.

Websites

AFL-CIO (undated) (The American Federation of Labor and Congress of Industrial Organizations). <www.aflcio.org>.

American Rights at Work. <www.americanrightsatwork.org/>.

Association of Labor Relations Agencies (ALRA). <www.alra.org>.

Bureau of Labor Statistics (BLS). <www.bls.gov>.

Center for Union Facts. <www.unionfacts.com/>.

Change to Win (undated). <www.changetowin.org/>.

Cornell Law School, Legal Information Institute (LII). <www.law.cornell.edu/wex/index.php/Employment_discrimination>.

Change to Win (undated). <www.changetowin.org/>.

Department of Labor. <www.dol.gov>.

Equal Employment Opportunity Commission (EEOC). <www.eeoc.gov>.

Federal Labor relation Authority (FLRA). <www.flra.gov>.

Federal Mediation and Conciliation Service (FMCS). <www.fmcs.gov>. 2004.

HR Policy Association. <www.hrpolicy.org>.

National Labor Relation Board (NLRB). <www.nlrb.gov>.

National Mediation Board. <www.nmb.gov>.

National Right-to-Work Committee. <www.right-to-work.org/>.

State of California, Employment Development Department, Paid Family Leave Insurance. <www.edd.ca.gov/direp/pflfaq1.asp#ELIGIBILITY>.

United States Department of Labor, Bureau of Labor Statistics (undated). Collective Bargaining. <www.bls.gov/cba/home.htm>.

United States Department of Labor, Bureau of Labor Statistics (undated). 'Wages, Earnings, and Benefits'. <www.bls.gov/bls/wages.htm>.

United States Federal Mediation and Conciliation Service (undated). <www.fmcs.gov>.

United States Department of Labor, Bureau of Labor Statistics (5 March 2010). Collective Bargaining. <www.bls.gov/cba/home.htm>.

Collective Bargaining Agreements File: Online Listings of Private and Public Sector Agreements. <www.dol.gov/esa/regs/compliance/olms/cba/index.htm>.

United States Department of Labor, Bureau of Labor Statistics (undated). Wages, Earnings, and Benefits. <www.bls.gov/bls/wages.htm>.

United States Federal Mediation and Conciliation Service, <www.fmcs.gov>.

Canada

Cranford C.J., J. Fudge, E. Tucker & L.F. Vosko. *Self-Employed Workers Organize.* Montreal: McGill-Queen's University Press, 2005.

Adell B.L., M. Grant & A. Ponak. *Strikes in Essential Services.* Kingston: IRC Press, 2001.

Arthurs, H.W. 'Fairness at Work: Federal Labour Standards for the 21st Century'. *Federal Labour Standards Review*, Gatineau: Human Resources and Skills Development Canada, 2006.

Bernier, J., G. Vallée & C. Jobin. *Social Protection Needs of Individuals in Non-standard Work Situations.* Quebec: Ministère du Travail, 2003.

Carter, D.D. *Labour Law in Canada.* 5th edn. Toronto: Butterworths of Canada, 2002.

Chaykowski, R. & A. Verma. *Industrial Relations in Canadian Industry*. Toronto: Dryden, 1992.

Fudge, J. 'The Supreme Court of Canada and the Right to Bargain Collectively: The Implications of the Health Services and Support Case and Beyond'. *Industrial Law Journal* 37, no. 1 (2008): 25–48.

Godard, J. *Industrial Relations, the Economy, and Society*. 3rd edn. North York, Ontario: Captus Press, 2005.

Gunderson, M. & D.G. Taras. *Canadian Labour and Employment Relations*. 6th edn. Toronto: Pearson/Addison Wesley, 2004.

Gunderson, M. & A. Sharpe. *Forging Business-Labour Partnerships: The Emergence of Sector Councils in Canada*. Toronto: University of Toronto Press, 1998.

Hébert, G. et al. *La convention collective au Québec*. Montréal: Gaetan Morin, 2003.

Kumar, P. & C.R. Schenk. *Paths to Union Renewal: Canadian Experiences*. Peterborough: Garamond Press/Broadview Press, 2006.

Kumar, P. *Uniformity or Divergence? Industrial Relations in Canada and the United States*. Kingston: IRC Press, 1993.

Macdonald, D.S. *Report/Royal Commission on the Economic Union and Development Prospects for Canada*. Ottawa: Supply and Services Canada, 1985.

Murray, G., M.L. Morin & I. Da Costa. *L'état des relations professionnelles: traditions et perspectives de recherché*. Quebec/Toulouse: Presses de l' Université Laval/Octares, 1996.

Murray, G. & P. Verge. *La représentation syndicale: visage juridique actuel et futur*. Quebec: Presses de l'Université Laval, 1999.

Swimmer, G. & M. Thompson. *Public Sector Collective Bargaining in Canada: Beginning of the End or End of the Beginning?*. Kingston: IRC Queen's University, 1995.

Task Force on Labour Relations. *Canadian Industrial Relations: The Report of the Task Force on Labour Relations*. Ottawa: Privy Council Office, 1968.

Thompson, M., J.B. Rose & A.E. Smith. *Beyond the National Divide: Regional Dimensions of Industrial Relations*. Kingston: McGill-Queen's University Press, 2003.

Vosko, L.F. *Precarious Employment: Understanding Labour Market Insecurity in Canada*. Kingston: McGill-Queen's University Press, 2006.

Weiler, P.C. *Reconcilable Differences: New Directions in Canadian Labour Law*. Toronto: Carswell, 1980.

Journals/Periodicals

Canadian Labour & Employment Law Journal.

Just Labour. Centre for Research on Work and Society, York University.

Labour/Le Travail: Journal of Canadian Labour Studies/Revue d'Études Ouvrières Canadiennes. Memorial University of Newfoundland.

Perspectives on Labour and Income. Statistics Canada.
Relations industrielles/Industrial Relations. Industrial Relations Department, Université Laval.
Workplace Gazette/Gazette du travail. Human Resources and Skills Development Canada.

Websites

Canada Industrial Relations Board. <www.cirb-ccri.gc.ca/>.
Canada Labour Code. <laws.justice.gc.ca/en/L-2/index.html>.
Canadian HR Reporter. <www.hrreporter.com/>.
Canadian Labour Congress. <canadianlabour.ca/>.
Confédération des syndicats nationaux. <www.csn.qc.ca/>.
Human Resources and Social Development Canada – Labour. <www.hrsdc.gc.ca/en/labour/index.shtml>.
Labour Standard in Quebec. <www.cnt.gouv.qc.ca/en/index.asp>.
Lancaster House. <www.lancasterhouse.com/>.
Ministère du Travail du Québec. <www.travail.gouv.qc.ca/>.
Ontario Labour Relations Board. <www.olrb.gov.on.ca/>.

New Zealand

Blackwood, L., G. Finberg-Danieli & G. Lafferty. 'Unions and Union Membership in New Zealand: Annual Review for 2005'. *New Zealand Journal of Employment Relations* 31, no. 3 (2006): 78–89.
Boston, J., J. Martin, J. Pallot, et al. (eds). *Reshaping the State.* Auckland: Oxford University Press, 1991.
Boston, J., J. Martin, J. Pallot, et al. *Public Management.* Auckland: Oxford University Press, 1996.
Burgess, J., J. Connell & E. Rasmussen. 'Agency Work and Employment Precariousness in Australia and New Zealand'. *Management Revue* 16, no. 3 (2005): 351–369.
Dannin, E. *Working Free: The Origins and Impact of New Zealand's Employment Contracts Act.* Auckland: Auckland University Press, 1997.
Davenport, G. & J. Brown. *Good Faith in Collective Bargaining.* Wellington: Lexis Nexis Butterworth, 2002.
Deeks, J. & E. Rasmussen. *Employment Relations in New Zealand.* Auckland: Pearson Education, 2002.
Department of Labour. 'Achieving Balanced Lives and Employment, What New Zealanders Are Saying about Work-Life Balance'. July 2004 (2005). <www.dol.govt.nz/PDFs/wlb-consultation-summary.pdf>.
Geare, A.J. & F.J. Edgar. *Employment Relations. New Zealand and Abroad.* Dunedin: Otago University Press, 2006.
Harbridge, R. (ed.). *Employment Contracts: New Zealand Experiences.* Wellington: Victoria University Press, 1993.

Haworth, N. 'Beyond the Employment Relations Act: The Wider Agenda for Employment Relations and Social Equity in New Zealand'. In *Employment Relationships: New Zealand's Employment Relations Act*, edited by E. Rasmussen. Auckland: University of Auckland Press, 2004, 190–205.

Haynes, P., P. Boxall & K. Macky. 'Non-union Voice and the Effectiveness of Joint Consultation in New Zealand'. *Economic and Industrial Democracy* 26, no. 2 (2005): 229–256.

Kelsey, J. *The New Zealand Experiment: A World Model for Structural Adjustment?*. Auckland: Auckland University Press, 1997.

Rasmussen, E. *Employment Relations in New Zealand*. Auckland: Pearson, 2009.

Rasmussen, E. (ed.). *Employment Relationships: New Zealand's Employment Relations Act*. Auckland: University of Auckland Press, 2004.

Rasmussen, E., V. Hunt & F. Lamm. 'New Zealand Employment Relations: Between Individualism and Social Democracy'. *Labour & Industry* 17, no. 1 (2006): 19–40.

Rasmussen, E. & F. Lamm. 'New Zealand Employment Relations'. In *Employment Relations in the Asia-Pacific: Changing Approaches*, edited by G.J. Bamber et al. Sydney: Allen & Unwin, 2000, 46–63.

Rasmussen, E., J. Lind & J. Visser. 'Flexibility Meets National Norms and Regulations: Part-time Work in New Zealand, Denmark and the Netherlands'. *British Journal of Industrial Relations* 42, no. 4 (2004): 637–658.

Rasmussen, E. & C. Ross. 'The Employment Relations Act through the Eyes of the Media'. In *Employment Relationships: New Zealand's Employment Relations Act*, edited by E. Rasmussen. Auckland: University of Auckland Press, 2004, 21–38.

Thickett, G., P. Walsh & R. Harbridge. 'Collective Bargaining under the Employment Relations Act'. In *Employment Relationships: New Zealand's Employment Relations Act*, edited by E. Rasmussen. Auckland: University of Auckland Press, 2004, 39–58.

Tucker, D. *'Precarious' Non-standard Employment – A Review of the Literature*. Report, Labour Market Policy Group, Wellington: Department of Labour, 2002, <www.dol.govt.nz>.

Waldegrave, T., D. Anderson & K. Wong. *Evaluation of the Short Term Impacts of the Employment Relations Act 2000*. Wellington: Department of Labour, 2003, <www.dol.govt.nz>.

Journals/Periodicals

New Zealand Journal of Employment Relations. <www.nzjournal.org.nz>.
New Zealand Journal of Human Resources. <www.humanresources.co.nz/articles>.
Political Science. Victoria University, Wellington.

Websites

Business New Zealand. <www.businessnz.org.nz>.
Department of Labour. <www.dol.govt.nz>.

NZ Council of Trade Unions. <www.nzctu.org.nz>.
New Zealand Work and Labour Market Institute. <www.aut.ac.nz/research/ research_institutes/nzwalmi>.
Statistics New Zealand. <stats.govt.nz/people/work-income/default.htm>.
Statistics New Zealand. <www.stats.govt.nz>.

Australia

Barry, M., M. Michelotti & C. Nyland. 'Protectionism, Common Advocacy and Employer Interests: Business Contribution to Labour Market Regulation in Australia'. In *Labour Law and Labour Market Regulation*, edited by C. Arup, et al. Sydney: Federation Press, 2006, 43–66.
Business Council of Australia (BCA). *Aspire Australia 2025*. Melbourne: Business Council of Australia, 2004.
BCA. *The BCA Workplace Relations Action Plan*. Melbourne: Business Council of Australia, 2005.
Clegg, H. *Trade Unionism under Collective Bargaining: A Theory Based on Comparisons of Six Countries*. Oxford: Basil Blackwell, 1976.
Creighton, B. 'One Hundred Years of the Conciliation and Arbitration Power: A Province Lost?' *Melbourne University Law Review* 24, no. 3 (2000): 839–865.
Deery, S. & D. Plowman. *Australian Industrial Relations*. 3rd edn. Sydney: McGraw-Hill, 1993.
Fox, C., W. Howard & M. Pittard. *Industrial Relations in Australia: Developments, Law and Operation*. Melbourne: Longman, 1995.
Macintyre, S. & R. Mitchell. 'Introduction: The Debate over Arbitration'. In *Foundations of Arbitration: The Origins and Effects of State Compulsory Arbitration 1890–1914*, edited by S. Macintyre & R. Mitchell. Melbourne: Oxford University Press, 1989, 1–21.
Mackinnon, B. 'Employer Matters in 2004'. *Journal of Industrial Relations* 47, no. 2 (2005): 212–225.
Peetz, D. *Unions in a Contrary World: The Future of the Australian Union Movement*. Cambridge: Cambridge University Press, 1998.
Peetz, D. *Brave New Workplace: How Individual Contracts Are Changing Our Jobs*. Sydney: Allen & Unwin, 2006.
Peetz, D., A. Preston, & J. Doherty (eds). 'Workplace Bargaining in the International Context'. First Report of the Workplace Bargaining and Research Project, Industrial Relations Research Monograph no. 2. Canberra: Department of Industrial Relations, 1992.
Pusey, M. 'Economic Rationalism versus Social Democracy: The Battle for the Industrial Relations System and the Public Sector'. Discussion Paper 35. Public Sector Research Centre, Sydney: University of New South Wales, 1994.
Richardson, S. 'Regulation of the Labour Market'. In *Reshaping the Labour Market: Regulation, Efficiency and Equality in Australia*, edited by S. Richardson. Cambridge: Cambridge University Press, 1999, 1–37.

Japan

Araki, T. *Labor and Employment Law in Japan*. Tokyo: Japan Institute of Labour, 2002.

Abegglen, J.C. *The Japanese Factory: Aspects of Its Social Organization*. Glencoe, IL: Free Press, 1958.

Aoki, M. & R. Dore (eds). *The Japanese Firm; Sources of Competitive Strength*. Oxford: Clarendon Press, 1994.

Debroux, P. *Human Resource Management in Japan: Changes and Uncertainties*. Aldershot: Ashgate, 2003.

Dore, R. *British Factory-Japanese Factory: The Origin of National Diversity in Industrial Relations*. London: George Allen & Unwin, 1979.

Dore, R. 'Three Lectures'. In *Work in the Global Economy*, edited by J.P. Laviec, M. Horiuchi & K. Sugeno. Geneva: International Institute for Labour Studies, 2003.

Jacoby, S. *The Embedded Corporation: Corporate Governance and Employment Relations in Japan and the United States*. Princeton, NJ: Princeton University Press, 2005.

Japan Institute for Labour Policy and Training, 'Law for Securing the Proper Operation of Worker Dispatching Undertakings and Improved Working Conditions for Dispatched Workers', Law No. 88 of 5 July 1985, <www.jil.go.jp/english/laborinfo/library/documents/llj_law6.pdf>.

Japan Institute for Labour Policy and Training. *Japan Labor Review* (Special edition) 4, no.1 (2007).

Koike, K. & T. Inoki 'College Graduates in Japanese Industries'. The Japanese Institute of Labour. *Japanese Economy & Labor Series*, no. 8, 2003.

Kuwahara, Y. 'Employment Relations in Japan'. In *International and Comparative Employment Relations*, edited by G.J. Bamber, N. Wailes & R.D. Lansbury. 4th edn. London/Sydney: Sage/Allen & Unwin, 2004.

Ministry of Health, Labour and Welfare, 'General Survey of Working Conditions'. 2006.

Ministry of Health, Labour and Welfare. Law Concerning the Welfare of Workers Who Take Care of Children or Other Family Members Including Child Care and Family Care Leave, Law No. 76 of 1991, <www.mhlw.go.jp/general/seido/koyou/ryouritu/english/e1.html>, Survey on the diversification of employment patterns 2003, 2007.

Nakamura, K. & M. Nitta. 'Developments in Industrial Relations and Human Resource Practices in Japan'. In *Employment Relations in a Changing World Economy*, edited by R. Locke, T. Kochan & M. Piore. Cambridge, MA: MIT Press, 1995.

Sako, M. & H. Sato. *Japanese Labour and Management in Transition: Diversity, Flexibility and Participation*. London: Routledge/London School of Economics & Political Science, 1997.

Shirai, T. (ed.). *Contemporary Industrial Relations in Japan*. Madison: University of Wisconsin Press, 1983.

Shirai, T. 'Japanese Industrial Relations; Japan Institute of Labor'. *Japanese Economy and Labor Series*, no. 5, 2000.

Journals/Periodicals

Japan Labor Review. Japan Institute for Labour Policy and Training <www.jil.go.jp/english/JLR.htm>.
The Japanese Journal of Labour Studies. Japan Institute for Labour Policy and Training. <www.jil.go.jp/english/ejournal/index.html>.
Quarterly Labor Law. Roudou Kaihatsu Kenkyukai.

Websites

Japan Institute for Labour Policy and Training. <www.jil.go.jp/english/>.
Ministry of Health, Labour and Welfare. <www.mhlw.go.jp/english/>
Statistic Bureau. 'Annual Report on the Labour Force Survey 2005', <www.stat.go.jp/english/data/roudou/report/2005/dt/pdf/01.pdf>, <www.stat.go.jp/english/data/roudou/report/2005/ft/index.htm>, général, 'Employment status survey 2007'.
Statistic Bureau. 'Labour Force Survey 2008'. <www.stat.go.jp/english/>.

20. Roger Blanpain, Stephen Frenkel & Oliver Clarke, *Economic Restructuring and Industrial Relations in Industrialised Countries*, 1990 (ISBN 90-654-4488-2).

21. Roger Blanpain & Friedrich Fürstenberg, *Structure and Strategy in Industrial Relations*, 1991 (ISBN 90-654-4559-5).

22. Roger Blanpain, Amira Galin & Ozer Carmi, *Flexible Work Patterns and Their Impact on Industrial Relations*, 1991 (ISBN 90-654-4572-2).

23. Roger Blanpain, *Workers' Participation: Influence on Management Decision-Making by Labour in the Private Sector*, 1992 (ISBN 90-654-4600-1).

24. Roger Blanpain, Brian Brooks & Chris Engels, *Employed or Self-Employed*, 1992, (ISBN 90-654-4613-3).

25. Roger Blanpain Tiziano Treu, *Industrial Relations Developments in the Telecommunications Industry*, 1993 (ISBN 90-654-4642-7).

26. Roger Blanpain & Marco Biagi, *Industrial Relations in Small and Medium Sized Enterprises*, 1993 (ISBN 90-654-4696-6).

27. Roger Blanpain & Marco Biagi, *Participative Management and Industrial Relations in a Worldwide Perspective*, (ISBN 90-654-4769-5).

28. Roger Blanpain, Jacques Rojot & Hoyt N. Wheeler, *Employee Rights and Industrial Justice*, 1994 (ISBN 90-654-4804-7).

29. Roger Blanpain & Ruth Ben-Israel, *Strikes and Lock-Outs in Industrialized Market Economies*, 1994 (ISBN 90-654-4841-1).

30. Roger Blanpain, Kazuo Sugeno & Yasuo Suwa, *The Harmonization of Working Life and Family Life*, 1995 (ISBN 90-411-0064-4).

31. Roger Blanpain & Laszio Nagy, *Labour Law and Industrial Relations in Central and Eastern Europe*, 1996 (ISBN 90-411-0298-1).

32. Roger Blanpain, *Labour Law and Industrial Relations in the European Union*, 1997 (ISBN 90-411-0527-1).

33. Taco Van Peijpe, *Employment Protection under Strain*, 1998 (ISBN 90-411-0528-8).

34. Roger Blanpain, Takashi Araki & Ryuichi Yamakawa, *The Process of Industrialization and the Role of Labour Law in Asia*, 1999 (ISBN 9-041-1104-7-X).

35. Roger Blanpain & Marco Biagi, *Non-standard Work and Industrial Relations*, 1999 (ISBN 90-411-1117-4).

36. Roger Blanpain, *Private Employment Agencies: The Impact of ILO Convention 181 (1997) and the Judgment of the European Court of Justice of 11 December 1997*, 1999 (ISBN 90-411-1118-2).

37. Roger Blanpain, *Multinational Enterprises and the Social Challenges of the XXIst Century: The ILO Declaration on Fundamental* Principles at *Work, Public and Private Corporate Codes of Conduct*, 2000 (ISBN 90-411-1280-4).

38. Roger Blanpain, Ryuichi Yamakawa & Takashi Araki, *Deregulation and Labour Law: In Search of a Labour Concept for the 21st Century*, 2000 (ISBN 90-411-1370-3).

39. Roger Blanpain, *The Council of Europe and the Social Challenges of the XXIst Century*, 2001 (ISBN 90-411-1543-9).
40. Roger Blanpain, *On-Line Rights for Employees in the Information Society, Use & Monitoring of E-Mail & Internet at Work*, 2002 (ISBN 90-411-1626-5).
41. Roger Blanpain, *The Evolving Employment Relationship and the New Economy: The Role of Labour Law & Industrial Relations*, 2001 (ISBN 90-411-1691-5).
42. Roger Blanpain, *Involvement of Employees in the European Union, Works Councils, Company Statute, Information and Consultation Rights*, 2002 (ISBN 90-411-1760-1).
43. Michele Colucci, *The Impact of the Internet and New Technologies on the Workplace: A Legal Analysis from a Comparative Point of View*, 2002 (ISBN 90-411-1824-1).
44. Roger Blanpain, *White Paper on the Labour Market in Italy: The Quality of European Industrial Relations and Changing Industrial Relations*, 2002 (ISBN 90-411-1841-1).
45. Roger Blanpain, Russell D. Lansbury & Young-Bum Park, *Impact of Globalisation on Employment Relations: A Comparison of the Automobile and Banking Industries in Australia and Korea*, 2002 (ISBN 90-411-1850-0).
46. Roger Blanpain & Antoine Jacobs, *Employee Rights in Bankruptcy: A Comparative-Law Assessment*, 2002 (ISBN 90-411-1942-6).
47. Roger Blanpain, Takashi Araki & Shinya Ouchi, *Corporate Restructuring and the Role of Labour Law*, 2003 (ISBN 90-411-1949-3).
48. Roger Blanpain, *Collective Bargaining, Discrimination, Social Security and European Integration*, 2003 (ISBN 90-411-2010-6).
49. Roger Blanpain & Luis Aparicio-Valdez, *Labour Relations in the Asia-Pacific Countries*, 2004 (ISBN 90-411-2239-7).
50. Roger Blanpain & Ronnie Graham, *Temporary Agency Work and the Information Society*, 2004 (ISBN 90-411-2252-4).
51. Roger Blanpain, *The Actors of Collective Bargaining: A World Report*, 2004 (ISBN 90-411-2253-2).
52. Roger Blanpain & Michele Colucci, *The Globalisation of Labour Standards: The Soft Law Track*, 2004 (ISBN 90-411-2303-2).
53. Roger Blanpain, Takashi Araki & Shinya Ouchi, *Labour Law in Motion: Diversification of the Labour Force & Terms and Conditions of Employment*, 2005 (ISBN 90-411-2315-6).
54. Roger Blanpain, *Smoking and the Workplace*, 2005 (ISBN 90-411-2325-3).
55. Roger Blanpain, *Confronting Globalization: The Quest for a Social Agenda*, 2005 (ISBN 90-411-2381-4).
56. Roger Blanpain, Thomas Blanke & Edgar Rose, *Collective Bargaining Wages in Comparative Perspective: Germany, France, the Netherlands, Sweden and the United Kingdom*, 2005 (ISBN 90-411-2388-1).
57. Roger Blanpain & Anne Numhauser-Henning, *Women in Academia & Equality Law: Aiming High – Falling Short?*, 2006 (ISBN 978-90-411-2427-6).

58. Roger Blanpain, *Freedom of Services in the European Union: Labour and Social Security Law: The Bolkestein Initiative*, 2006 (ISBN 978-90-411-2453-5).
59. Roger Blanpain, Frans Pennings & Nurhan Sural, *Flexibilisation and Modernisation of the Turkish Labour Market*, 2006 (ISBN 978-90-411-2490-X).
60. Roger Blanpain & Boel Flodgren, *Corporate and Employment Perspectives in a Global Business Environment* 2006 (ISBN 978-90-411-2537-X).
61. Roger Blanpain, Shinya Ouchi & Takashi Araki, *Decentralizing Industrial Relations and The Role of Labor Unions and Employee Representatives*, 2007 (ISBN 978-90-411-2583-3).
62. Roger Blanpain, *European Framework Agreements and Telework: Law and Practice: A European and Comparative Study*, 2007 (ISBN 978-90-411-2560-4).
63. Roger Blanpain, Jim Kitay, Leanne Cutcher & Nick Wailes, *Globalization and Employment Relations in Retail Banking*, 2007 (ISBN 978-90-411-2620-1).
64. Roger Blanpain, Russell Lansbury, Jim Kitay, Nick Wailes & Anja Kirsch, *Globalization and Employment Relations in the Auto Assembly Industry: A Study of Seven Countries*, 2008 (ISBN 978-90-411-2698-6).
65. Roger Blanpain & Michele Tiraboschi, *The Global Labour Market: From Globalization to Flexicurity*, 2008 (ISBN 978-90-411-2722-8).
66. Roger Blanpain, Michele Colucci & Frank Hendrickx, *The Future of Sport in the European Union: Beyond the EU Reform Treaty and the White Paper*, 2008 (ISBN 978-90-411-2761-7).
67. Roger Blanpain, Linda Dickens, *Challenges in European Employment Relations: Employment Regulation, Trade Union Organization, Equality, Flexicurity, Training and New Approaches to Pay*, 2008 (ISBN 978-90-411-2771-6).
68. Roger Blanpain, Hiroya Nakakubo & Takashi Araki, *New Developments in Employment Discrimination Law*, 2008 (ISBN 978-90-411-2782-2).
69. Roger Blanpain, Andrzej Marian Świątkowski, *The Laval and Viking Cases: Freedom of Services and Establishment v. Industrial Conflict in the European Economic Area and Russia*, 2009 (ISBN 978-90-411-2850-8).
70. Roger Blanpain, William Bromwich, Olga Rymkevich, Silvia Spattini, *The Modernization of Labour Law and Industrial Relations in a Comparative Perspective*, 2009 (ISBN 978-90-411-2865-2).
71. Roger Blanpain, Juan Pablo Landa & Brian Langille, *Employment Policies and Multilevel Governance*, 2009 (ISBN 978-90-411-2866-9).
72. Roger Blanpain, European Works Councils; *The European Directive 2009/38/EC of 6 May 2009, 2009* (ISBN 978-90-411-3208-6).
73. Roger Blanpain, William Bromwich, Olga Rymkevich & Silvia Spattini, *Labour Productivity, Investment in Human Capital and Youth Employment: Comparative Developments and Global Responses*, 2010 (ISBN 978-90-411-3249-9).
74. Greg J. Bamber & Philippe Pochet, *Regulating Employment Relations, Work and Labour Laws: International Comparisons between Key Countries*, 2010 (ISBN 978-90-411-3199-7). General Editor: Roger Blanpain.

LaVergne, TN USA
10 December 2010

208204LV00002B/4/P